CHURCH
PLANTING

CHURCH
PLANTING

LAYING FOUNDATIONS

North American Edition

Stuart Murray

Foreword by J. Nelson Kraybill

Herald
Press

Scottdale, Pennsylvania
Waterloo, Ontario

Library of Congress Cataloguing-in-Publication Data
Murray, Stuart, 1956-
    Church planting: laying foundations.— North American ed.
      p. cm.
    Includes bibliographical references.
    ISBN 0-8361-9148-X (trade pbk. : alk. paper)
      1. Church development, New—Anabaptists. 2. Church growth—
      Anabaptists. I. Title.

BV652.24 .M87 2001
254'.5—dc21   00-046089

All Bible quotations are used by permission, all rights reserved and are from *The Holy Bible, New International Version*, copyright © 1973, 1978, 1984 International Bible Society, Zondervan Bible Publishers.

This North American edition of *Church Planting* is based on the version first published in 1998 by Paternoster Press, an imprint of Paternoster Publishing, P. O. Box 300, Carlisle, Cumbria, CA3 0QS, U.K. This edition is published by agreement with Paternoster Press. In relation to the UK edition, the right of Stuart Murray to be identified as the Author of this Work has been asserted by him in accordance with the Copyright, Designs and Patents Act 1988.

To order or request information, please call 1-800-245-7894 or visit www.heraldpress.com.

To my parents,
Norman and Hazel Murray

CONTENTS

FOREWORD

I like to read sailing books by people who have circumnavigated the globe; I prefer history from the pen of eyewitnesses who participated when the tide turned for a nation; and I want to read church planting books by people who have been down the alleyways of neopagan Western society and know what it means to call together a new body of believers in Jesus Christ. Although he brings the discipline of scholarly reflection to his discussion of witness, Stuart Murray is no armchair church planter. Having given primary leadership to an innovative and thriving new church in culturally diverse East London, Murray went on to become teacher, coach, and mentor to a generation of church planters in England and beyond.

What an array of skills and experiences he brings to the task! Trained first as a lawyer, Murray tracks clues and arguments through to logical and satisfying conclusion. Still bearing the spiritual battle scars of a frontline church planter, he brings a generous dose of realism to his observations. Having drawn from the Anabaptist stream of church renewal for much of his own theological framework, he also incorporates insights from church planters and theologians in a wide range of denominations.

Those who meet Murray notice his gentle, unpretentious personality—and discover that he writes in the same understated style. So much dust and noise have issued from our generation's wrestling with church planting that mere mention of the term elicits response ranging from sneezing to louder drumbeating. In his measured yet passionate way, Murray looks at church planting from theological, biblical, historical, and structural perspectives. He is critical but not cynical, seeking out the thread of truth in almost any church planting strategy. Deeply committed to speaking the gospel, he also has a keen eye to spot naïve or manipulative approaches that have discredited church planting in some circles.

Church planters seeking a bag of tricks or sure-fire strategies for quick results will need to look elsewhere. This is a well-seasoned volume of ecclesiology, not a how-to manual. The title of the book includes the words "laying foundations," and indeed this volume addresses the kinds of issues that often are under the surface in church planting. Murray insists, for example, that mission is more about the kingdom of God than about the church. This perspective points the reader to Jesus, who modeled the startling reversals of economic, social, and political power that come with the kingdom. Mere ticket-to-eternity evangelism will not be very satisfying to people who get a wholistic view of the kingdom in the Sermon on the Mount. The treatment of foundational concepts of mission is what will make this book valuable both for church planters and for people who simply care about keeping any congregation or denomination on strong footing.

Daughter congregations often transform the mother church, and well-established churches that engage questions raised by this book will experience creative change. Multivoiced worship, commitment to social concerns, leadership training, gender roles, and other topics Murray addresses are urgent agenda for most congregations, whether newer or older.

Most churches in Western society witness in a context of astounding cultural and ethnic diversity. If sometimes hostile to the gospel, our diverse world also creates opportunity for something new. The gospel of Jesus Christ is radically different from the values and belief systems of the Western world. It will take more than individuals to penetrate and transform society with the good news of the resurrection; it will require new communities empowered by the Holy Spirit. Like colonies of resident aliens returning back from God's future, church plants will continue to embody and proclaim the healing, empowerment, forgiveness, and liberation that come with the kingdom of God. Stuart Murray has been an ambassador of this good news, and his reflections on church planting will serve God's people well.

—*J. Nelson Kraybill*
  President, Associated Mennonite Biblical Seminary
  Elkhart, Indiana

PREFACE

*D*escribing his church planting ministry, the apostle Paul writes,

> "I planted the seed, Apollos watered it, but God made it grow. . . . For we are God's fellow-workers; you are God's field, God's building. By the grace God has given me, I laid a foundation as an expert builder, and someone else is building on it. But each one should be careful how he builds. For no-one can lay any foundation other than the one already laid, which is Jesus Christ."[1]

Mixing his metaphors, Paul speaks of the church in Corinth as both a field and a building. Church planters are co-workers with God, planting seeds from which churches grow and laying foundations on which they are built. God is the life source of these churches. Jesus Christ is their foundation. Other workers, like Apollos, water the seed which has been planted and build on the foundations which have been laid. The role of the church planter is to ensure that good seed has been sown and firm foundations laid.

Church planting involves laying foundations. The quality of these foundations has profound implications for what can be built on them. Strong and secure foundations provide the basis for healthy churches and effective mission. Weak and inadequate foundations jeopardize these prospects. Enthusiasm alone is not enough. Nor is slavish dependence on guidelines in training manuals any guarantee of success. Effective church planting, according to Paul, requires the grace of God, appropriate expertise and considerable care.

And the practice of church planting itself requires foundations. Why do we need to plant churches in Western societies[2] at the beginning of the twenty-first century? What theological and biblical foundations undergird this practice? How does church planting relate to the mission of the churches in a postmodern and pluralistic culture? What kinds of churches should we plant? What strategies and methods are appropriate?

This book is not a training manual. It does not engage with all the practicalities of church planting. But it is written for practitioners rather than theorists. Nor is it intended to be unduly prescriptive about the kinds of churches that need to be planted. It contains many questions and considers various possible answers. What it does attempt to do is to lay some theological foundations for church planting, to invite church planters to think seriously about missiology and ecclesiology, to reflect on their assumptions and expectations, and to take care that they lay strong foundations for the churches they are planting.

I am grateful to people who read draft versions of sections of this book and whose comments helped me to sharpen my thinking and clarify what I was trying to communicate: Arthur Rowe, John Colwell, Peter Stevenson, Peter Brierley, Iain Clark, John Treby, Keith Neville, Helen Wordsworth, and Paul Whiting. I am particularly grateful to my secretary, Elaine Newey, for her patient help proofreading and checking the text.

Many of the ideas contained in this book were refined in the crucible of thoughtful and sometimes animated discussion with students of the Spurgeon's/Oasis Church Planting and Evangelism course over the past eight years. To these students and others like them, who are committed to the task of planting the kinds of churches that will be good news in contemporary society, I offer what follows as a stimulus to further debate and to courageous and creative initiatives.

—Stuart Murray
    London, England

CHURCH
PLANTING

1. CHURCH PLANTING: LISTENING TO THE CRITICS

*T*here are many reasons *not* to plant churches at the beginning of the twenty-first century. This is not immediately apparent from the plethora of conferences, books, and strategies advocating church planting as a crucial component in evangelistic strategies associated with the year 2000. Many local churches have not been involved in church planting within living memory. Until recently, most denominations have been more concerned with reorganization and survival than with establishing new churches.

Not surprisingly, there has been a need to enthuse about church planting, to promote this strategy, and to draw attention to successful examples. Such advocacy of church planting has been effective. Church planting policies, strategies, and targets have been adopted by many denominations and church networks. Thousands of new churches have been planted, and many more are planned. The language of church planting has become familiar and the practice has achieved respectability.

But not everyone is fully persuaded. Critics of church planting have voiced various objections. Some are opposed to any church planting, regarding this as no more than the latest ecclesiastical bandwagon. Others welcome church planting in principle, but are concerned about some of the strategies being adopted, or about the priority given to church planting over other dimensions of mission and ministry. And there are a growing number who have been actively involved in church planting ventures, where they encountered unexpected problems, who are now more cautious.

It is tempting to ignore or dismiss these objections and concerns. Policies embracing church planting have only recently been adopted. Church planting initiatives are in their infancy. Many opportunities for church planting have been identified. And for thousands of churches, the issue of church planting is not even on the agenda. Much more advocacy and encouragement is needed, if the trickle of church planting that has become a stream is to develop into the flood that many believe is vital, if our society is to be effectively evangelized. Surely this is not the time to become immured in arguments about the validity of the strategy, or to examine too closely situations where difficulties have impeded or thwarted the establishment of new congregations? Indeed, some of these arguments *cannot* be effectively answered until more time has elapsed and the impact of church planting policies and initiatives can be assessed.

In fact, in most of the literature, at conferences, and in serious conversations about church planting, consideration *is* given to such concerns and criticisms. Integrity demands this, and even the most ardent advocates of church planting acknowledge that indeed there are problems and issues to be faced, locally and at a strategic level. Seminars have explored practical difficulties, such as maintaining momentum after the initial enthusiasm has waned, strained relationships between planting churches and planted churches, and decisions about buildings. Most books about church planting consider familiar objections and offer practical advice and encouragement to those who are grappling with the realities of establishing new congregations. Those in the forefront of what is becoming a church planting movement are not theorists, but experienced practitioners, who are aware of the struggles and setbacks involved.

But are the objections and criticisms being taken seriously enough? Is the concern to motivate and mobilize precluding this? In the final years of the twentieth century, did the pressure of attaining goals which had been set in relation to what could be accomplished by the year 2000 squeeze out careful reflection on important issues that could affect the future of church planting for many years into this new century?

If one reason for not taking the objections too seriously is concern lest the wheels might come off a bandwagon that has only just begun to roll, another reason may be suspicion about the presuppositions and priorities of those raising the objections. Who is opposed to church planting, and why?

Some object to church planting because they object to evangelism. Some are so locked into a maintenance mentality that they cannot relate to the idea of establishing new congregations. Some are protecting vested interests or denominational loyalties at the expense of those who are beyond the churches. Some are appalled at the risks involved and have frankly lost their nerve. Some continue

equate church planting with erecting new church buildings and be-
moan the resources required for this.

These are *bad* reasons for not planting churches at the beginning
of this new century. If this is all the objections amount to, the church
planting movement will not want to spend too much time or energy
responding to its detractors and critics.

But this is not all that the objections amount to, nor do many of
the most significant concerns and criticisms come from such sources.
There are advocates and practitioners of church planting who are
dissatisfied with the hype, unrealistic expectations, and glib answers
sometimes associated with church planting conferences. And there
are those who, having been involved in church planting which has
not been effective, have questions to ask and concerns to raise.

I should identify my own stance rather than hiding behind anonymous critics. I have been involved in church planting in various ways
for most of the past two decades: establishing a church in East London that now has three congregations; participating in a failed attempt to plant a church in another part of London; acting as a consultant to numerous church planting initiatives; directing the first university accredited course in the United Kingdom for training church
planters; overseeing students in church planting placements; and
developing church planting teams. I am committed to church planting as an important contribution to the mission of the church. I am
grateful for the creativity, faith, perseverance, and resourcefulness I
have encountered among church planters. I believe new churches
are needed to incarnate the gospel into twenty-first-century society.

But I have concerns about the ways we are planting churches,
the kinds of churches we are planting, and especially about the lack
of theological reflection among church planters. I want to voice these
concerns and engage in reflection, not because I am disillusioned
about church planting, but because I believe it is vital and that we
can do it more effectively.

I am troubled by the many conversations I have had with men
and women involved in church plants that are struggling, failing to
thrive, or on the point of closing. I regularly receive telephone calls
from people I have never met, desperate for help in situations where
church planting seems to have turned sour. Many of these situations
exhibit very similar characteristics. Some can be saved, others cannot. Most have encountered difficulties related to unclear vision, in-
secure foundations, unrealistic expectations, inadequate leadership,

limited training, and lack of ongoing supervision. I am concerned about the pastoral implications of church planting "failures." I am also concerned about the mission implications of some apparent church planting successes.

I recognize that there is no foolproof way of planting churches, that there are remarkable success stories that defy human explanation, and that some initiatives that seemed bound to thrive have foundered. I do not want to remove the mystery from church planting nor reduce it to formulas. Indeed, overemphasis on methodology may contribute to failure in some situations. But there is enough contemporary church planting experience now available to engage in preventive rather than remedial treatment of church planting that is unlikely to flourish. There are ways not to plant churches!

My intention is not to engage at this very practical level, since several books already provide helpful counsel on these issues.[1] Instead, I want to explore some of the theological, missiological, and ecclesiological issues raised by church planting. We will return to questions of methodology at the end of the book, but not until we have examined more fundamental issues. I suspect many practical difficulties encountered in church planting are actually symptoms of underlying weaknesses in direction and strategy. I also believe that, measured against theological and missiological criteria we will consider in subsequent chapters, many church planting situations that seem successful may in fact be less effective than they appear.

My aim is to construct a theological framework for church planting that will provide a more secure foundation for action, and a more sensitive basis for evaluation and planning, than currently appear to be available. A useful starting point may be sympathetic consideration of some objections to church planting.

Objections to church planting arise from three main sources: members of a local church that is considering planting a new church; leaders of another local church in the vicinity of a proposed church plant; and representatives of the wider church who are concerned about certain aspects of church planting as a policy, rather than about a specific venture. The concerns raised overlap sufficiently to allow us to consider them together, rather than under separate headings, but some are more sharply focused at the local level, whereas others relate to strategic issues.

Our concern here is to listen carefully to these objections, assess their significance, and consider their implications for church planting. No doubt many others have engaged in this kind of listening process, but adequate documentation of the discussion appears to be missing from church planting literature. What is apparent is a degree of frustration on both sides. Advocates of church planting are wary of being distracted from their vision and task by objections with which they have little patience. Critics of church planting are irritated that their concerns are not being taken seriously or that their motives are being questioned. This is fertile ground for caricature, polarization, and entrenchment.

A common perception of church planters is that they are activists and entrepreneurs—not personalities who find it easy to engage with objections and concerns that might distract them from tasks they are single-mindedly pursuing. Their response may be similar to that of Nehemiah, who retorted repeatedly to his critics, "I am carrying on a great project and cannot go down. Why should the work stop while I leave it and go down to you?" (Neh. 6:3). The context indicates that these critics were making mischief and that Nehemiah's response was entirely appropriate.

But not all criticism is so motivated and not all should be so easily dismissed. There are other biblical incidents where critics played an invaluable role in helping trailblazers assess their activities and improve their effectiveness. Jethro's advice to Moses (Exod. 18:17-23) to delegate some of his work significantly reduced the waiting time for judicial decisions and arguably saved Moses from burnout.

The church planting movement needs to listen to its critics. Whether such critics are friendly or hostile, we need to heed their concerns and weigh their comments carefully. Almost invariably there are elements of truth and value even in arguments that may be untenable as a whole. Effective church planting does need entrepreneurs who will not be distracted or bogged down in endless discussions. But it also requires people capable of strategic thinking, theological reflection, and contextual awareness, all of which might be enhanced by engagement with critics.

Objections to church planting are many and varied, but we will concentrate on three of the main objections rather than undertaking an exhaustive treatment. Our aim is to identify their underlying assumptions and explore their implications. We will take very seriously the concerns contained within these objections and assess whether the objections can be answered without abandoning church planting as a contemporary mission strategy. In the course of this discussion, we will discover many issues that will be explored in greater detail throughout this book. Our intention is not to provide a thorough refutation of the objections and so defend the policy of church planting. We will suggest that none of these objections, alone or in combination, provide convincing reasons to abandon church planting. But they do raise vital questions which, if ignored, may significantly diminish the effectiveness of church planting initiatives.

***Objection 1*: There are enough churches already. We should concentrate on improving existing churches rather than planting new churches.**

This apparently straightforward objection contains several issues that need to be identified and evaluated. There is no doubt that there are very many churches in those nations where Christianity has long been established, whether we calculate the number of church buildings or use the more relevant measure of the number of congregations. Indeed, it is arguable that in the current spiritual and sociological climate there may be too many churches.

Figures for England exemplify this. The 1989 English Church Census[2] counted nearly 39,000 churches in England. Those responsible for this census were aware of other groups they had not located (primarily recently formed congregations or congregations without their own buildings). The true figure was probably closer to 40,000 churches. In the United Kingdom as a whole, a figure of 50,000 is indicated in the *UK Christian Handbook*. Are more churches really needed?

But, impressive though this figure looks, there were rather fewer churches in 1989 than there had been in 1979 or 1969. Since church attendance and church membership have been declining over recent decades,[3] it is not surprising that some congregations have ceased to function and many church buildings have been closed. It has seemed sensible to combine parishes, amalgamate congregations, reduce the number of paid church staff, and dispose of unwanted premises. This process has been necessary as churches of all denominations have been forced to come to terms with the end of Christendom,[4] where church attendance was culturally normal, albeit not as extensive as sometimes assumed, and the emergence of a post-Christian society where it is not. The closure and disposal or demolition of church buildings acts as a salutary reminder that previous generations of church planters enthusiastically erected too many buildings, some never effectively used.[5]

The still large number of existing churches, the continuing experience of declining attendance and church membership, and the harsh realities of life in a post-Christian culture, all lend weight to the argument that establishing more churches is an unwise policy. The alternative option of attempting to make more effective use of existing resources may be regarded as a wiser policy than spreading these resources more thinly. The response of the church planting movement to this objection is twofold.

First, church planting is predicated not on a history of decline but on expectations of growth. Planting thousands of new churches in a situation of continuing decline manifestly does not make sense and will sooner or later stretch resources past breaking point. But planting new churches in a situation where the decline has stopped or will shortly stop—to be replaced by steady or rapid growth—is vital. If the number of church attenders increases, more churches will be needed to replace those that have closed during the decades of decline. Many would go farther, arguing that planting new churches is proactive rather than reactive, that establishing new congregations is a way to attract new church members and reverse the trend of decline. But the essential point is that church planting assumes a context of growth rather than decline in church attendance.

Second, what is important is not how many churches there are but whether they are in the right places. Population shifts, new housing developments, changes in transport systems, and various other factors mean that some churches are now poorly located and appear to have little future where they are, and some areas of the country are effectively devoid of local churches. Even if it were conceded that there are enough churches in absolute terms, church planting would still be necessary to address these locational issues. Few of those who object to church planting oppose the establishing of new congregations in areas where there is clearly no local church of any description. What is much more contentious is the establishing of new churches in areas where there are already churches.

But advocates of church planting need to reflect carefully on this matter of how many churches are needed. It should be candidly acknowledged that current initiatives to plant thousands of new churches are ill-conceived unless these are accompanied by a significant reversal of the decades of decline that have characterized Christianity in many Western nations this century. There is no empirical evidence to support such an expectation at present.[6] There are many signs of renewed interest in spirituality, but in a post-Christian society the churches are not often perceived as having much to contribute in this area.

Furthermore, even where spiritual interest leads to Christian faith, "believing without belonging" is common,[7] which might suggest the need for evangelistic strategies which are less dependent on people joining churches. Wariness about belonging to institutions is not restricted to the churches. In a postmodern environment, many organizations, including political parties, trade unions, voluntary agencies, and other religious groups struggle to gain and retain the allegiance of members, especially where allegiance requires regular attendance. Church planting is attempting to "buck a sociological trend."[8]

Objectors are right to argue that for current and projected church attendance figures there are sufficient churches, even if some are in the wrong locations. Relocation rather than increased numbers is a more appropriate strategy. So on what grounds are contemporary church planting strategies based, which advocate planting thousands of new churches? Presumably, a conviction that there will be a reversal of the trend and that thousands of new churches will be needed for tens or hundreds of thousands of new Christians. And the conviction that church planting itself has a dynamic that will contribute toward the trend reversal that is needed.

In a nation where a significant percentage of the population does not attend church, it is easy to argue there is plenty of room for more churches. But planting new churches on the basis of this argument is only valid if either the spiritual climate changes and enough nonattenders decide to attend church to justify planting more churches, or the planting of new churches will attract those who do not attend existing churches. Both propositions depend on faith convictions rather than empirical evidence, and the latter requires that new kinds of churches are planted, rather than more of the same kind.

Advocates of church planting may point to the experience of some nations where vibrant church planting strategies have coincided with, responded to, or acted as catalysts for significant increases in the number of people becoming Christians and joining the churches. But there is no guarantee that a similar strategy will achieve comparable results in every situation. As we will argue later, other spiritual and/or sociological factors may have been involved in these contexts.

None of this is sufficient to justify abandonment of strategies to plant new churches. But the objection helps to clarify the basis on which such strategies must operate: a basis of faith rather than statistics, of expectation rather than recent history. This is an acceptable basis for church policies to rest on, provided it is acknowledged for what it is. There are sufficient churches in most Western nations at present for the churchgoing population—in fact, too many—and thus the objection contains a valid assessment of the status quo. But this does not invalidate the adoption of church planting policies designed to provoke or respond to changes in the situation.

A further issue raised within this objection is that attention should be given to improving the quality of life and witness in existing churches rather than establishing new churches. The energy and resources required to plant new congregations, it is argued, could be more effectively invested in renewing and strengthening churches that are struggling. These churches usually already have a profile in their local community; buildings; a congregation; financial resources; and the general infrastructure of church life. Surely it would be more sensible to build on these existing foundations rather than starting all over again?

Responses to this argument from those advocating church planting include assessments of such churches that are often blunt rather than diplomatic. The very features that might be regarded as advantages are sadly often the reasons why no amount of investment of energy and personnel will achieve the wanted goals. Many struggling churches face inadequate or inappropriate buildings, indebtedness, poor community relations, debilitating traditions, intransigent leaders, and low morale. The loyalty and perseverance of members of these congregations may be undeniable, but attempts to prolong the life of such churches may be based more on sentimentality and a maintenance orientation than on seeking first the kingdom of God and reaching out effectively in mission to the surrounding community. A dismissive but expressive summary of the options is that "it is easier to have babies than to raise the dead!"[9]

However, advocates of church planting do not conclude that it is always preferable to start new churches. Each church and community should be carefully and prayerfully examined. In some situations there may be so many drawbacks with existing churches that planting a new church seems the only feasible way forward. In others, an existing church may be an appropriate base for mission, and investing personnel and resources there could be the wiser strategy. Church planting literature does include consideration of these scenarios, with two kinds of remedial action recommended for working with existing churches.

Planting by adoption requires a local church with sufficient resources to adopt a struggling church and work with its leaders and members to strengthen its life and witness. This may involve varying degrees of restructuring, the transfer of people from the stronger church, and sometimes temporary or permanent loss of independence for the adopted church. Much depends on the readiness of the adopted church to embrace changes.[10]

Replanting involves one or more individuals—rather than another local church—committing to a struggling church with a view to renewing its ministry and witness. This strategy is not an easy option. Indeed, it may be harder work than establishing a new church. But there do seem to be individuals who are gifted for such an approach and able to work through the difficulties involved.[11]

Thus, planting new churches and renewing existing ones should not be seen as competitive but complementary approaches. There are mission opportunities that will be more appropriately seized by employing one or other of these strategies. Within the churches are people whose calling, gifts, and personality may be better suited for either option. But, just as church planting should not normally be undertaken without careful research into the community into which planting is to take place, so those considering adoption or replanting should investigate carefully whether there are sufficient positive features in the situation to justify the investment that will be required. The fact that a church exists is not enough in itself. If enthusiasm sometimes blinds those advocating church planting to the realities of a situation, sentimentality may equally obscure the view of those advocating the investment of further resources in existing churches.

Furthermore, in linking together the number of churches required and the issue of what to do with existing churches that are struggling, the objection helps focus attention on something that is generally neglected within church planting policies: *church pruning*. In the current context, where most church planting ventures are initiated by local churches, rather than resulting from regional or denominational policies, such neglect is unsurprising. It is neither appropriate nor feasible for one local church to advocate the closure of another. But, as we will argue,[12] a more strategic approach to church planting is needed, that does not rely so heavily on local church initiatives, and in that context the contentious issue of closing existing churches as well as opening new churches needs to be addressed, if the available resources are to be effectively deployed. Adopting a church planting policy without an accompanying church pruning policy is irresponsible.

There are good reasons for closing churches. To regard this as always indicating failure or defeat is unhelpful. None of the churches established by the apostle Paul exist today, but this invalidates neither his ministry as a church planter nor the life and witness of those churches during the years in which they operated. Whether the closure of a church is precipitated by persecution, by demographic changes, or by internal decay, the significant issue is not the perpetuation of a particular structure or organization but the provision of an effective base for mission and ministry in a community.

Attempting to prolong indefinitely the life of a church that is no longer able to provide such a base is akin to keeping on a life support machine a patient in a persistent vegetative state with no hope of recovery. Euthanasia may be problematic in the case of human lives, but it should be regarded as a sensible policy for churches, since all that will "die" is a structure.

There is a fundamental issue underlying this objection and responses to it. How can the mission of the church in contemporary society be accomplished? If this mission can be accomplished through the churches that already exist, then church planting is unnecessary. But if this is not feasible, because of the location of these churches, their inability to communicate with the surrounding community, or simply because there are not enough of them, then church planting is crucial.

However, simply planting churches of the kind we already have is not the answer. Churches have been leaking hundreds of members each week for many years. Planting more of these churches is not a mission strategy worth pursuing. But planting new kinds of churches may be a key to effective mission and a catalyst for the renewal of existing churches.

Objection 2: Church planting weakens the mission and ministry of the churches by dividing their resources and minimizing their impact.

As with the previous objection, this statement contains several related issues that we will explore in turn. It challenges the claim made by advocates of church planting: that establishing new congregations tends to increase the impact of the church on society. It questions the assertion that church planting makes more effective use of the gifts of church members. The underlying concern is that church planting may hinder rather than enhance the ability of churches to engage effectively in ministry and mission.

Within the church planting movement, the conviction is strongly held that planting more congregations will enable churches to impact the surrounding community more effectively. Advocates argue that locating churches closer to where people live will make them more accessible, that new churches offer fresh opportunities to people who have not found existing churches attractive, and that new churches tend to be more outward-looking and welcoming to newcomers. "More effective penetration of the parish" is the predominant reason for planting new Anglican churches in Britain, according to a recent report.[13] More churches, newer churches, more local churches, churches that are community-based and community-focused are expected to have greater impact than churches which have been part of the landscape for many years and which do not appear to have achieved the level of penetration hoped for.

Many examples can be given where church planting does seem to have accomplished this. Growth in numbers has not simply been by transfer from other churches, but by the addition of people coming to faith for the first time and others (quite a significant proportion) renewing their commitment to Christ and his church.[14] In some cases, the planting church has found that it has gained within months as many new members as it has given up to a church planting venture, so that church planting has not divided resources but has resulted in a significant net gain. The initial weakening was a step of faith that has resulted in strengthening and enlargement. Church planting may also enable a church to reach a segment of the local community that it had been unable to break into through other forms of outreach. In these ways, and others, church planting can increase the impact of a church and help its mission.

However, this is not always the outcome of church planting. Examples can also be given where there has been little or no growth, where the impact on the target community has been negligible, and where the effect on the planting church has been negative. There are situations where a relatively strong and healthy church has planted a new congregation that has failed to thrive and where, two or three years later, there are fewer people in the two congregations than there were in the original congregation.

There are situations where the success of a church plant has been detrimental to the church which planted it. What happened was that those with energy, vision, and enthusiasm established a vibrant new congregation, leaving the original church struggling to recover and feeling second-rate.

And there are other situations which *appear* to be successful, in that the new church has grown numerically and thrived in many ways, but where closer investigation reveals that this growth has not been from the target community and that the kind of church planted is alien to that community. "Successful" church planting may not actually enhance the impact of the church in the community with which it is trying to engage.

Again, we encounter the question of what kind of church is planted and how this relates to the culture, needs, and aspirations of unchurched people. The establishing of congregations that are very similar to existing churches may be effective in certain communities, but such planting is unlikely to enable the church to impact communities that are distant in culture and ethos from those churches. Since much church planting is currently restricted to areas where the churches are already doing well, establishing new congregations may increase the impact of the church in these areas, but it will not enable the church to penetrate areas of society where its impact has been historically weak.

Strategically, this may have serious implications. Church planting may increase the presence of the church in communities where it is already well-established (not in itself a negative result), but at the expense of further endorsing the popular image of the church as belonging to a certain culture and class. This may have the unintended consequence of hindering the mission of the church in communities where it is already regarded as an alien institution.

Most church planting currently is taking place in the more comfortable parts of society. Some of this is enabling the church to reach these areas more effectively; some of it is merely redistributing comfortable Christians. But the impact on other parts of society, where the church is already weak, is minimal and may even be counterproductive as the church increases its profile in comfortable areas and so seems less relevant than ever to many urban and rural communities.

One major exception to this trend is the planting, in many Western cities, of new ethnic churches. Growth within these churches has often been rapid, even spectacular, and many of them are located in areas of the country where few other churches are thriving. This is a significant and encouraging development, which we will examine in more detail in a later chapter.[15]

However, most of these churches are comprised of people from one ethnic group, and the ability of these churches to penetrate other communities is as yet uncertain. It is not impossible that in some cities what was once regarded as a "white man's religion" may soon be regarded as the preserve of African and Caribbean communities. The impact of this form of church planting may, therefore, also be mixed, alienating some while attracting and nurturing others.

Another dimension of the issue of a church's impact on society is size. Church planting, by its very nature, at least in the initial stage, reduces the size of participating churches. A church with 150 members may be replaced by two churches, one with 50 members and one with 100 members. Although this may enable the church to penetrate the local community more thoroughly, some have expressed concern lest the public profile of the church be minimized. Larger churches have a louder voice in the community, can organize events on a grander scale, and can initiate projects that smaller churches would balk at.

We will return in a later chapter[16] to this issue of church size and the effects of size on the nature and ministry of churches. The point here is that small local churches have a different kind of impact on the community than larger churches with a town center or regional profile. Church planting may either increase or diminish the overall impact of the church, but it will tend to affect the nature of this impact.

A related but distinct issue is the division of resources church planting requires. Running two congregations necessitates a degree of duplication in many aspects of church life, such as public ministry, administration, finance, and leadership. At the most basic level, two guitarists or pianists, two overhead projectors or sets of hymn books, and twice as many elders' or deacons' meetings are needed. The amount of time, energy, and money spent on such activities or equipment could have been invested in other ways, arguably more effectively. Despite an avowed intention to be mission-oriented, a new church may find that many of its members are tied up running the church rather than reaching out to the local community. Church planting may result in twice as many church members being immersed in church administration as previously.

This can be a serious problem in church planting, as groups with the best of intentions become enmeshed in organizing a new congregation and lose their vision for mission. Not all new churches are evangelistic. Some that are lose this dimension within six months as the organization takes over. To some extent, this is an issue that can be addressed by careful planning and wise leadership, and by streamlining the way in which the new church operates, but setting up a new church will inevitably involve giving time to internal arrangements that might otherwise have been spent in building relationships or engaging in mission beyond the church.

Advocates of church planting who acknowledge this as a problem argue, however, that it is more than offset by the tendency of church planting to motivate and mobilize church members to do more than they were in the planting church. The duplication of needs is also a duplication of opportunities, enabling people to discover gifts and make contributions not previously required. Church planting challenges and enables those who were underemployed to find a role within the church and exercise a ministry in the new situation.

This operates in two ways. People establishing a new church gain responsibilities they would not have had in a more settled situation and exercise faith in new ways. And people remaining in the planting church take on responsibilities laid down by those who have left, growing into tasks they would not have considered themselves competent to do while someone seemingly more able was around.

This is, without doubt, a frequent experience in church planting and one that most would broadly welcome as a further move toward the ministry of the whole people of God. Church planting can unblock congregations where limited job opportunities and leadership bottlenecks have caused frustration and restricted the development of gifts and ministries.

But we need to register concerns about the quality of such ministries, the demands on church members, and the focus of this activity. The proliferation of congregations may result in willing volunteers being asked to function in areas where they are neither competent nor confident. In church planting, the mentality often appears to be "all hands on deck," with people taking on responsibilities (from preaching to pastoral care to leading worship) for which they have neither experience nor ability. This may result in stress for the volunteers, low quality of ministry for the church, and general dissatisfaction. Inadequate pastoral care, uninspiring preaching, and inefficient administration sadly afflict many new churches. If church planting is to result in effective mission and ministry, more attention needs to be given to training and equipping participants, even if this means it takes longer to plant better churches. The mobilization of more church members is not an automatic blessing.

Such mobilization may also place unhelpful strains on people who are already under pressure in family and work environments. Planting new churches is demanding, and this should not be obscured by the vision and enthusiasm that often energizes participants in the early stages. Unless a new church grows reasonably quickly and attracts others who can share in the work (rather than those who will place further demands on the founding members[17]), the pressure on those who have taken on responsibilities in the new church can become intense. There is no easy answer to this, but it must be taken seriously if casualties are to be prevented.

Perhaps a limited time commitment should be required, rather than an indefinite sense of obligation, with an escape route if it becomes clear things are not progressing as hoped. Perhaps the popular model of planting independent churches should be reconsidered in favor of the less popular practice of establishing networks of interdependent congregations, where resources can be shared and pressures eased, and where some unnecessary duplication is removed.

The objection, as it stands, is overstated and untenable. Planting new churches often results in a release of energy and the multiplication of ministry. It may significantly increase the resources available and the impact on the surrounding community. But the objection does draw attention to some concerns that will be familiar to many who have been involved in church planting. It invites consideration of the models of church planting being employed, the importance of preparation and training, the balance between internal activity and mission beyond the church, and the very significant demands on those involved in church planting.

***Objection 3:* Church planting has become an end in itself rather than a means to an end. It has distorted the biblical understanding of the mission of the church.**

In his foreword to a recent book on church planting,[18] Nigel Wright commented facetiously that the Christian world is divided between those who think church planting is a good idea and those who are actually doing it. In fact, as he would no doubt acknowledge, the situation is somewhat more complex. Some sections of the church are blissfully unaware of church planting. Some, as we have seen, express concerns and objections. Some may already regard church planting as passé and be more interested in other mission strategies.

But there are fears within some sections of the church that advocates of church planting are wanting this subject to dominate the agenda. The charge potentially contained within this objection is that such dominance would be unhelpful and would result in other aspects of mission being marginalized. Church planting, it is argued, instead of being one means of fulfilling some aspects of the mission of the church, can acquire a status that is unwarranted and even unbiblical.

We touched on this issue in the previous section, when we considered the tendency in some new churches for mission to be neglected in favor of "doing church." Church planting does not ensure that the churches planted will be any more successful in avoiding self-absorption and a maintenance mentality than other churches.

Indeed, the challenge of constructing a new church may lead to church planting teams being more "churchy" than the members of the church from which they came. Not all church planting is motivated by evangelistic aims, but even that which is can find itself diverted into reinventing and perfecting internal church structures and activities. And churches that decide to plant a new congregation may invest so much energy and creativity in this venture that the ongoing mission of the planting church is threatened. Church planting has the potential to be a significant hindrance to evangelism, social action, and other aspects of the mission of the church.

Perhaps the best safeguard against this tendency is to insist that the planting of a new church is not an end in itself but a means to an end, or that the establishing of a new congregation is a penultimate rather than ultimate goal. Questions can then be asked about what the new church is doing and why, about its terms of reference, and about how its ministry is evaluated. Questions can also be raised concerning the resources being invested in planting a new church and whether these might be more effectively invested in other ways of engaging in mission. The planting of thousands of new churches that are not contributing toward the fulfillment of the church's mission is not a prospect that we should welcome. There are enough moribund and introverted congregations already.

Whenever church planting becomes an end in itself, not only does the focus on mission become unclear, but other features can appear that have blighted church planting initiatives in the past. Competition, denominationalism, sheep-stealing and empire-building have been some of the less welcome accompaniments of church planting. In *Transforming Mission*, his magisterial work on mission through the past twenty centuries, David Bosch identifies *plantatio ecclesiae* (church planting) as a legitimate missionary motive but cautions against it becoming the predominant aim. He writes, in relation to nineteenth century developments, that

> there was something incongruous about the heavy emphasis on church planting as the goal of missions . . . the church had, in a sense, ceased to point to God or to the future; instead it was pointing to itself. Mission was the road from the institutional church to the church that still had to be instituted. . . . The relationship of these churches to society and to the wider ecumenical and eschatological horizons was largely ignored.[19]

A welcome feature of the contemporary church planting movement is its cooperative spirit. So much church planting in the past has been fragmented and competitive, that it is a cause for celebration that many contemporary church planting initiatives have been inclusive, consultative, and complementary. Through national gatherings, regional planning groups, and local consultations, attempts have been made to work together rather than in isolation and to set local ventures into a broader framework.

Accusations that church planting is antagonistic to ecumenical development[20] are increasingly hard to substantiate—unless ecumenism is understood very woodenly in terms of official structures rather than developing friendship and cooperation. Indeed, since church plants often have more in common with church plants from other denominations than with longer-established churches of their own denomination, the proliferation of new churches has the potential to erode denominational distinctives and to produce a grassroots ecumenicity that may be quite chaotic but may also achieve more than a hundred official unity commissions.

If one aspect of the mission of the church is to pray and work toward the unity for which Jesus prayed in John 17, so that the world might see the reality of God's love expressed in the love of God's people for one another, then church planting may have a contribution to make to ecumenical progress as well as to evangelistic potency.[21]

However, not all church planting in recent years has been carried out in this spirit. There are many churches and church leaders who have been hurt deeply by the attitudes and activities of insensitive church planters. Sometimes consultation has not taken place. Sometimes it has been nominal and an occasion for criticism and dismissive comments. Sometimes objections and concerns have not been taken seriously. Church planting has at times been divisive, imperialistic, and antagonistic. Expanding the number of outlets of a particular brand of church has taken precedence over careful assessment of strategic considerations. However this is justified, questions remain about motivation and long-term efficacy.

Church planting operates well when the focus is not on planting new churches *per se* but on fulfilling the mission of the church or, better still, participating in the mission of God. Planting a new church is then not self-evidently the correct policy, but one of a number of possible methods of fulfilling some aspect of that mission. This objection contains an important warning: considered in isolation, church planting can attain an unhelpful status and discourage engagement with the scope and complexity of mission in contemporary society.

Church planting initiatives need to be evaluated in the light of a strategic consideration of the context within which they are being proposed and the steps that need to be taken to address its diverse mission needs. Planting a new church may be the crucial means of addressing those needs, a significant step alongside other initiatives, a necessary first step but only the first step, or even a step in the wrong direction. Setting church planting initiatives within the framework of a strategic discussion of mission is vital.

In the next two chapters we argue that church planting also needs to be set within a biblical and theological framework. In some recent church planting literature, the scope and level of theological discussion and engagement with biblical teaching has been disappointing. Responding to the objection we are considering here requires advocates of church planting to move beyond selected proof-texts and develop a hermeneutically responsible and theologically coherent framework for the practice they are advocating. Our intention in the

next chapter is to sketch out theological perspectives that might contribute toward construction of such a framework. This framework is
not intended to minimize the significance of church planting but to
clarify the role of church planting within a theological understanding
of mission.

Nevertheless, some advocates of church planting may be suspicious of what appears to be theoretical discussion. Would setting
church planting more explicitly into such a theological framework
result in more or fewer churches being planted? For some advocates
of church planting, this has been the main concern when theological
issues have been raised. The answer may be that both more and
fewer churches will be planted. Some attempts to plant a new church
may be reevaluated or abandoned in the light of questions about ultimate mission goals. In other situations, a deeper understanding of
theological priorities may lead to church planting initiatives. But the
way in which this question is phrased may betray a continuing and
dangerous obsession with church planting as the ultimate issue rather
than one means to a larger end.

The danger identified in the objection is that an exclusive focus
on church planting may distort the church's understanding of the
mission of God and its role in this. However much members of a
church planting team may acknowledge their dependence on God
and commitment to his mission as they embark on a new venture,
unless church planting is set within a broader context and theological framework of mission, there will be a persistent tendency toward
a reductionist stance that equates a successful church plant with the
fulfillment of their mission.

A nation could be covered with churches within reach of every
man, woman, and child—yet the mission of God might not have
significantly advanced. Or it might have advanced only in certain
ways, so that the result is unstable and lopsided. Success in church
planting might have been achieved at the expense of serious neglect
of other aspects of mission, or be accompanied by an evasion of the
church's prophetic role in society.

In a later chapter we will reflect on the Christianization of Europe
that followed the adoption of Christianity by the Roman emperor
Constantine and his successors. This involved the multiplication of
churches and the pervasion of Christian thinking and practices in all
areas of society. But it is arguable that what emerged was a domestication and distortion of Christianity and a distraction from the ad-

vance of the mission of God. Church proliferation and church growth are not necessarily signs of progress.

Agreement on the dimensions of the mission of God may not be easy to reach. Some will focus on sociopolitical aspects of mission and see the justice of God experienced in society as a sign of God's mission progressing. Others will look for examples of sick people receiving healing and the demonized being set free as indicators that the mission of God is being fulfilled. Concerns for peace, environmental action, human rights, liberation from oppression, material welfare, and a host of other possible dimensions of mission may be included. Still others will be wary of such an expansive agenda and will argue for evangelism as the primary mission mandate.

There is room for diversity of opinion, for the mission of God is rich and multifaceted. Not every church may wish to embrace every aspect of mission. And no local church will have the resources to engage in every area where the mission of God impacts society. What is important is that church planting be evaluated in the light of this and other theological perspectives. In what ways will the planting of a new church in a given context contribute to the advancing mission of God? In what aspects of mission will this new church engage? If a church or denomination is considering church planting as a strategy, how will this relate to other dimensions of its mission?

Church planting *may* be a significant way to advance the mission of God. It *may* help evangelism, peace making, action for justice, environmental concern, community development, social involvement, and other mission ventures. But it is likely to function in this way only if it is set within the right framework. Church planting seen as an end in itself, or simply as an evangelistic methodology, may fall short of its potential and distort our understanding of God's mission and the nature of God's kingdom, as the objection suggests.

If this happens, an opportunity will have been missed. Church planting has the capacity to recall the church to its essentially missionary character and calling, to engender creativity and fresh initiatives, and to help churches take risks and break out of a maintenance mentality. Perhaps where this objection is helpful is to remind us that this will not happen automatically and that, unless church planting is established within a more wholistic context, the planting of hundreds (or even thousands) of churches in the next few years may not mark a significant advance for the mission of God, and might even represent a setback.

2. CHURCH PLANTING:
A THEOLOGICAL FRAMEWORK

*D*uring the process of gestation that eventually resulted in this book being written, a tentative subtitle was "a theology of church planting." Such a subtitle conveys both authority and humility: authority, because this is not just a methodological treatment of a popular subject but an examination of the practice of church planting in relation to theological and biblical principles, with the implication that such principles should influence church planters; and humility, because the use of an indefinite article suggests that this is not a definitive statement of theological principles applying to church planting, but a contribution to an ongoing discussion.

As the writing continued, the dual concern to examine underlying principles and to stimulate further reflection remained, but the phrase "a theology of church planting" seemed increasingly problematic. Such phrases abound in contemporary literature, offering "a theology of" all kinds of issues. A survey of the library of Spurgeon's College, London, where I teach, revealed, among others, "a theology of the family," "a theology of professional care," "a theology of speech," "a theology of force and violence," "a theology of church growth," "a theology of death," "a theology of ministry," "a theology of work" and "a theology of pastoral care." But is this terminology legitimate or even helpful? What does this phrase actually mean? Can any and every human activity be treated in this way (a theology of adolescence, a theology of mowing the lawn, a theology of car maintenance)?

Theology refers primarily to the study of God and by extension to the activities of God within creation. Systematic theological treatises draw the boundary lines in different places and give greater or lesser attention to various components, but they typically include such foundational subjects as the Trinity, the doctrine of God, Christology, pneumatology, soteriology, epistemology, anthropology, missiology, ecclesiology, and eschatology. Theological reflection oper-

ates in two directions. Study of these central beliefs, and
text from which it is argued that they are derived, leads tc
nition of practical implications for a wide range of human activities,
relationships, and structures. Study of the context within which
human beings are set, and the challenges and struggles faced by individuals and communities, prompts renewed wrestling with the biblical text and the refining or reshaping of theological statements and
systems.

Attempts to develop "a theology of" in various disciplines are
welcome, insofar as they represent efforts to engage in theological
reflection in either or both directions and help practitioners to resist
the prevailing pragmatism of contemporary culture. But this phrase-
ology, though popular and superficially impressive, may in fact hinder such theological reflection and accord to certain structures,
methods, and activities a status that is undeserved and difficult to
challenge. The use of the phrase, "a theology of," may discourage
the creative interaction between experience, analysis, and theological reflection that is required in all areas of Christian discipleship.

Designating an approach as "a theology of" an issue may represent careful reflection on experience and an attempt to engage theologically with contemporary issues, but sometimes it is little more
than an attempt to provide theological justification (or a few biblical
proof texts) for practices or structures that are already established on
other foundations. This approach may also suggest that the topic
under consideration deserves incorporation among those things that
are of universal significance for Christians. Secondary issues may
thereby be accorded primary status.

Church planting does not generally comprise even a subsection
of systematic theological treatises. This omission may be regarded
as lamentable and interpreted as evidence that generations of theologians have been operating within a static ecclesiological context.
It may be noted as a further example of the weakness of much systematic theology in the areas of missiology and ecclesiology. Or it
may be welcomed as an opportunity to engage in theological reflection on a practice that has been, and will continue to be, significant
for the mission and renewal of the church, without the assumption
that church planting *per se* needs a theology. The static ecclesiology
and marginalization of missiology evident in much theological discussion certainly needs to be challenged, and church planting may
stimulate and guide such challenges. Within a systematic theological

treatise there may be occasions to refer to church planting to illustrate certain theological assertions. But to suggest that there is a theology of church planting is surely to confuse strategy with theology and processes with principles.

There are simple alternatives to the language of "a theology of," which avoid some of the confusion and dangers we have identified. Why not talk about "theological perspectives on," or "theological reflections on"? This is a more accurate use of language, which reserves the term *theology* for the central task of reflection on God, and encourages creativity rather than premature finality. It avoids unwarranted assumptions about the status of an issue and enables us to explore any aspect of human experience by examining it in relation to what we believe about God and to make connections between our area of interest and foundational theological principles.

In this chapter, then, we will not attempt to construct a theology of church planting but instead to reflect theologically on the practice of church planting and enquire whether there are theological perspectives that impinge on and might help guide church planting strategies and policies. This may appear to some a pedantic distinction, but there are serious implications if church planting is accorded a status that is not warranted biblically or theologically.

Church planting movements are always in danger of elevating church planting to such a status, to the detriment of other components of mission and ultimately to the detriment of church planting itself. The construction of a theology of church planting risks exacerbating this problem. Our concern rather is to set church planting within a theological framework, and to engage in theological reflection on the experience and implications of church planting.

A Theological Framework for Church Planting

Church planting can legitimately be subsumed under theological disciplines of either missiology or ecclesiology. Some instances of church planting emerge for missiological reasons, as evangelism penetrates new communities, and churches are established to nurture converts. Other church planting initiatives represent attempts to express ecclesiological convictions through the development of new kinds of churches. Where churches are planted for evangelistic reasons, theological reflection may be less evident than where ecclesiological renewal is the motivation. However, even where new kinds of churches are consciously being planted, pragmatic and cultural factors rather than theological factors may be primary.

All church planters operate within theological frameworks, but often these are assumed rather than articulated and adopted uncritically rather than as the result of reflection. Theological principles may influence strategy and practice less than unexamined tradition or innovative methodology. Some church planters are openly impatient with what they regard as theoretical considerations, and most literature on church planting contains little theological discussion.

An inadequate theological basis will not necessarily hinder short-term growth, or result in widespread heresy among newly planted churches. But it will limit the long-term impact of church planting, and may result in dangerous distortions in the way in which the mission of the church is understood. Church planting is not an end in itself, but one aspect of the mission of God in which churches are privileged to participate. We can understand the scope and implications of this mission, and the place of church planting within it, in relation to three important theological concepts.

Missio Dei

The first and fundamental theological concept is *missio Dei*. Missiologists have increasingly been drawn to this phrase to express the conviction that mission is not the invention, responsibility, or program of human beings, but flows from the character and purposes of God.[1] Historically, the term *mission* was first used by theologians to refer to the acts of God, rather than the activities of the churches. God is the Missionary, who sent his Son and sends his Spirit into the world, and whose missionary purposes are cosmic in scope, concerned with the "restoration of all things,"[2] the establishment of *shalom*, the renewal of creation, and the coming of the kingdom of God, as well as the redemption of fallen humanity and the building of the church. Mission has a trinitarian basis and is theocentric rather than anthropocentric. Mission is defined, directed, energized, and accomplished by God.

All that the church does in mission must be related to the missionary work of God. The church has a vital role in missio Dei, but it dare not allow its status as a mission agent to result in an inflated view of its own importance. The marginalization of the church in some missiological discussions does not justify the opposite imbalance, whereby the planting of churches dominates mission strategies. Dutch missiologist Hans Hoekendijk uses the phrase missio Dei in a way that seems to bypass the church and concentrate solely on God at work in the world, and he has been accused of depreciating the church as the agent of God's mission. But his warning that "church-centric missionary thinking is bound to go astray," because this represents an "illegitimate centre" for mission,[3] deserves to be taken seriously. Church planting is not an end in itself, because the church is an agent of God's mission.

For church planting this has considerable significance. First, the inevitable interest in internal church structures which characterizes church planting initiatives, as plans are developed for the formation of a new congregation, must not subvert the primary focus on the mission to which this new church is being called. Missio Dei is toward the world rather than the church. Robert Warren writes: "A church effectively engaged in mission will see that participating in the *missio Dei* will involve shifting emphasis from a focus on the life of the local church . . . to a concern for the world in its need, joys and struggles."[4]

Adequate attention to internal matters is important for the development of healthy and sustainable churches. But if this predominates, it will distract the church from its *raison d'être* and jeopardize the attainment of a church that is either healthy or sustainable.

Second, the broad scope of missio Dei must not be reduced to evangelism or church planting. Church planting is legitimate only if set within a broader mission context. Divorced from this context, church planting may represent little more than ecclesiastical expansionism. Church planting can too easily embody a limited vision of mission[5] that concentrates on one or two aspects of this mission (usually evangelism and church growth) to the neglect of other vital aspects (including working for justice and peace within society, concern for the environment, and engagement with culture). Since most church planting initiatives are currently emerging from churches and networks that already concentrate mainly on these familiar areas, church planting without theological reflection may lead to further imbalance in mission. Planting more churches with limited missiological understanding is not a helpful development.

Third, church planting shares with other aspects of mission the need for divine energy and direction. Church planting literature, conferences, and training courses have not ignored this imperative, and the experience of many churches is that planting a new church stimulates spiritual growth and deepened dependence on God. But there is a temptation in movements advocating new strategies and methodologies to focus on skills and practical issues rather than spirituality. This temptation becomes stronger as church planting attains popularity and the experience and accumulated wisdom of church planting pioneers is mediated through manuals. It is not that this experience is unhelpful (indeed, many church planters make unnecessary mistakes by failing to draw on such resources), but there is a danger of copying methods rather than recognizing principles. Methodology begins to marginalize spirituality.

If church planting is set consciously within the context of missio Dei, attention can be given to such issues as the spirituality of church planters, spiritual resources for new churches, spiritual warfare, and prayerful discernment of the purposes of God for churches and their communities. Research into demographics may be accompanied by prayer-walking;[6] strategic discussions may be informed by prophetic revelation as well as by contextual studies; and decisions to plant new churches may be prompted by an awareness of divine purpose rather than by the pressure of numerical growth on church premises.

Fourth, church planting presents an opportunity to express something of the nature of our missionary God. Church planters who reflect theologically on their mission may, for example, consciously engage in church planting as fellow workers[7] with God and with others. This may mean commitment to creativity in church planting, in the belief that the God who has created diverse profusion in the natural world is unlikely to desire monochrome uniformity in the creation of new churches. It may also underscore the teamwork which characterizes church planting initiatives. Church planting frequently involves the formation and deployment of planting teams, whose shared gifts and experiences enable new churches to be planted.

Churches that are unfamiliar with team ministry discover through church planting the benefits of teamwork and may adapt their own style of ministry as a result. Team ministry may be endorsed primarily for practical reasons, and encouragement may be drawn from New Testament examples of church planting teams,[8] but the theological basis for such teamwork is the teamwork revealed in the doctrine of the Trinity. Although Western theology generally has been weak on this issue, there has been greater emphasis recently on the "threeness" of God, who exists as eternal, relational community. Models of ministry where a single individual dominates are not just unwise pastorally and ineffective for mission. They are inconsistent with the nature and modus operandi of the God whose mission constitutes the context for all ministry. Church planting is contributing toward the rediscovery of team ministry. Setting church planting in the context of missio Dei would provide theological underpinning for the practice of team ministry embodied in many church planting initiatives.

Incarnation

A second theological principle that might helpfully undergird church planting is that of *incarnation*. If mission originates in the character and activity of God, the means by which God engages in mission are paradigmatic for those who participate in this mission. The biblical records of God's dealings with humanity reveal a startling flexibility in the divine mission, as diverse individuals, structures, models and methods are employed to advance the purposes of God. Appreciation of and reflection on this creativity and diversity might stimulate similar flexibility in planting new churches. There is no uniform approach or stereotypical strategy. Indeed, there are indications that divinely inspired initiatives that transformed one generation or one context may be inappropriate in another time or place. These serve as warnings that the mission of God cannot be reduced to a missiological manual, and will not be advanced effectively by copying methods and programs.

But the focal point of missio Dei is the incarnation. Although God spoke to previous generations "at many times and in many ways," the writer to the Hebrews reminds his readers as he reflects on the diverse means of God's revelation in Jewish history, "in these last days he has spoken to us by his Son," who is "the radiance of God's glory and the exact representation of his being."[9] Jesus Christ, God in the flesh, is the one who defines authoritatively the scope and purpose of God's mission and the one through whom this mission will be fulfilled. This has significance for church planting in a number of ways.

First, Jesus rather than the early church is the source of inspiration for church planters. The New Testament introduces us to a range of recently planted churches and the issues with which they were grappling, and to church planting teams and strategies. There are resources here for contemporary church planters, provided significant contextual differences are recognized, but the primary resource is the life and ministry of Jesus and his mission agenda. We will return to this on several occasions in later chapters. For church planting that fails to engage with the mission agenda of Jesus can easily become church-centered rather than kingdom-oriented. The result may be proliferation of churches rather than significant advance in the mission of God. In a classic passage defining his mission[10] Jesus used the socially and politically charged language of the Year of Jubilee as he spoke of bringing good news to the poor, freedom for prisoners, sight for the blind, and release for the oppressed.

The theme of the kingdom of God which permeated his teaching, and the wholistic nature of his ministry, require church planting strategies to be set firmly within this broader understanding of mission. Jesus later told his hesitant followers: "As the Father sent me, I am sending you."[11] Their mission was defined by his. Church planting, or any other aspect of the mission of the church, cannot be pursued in isolation but must be related to the mission of Jesus.

A second implication of the principle of incarnation for church planting is that God speaks to people through making his word flesh. Globally, this provides theological underpinning for the planting of churches wherever the word is proclaimed, if there are no churches already in existence. But in most parts of the world, where churches already exist, the principle has to be applied with greater caution. Irresponsible church planting may appear to be tearing apart the body of Christ rather than incarnating good news. It is important to affirm that both *word* and *flesh* are involved in incarnation.

Evangelism is rightly understood, on etymological and theological grounds, as the announcement of good news. Attempts have been made in recent decades to redefine evangelism in ways that minimize this element of proclamation and emphasize instead Christian presence within society. In a culture where religion is relegated to the private domain and where pluralism is celebrated, this is understandable. The language of proclamation is regarded as problematic and potentially confrontational. It is also widely accepted that "who you are speaks more loudly than what you say." The testimony of a consistent Christian lifestyle is vital if Christian faith is to be commended to others. But if evangelism is to be understood in relation to missio Dei, rather than tailored to social sensibilities, it is not possible to eradicate or minimize the element of proclamation. The God who sends his people into the world to participate in his mission is a God who speaks, whose Son is the Word, and whose

Spirit leads people into truth. Silent presence does not accurately describe the mission or ministry of Jesus, whose words unsettled, challenged, and disturbed his hearers.

But there is no need for evangelism to consist of words alone. If presence without proclamation is unintelligible, proclamation without presence is unconvincing. The ministry of Jesus "fleshed out" his message in various ways: his miracles authenticated his claims; his lifestyle demonstrated his integrity; his prophetic actions underscored his teaching. And the band of disciples who lived, ate, talked, laughed, and prayed with Jesus were the prototype of communities planted all over the known world in subsequent decades.

The great commission may not have specifically mentioned church planting as the means of making disciples, but the necessity of such incarnating communities was recognized very quickly. The Word which had been made flesh uniquely in Jesus would be proclaimed not only by individual messengers but through incarnation in these new churches. The description of the church as the "body of Christ" provides a secure biblical foundation for applying (albeit cautiously) the language of incarnation to the church.

This impacts the practice of church planting in a number of ways. First, the presence of church buildings or even congregations in an area where church planting is being considered does not necessarily preclude the possibility of planting new churches. Introverted or socially isolated churches, churches concerned only with their own spiritual development, churches with nothing to communicate to their neighbors, churches speaking in terminology that cannot be understood, churches that speak much but do little, churches that fail to incarnate what they are proclaiming, may be making no positive contribution to missio Dei.

To the extent the local community is aware of them at all, they may be incarnating a message that contradicts the gospel: a message that suggests the God they worship is remote, unconcerned, silent, restricted to a holy building and religious issues. Such churches may be theologically conservative or liberal, dying or lively, small or large, from any denomination or none. From a church planting perspective, the crucial issue is whether such churches are incarnating the good news.

If there is no such incarnation of the good news, those concerned about mission in the locality are faced with a strategic choice between working within such churches to enable them to become missionary communities, or planting new churches. There may be contextual factors that support different conclusions in different situations, but the undergirding theological principle is that of incarnation. Effective mission into the local community must take precedence over ecclesiastical sensibilities.

But the same standard must be applied to new churches. Church planting cannot be equated with participation in missio Dei unless these churches are communicating good news to the wider community and incarnating the good news that they are proclaiming. Not all new churches do this. Some are as wordy and irrelevant as any older churches. Others are introverted and caught up with internal development. Church planting that does not evaluate what is planted in light of the principle of incarnation risks adding more ineffective congregations to the contemporary church scene and contributing little to the mission of the church.

The principle of incarnation raises further questions for church planters. An important tension in the relationship between churches (new and old) and the wider community to which they are bearing witness is the need for churches to be "in the world" but "not of the world," distinctive but not disconnected. Unless there are ways in which a church is "not of the world," there is nothing to proclaim or incarnate; unless the church is in some way "in the world," proclamation and incarnation cannot take place. All churches can be located somewhere on a continuum between the poles of isolated irrelevance and indistinguishable integration. In his exploration of what it would mean for churches to become missionary congregations, Robert Warren rejects as an unhelpful caricature the assumption that *parish church* and *gathered church* models necessarily represent these extreme positions. He urges emerging missionary congregations to be both *distinctive* and *engaged*.[12]

An encouraging feature of contemporary church planting is the increased attention that is given to community surveying and demographic research. Although some church planting involves little more than the transplanting of existing models into new locations, many church planters are concerned to plant churches that are contextually appropriate, that will engage dynamically with the target community. There are implications for the style of worship, the length and content of sermons, the kind of building used for meetings, the design of publicity material and many other aspects of church life. Some church planters have visited local residents before a new church is planted to ask what kind of church they would welcome in their community.

Valuable as this research may be, and welcome as the concern for contextualization is, there are some dangers here if the principle of incarnation is not kept clearly in view. Churches designed by reference to the perceived needs, aspirations and preferences of an unchurched community may be engaged but not sufficiently distinctive to function as missionary congregations. For Jesus, incarnation meant that he was a male, first-century Jew, immersed in the culture and customs of his day, speaking the language of his contemporaries. But it meant also that he was distinctive, that he challenged social norms and gender stereotypes, that he asked awkward questions, that he taught and modeled different values. Jesus was both engaged and distinctive. Church planting that takes the principle of incarnation seriously will struggle toward a similar and often uncomfortable position.

In later chapters we will examine in greater detail the implications of this for the shape and ethos of newly planted churches. Adopting the principle of incarnation does not resolve all the difficulties. But it does offer a perspective from which to identify and challenge practices or attitudes that represent an illegitimate shift away from this combination of distinctiveness and engagement.

The Kingdom of God

A third theological perspective that might helpfully undergird church planting is the *kingdom of God*. The theme of the kingdom of God has been recovered in recent decades at both theological and popular levels. Its meaning and implications have been debated, and some expositions of the kingdom have provided a framework within which a more wholistic understanding of mission has developed.[13]

Advocates of church planting are familiar with this debate and some have set church planting firmly within the framework of the kingdom of God.[14] It is rather disappointing, therefore, to find that church planting practitioners rarely embrace this perspective. Establishing new churches often appears to be a freestanding policy. It is as if planting a new church automatically implies the advance of the kingdom of God, and as if the kingdom advances primarily, if not exclusively, through church planting. This identification of church and kingdom is not justified biblically or contextually.

Merely using "kingdom" language or talking about the kingdom of God is not enough.[15] Martin Robinson has asked whether it is "unfair to observe that aggressive church planting follows in the wake of a radical preaching of the kingdom, whereas those who emphasize the importance of the church in relation to the kingdom are strangely slow off the mark in the field of church planting."[16] Although this observation is fair enough in itself, the examples given are of movements whose understanding of the kingdom was arguably lopsided, and whose church planting activities seemed to bear no relation to their understanding of the kingdom. Our concern here is to examine church planting in the context of the kingdom of God and to indicate ways in which this influences church planting.

The subject of church planting, as we will see in the next chapter, is peripheral rather than central in the New Testament, whereas the kingdom of God is arguably the central theme of Jesus' teaching and the integrating paradigm for the mission of the church. If the status and role of church planting are to be theologically assessed, the relationship between the kingdom of God and the church will need to be clearly understood. The church is not the kingdom. It is closely related, but distinct.

If they are functioning properly, churches will be agents of the kingdom, signposts to the kingdom, sacraments of the kingdom, provisional representations of the kingdom, proclaiming and demonstrating the kingdom, pointing to what is coming when the kingdom is fully established, but they can never be equated with the kingdom. There are several reasons for insisting on this distinction (in addition to the absence of any biblical evidence to equate the church and the kingdom).

First, the church is a community, whereas the kingdom is an activity: God extending his rule throughout creation. Failure to acknowledge this distinction can lead to static interpretations of the kingdom and ecclesiastical complacency, where it is assumed that the kingdom is in evidence because of the mere existence of churches in a region. An unwarranted identification of church and kingdom can insulate churches from the disturbing but vital challenge of the kingdom to their own inner life and values. Churches may be agents of the kingdom, but they need also to respond to the impact of the kingdom and to recognize the provisional status of all their structures and activities. The activity of church planting can stimulate reflection on the dynamic nature of the kingdom by challenging static conceptions of the church. The cost of church planting may also help churches assess the extent to which they are prepared to be disturbed by the implications of being committed to the kingdom.

If the kingdom is advancing rather than standing still, churches may also need to define their understanding of mission in dynamic rather than static terms. Despite the New Testament emphasis on mission as involving movement—"go"—the perennial temptation to reverse this thrust and to expect the world to "come" to the church is not resisted even by many apparently mission-minded churches. The Old Testament mission paradigm may have been largely *centripetal*, energized by the prophetic vision of the nations coming to Jerusalem, but the New Testament paradigm is *centrifugal* as the church is sent out from Jerusalem to the ends of the earth.

Some, but not all, church planting movements have represented a recovery of this centrifugal dimension. John Finney[17] contrasts the Celtic and Roman church planting missions in England in the sixth and seventh centuries. He argues that the Celts "saw movement as of the essence of the gospel" and that for them "evangelism is linked with a thrust from an area of safety into a potentially dangerous world." Roman church planting was much more cautious and Roman monks were discouraged from engaging in the wandering evangelism of the Celtic *peregrinati*. Contemporary churches may be equally cautious and attempt to engage in "mission without movement." Finney suggests that church planting represents a rediscovery of mission as movement, attempting to incarnate the gospel in new locations or cultures. However, this may be an unduly optimistic assessment of the missiological impact of church planting.

There are contemporary examples of church planting that represent the sense of adventure that Finney detects in Celtic missions. But there are examples also of church planting that are much closer to the rather ponderous ecclesiastic extension which characterized Roman missions. To help churches recover a sense of mission as movement, church planting needs to be set firmly within a theological framework that recognizes that the kingdom is dynamic, and that churches concerned to be agents of this kingdom must also be on the move.

Second, the kingdom is broader than the church. It is arguable that the church has a unique role within the kingdom, as the community where the King is worshiped and served, as the bride of Christ, as the "little flock" to whom the kingdom has been given,[18] as those who have been entrusted with the "keys of the kingdom."[19] Attempts by liberal missiologists, liberation theologians, and others to minimize the significance of the church, in favor of other agents of the kingdom, fail to do justice to these ecclesiological contributions to the coming of the kingdom. But the opposite temptation must also be resisted. God is at work outside the church as well as within it and through it. Not all the redeemed people of God are identifiable as members of local churches, any more than it is legitimate to claim that every person on a church membership roll has necessarily entered the kingdom of God.

One of the discoveries frequently made by church planting teams is that new churches attract Christians who have not recently been associated with other churches and some who are believers who have never belonged to a local church. Distinguishing the kingdom from the church prepares church planters and evangelists to encounter God already at work in people who have had no contact with the church, rather than assuming that they are in some way bringing God with them into situations where he has not been at work. This perspective makes church planting less humanistic and evangelism more sensitive.

Furthermore, God is not restricted to working through the churches but can use other instruments to advance his purposes in society. Although our hope is that the church will be especially sensitive to the prompting of the Spirit and responsive to the ways in which God is acting to advance his kingdom, honesty requires us to admit that quite often the church is sluggish and resistant. We can confuse human tradition with faithfulness to God and can be a reactionary institution rather than a revolutionary movement. Sometimes the church is in the vanguard of the advancing kingdom. On other occasions we may discern God at work in parallel ways in the church and in society. Not infrequently, if we have eyes to see this, God is advancing his kingdom through those who may not recognize this but whose quest for justice and wholeness, for liberty and community, is contributing toward the kingdom's advance.

Planting churches which are freed from ecclesiastical traditions and structures to explore the implications of the kingdom may help the church as a whole to catch up with what God is doing. Replicating churches that the Spirit of God has effectively bypassed to advance the kingdom is likely to present further obstacles to progress. Thus, for example, the multiplication of churches characterized by racism or sexism may contribute to church growth but also represent a strengthening of forces opposed to God's rule of justice and peace. Church growth and kingdom advance cannot simply be equated.

Third, the kingdom rather than the church defines the scope of God's mission. There is a persistent tendency in the history of the church for mission to be defined in ways that fail to do justice to the breadth and depth of biblical teaching on the kingdom of God.

Mission can be *reduced to "soul-winning,"* where a narrow, anthropocentric understanding of evangelism prevails. Such evangelism often calls only for changes of belief and certain aspects of personal morality. But the kingdom challenges political, social, and economic values and commitments, and leads to a radically new allegiance, a progressively transformed lifestyle, and different priorities.

Mission can be *relegated to the private sphere* of church, family and leisure interest, where larger issues of justice, peace, care for the environment, and the alleviation of human suffering are ignored. But the kingdom challenges any contemporary expression of the behavior of the Pharisees, who strained out gnats but swallowed the camels of justice, mercy, and faithfulness.[20]

Mission can be *restricted to proclamation*, marginalizing the demonstration of the power of the gospel that is evident in the wholistic evangelism of the New Testament as well as in many subsequent periods of mission. But the kingdom of God is a kingdom of power rather than mere words, advancing through the healing of the sick, the expulsion of demonic forces, and the raising of the dead.

And mission can be *regarded as a recruitment drive* or marketing exercise. But the kingdom involves conflict: "To preach the gospel of the kingdom is to be engaged in battle with the kingdom of this world. The triumph of God's kingdom is assured to those who see reality through eyes of faith. However, this does not make the conflict any less real. The conditions of our warfare call for unfailing loyalty, clarity of vision, depth of commitment, and willingness to suffer persecution.[21] Church planting, as a dimension of the advance of the kingdom, involves spiritual warfare rather than ecclesiastical expansion, as another community of the kingdom is established as a resistance cell in a world that is hostile to its Creator.

Defining mission in terms of the advance of God's kingdom makes such reductionist tendencies untenable. This then implies, however, that churches are planted with an agenda set by biblical teaching on the kingdom. This teaching calls churches to other forms of involvement in God's world than evangelism and church planting alone. Neither church growth nor church planting are ultimate goals. Both are subordinate theologically to the advance of the kingdom. Some church planting may significantly advance the cause of the kingdom: as communities of Christians incarnate the values and lifestyle of the kingdom in new ways and in new locations; as wholistic evangelism takes place; and as these churches function as salt and light in society, bringing a prophetic insight to their context, confronting injustice, championing the cause of the poor and marginalized, working with others to rebuild broken lives, and playing their part in the healing of individuals and communities. Such church planting is a sign of the coming kingdom.

Church planting divorced from the values and goals of the kingdom may actually hinder the coming of the kingdom: if it unwittingly reinforces the individualism that destroys communities; if it legitimizes the privatized notion of religion that emasculates the gospel and produces ghetto-churches; and if it engages in evangelism without prophecy. Mortimer Arias has insisted memorably that "there is no true evangelization without prophecy. . . . Our silence may be the countersign of good news, the negation of hope."[22]

Church planting can contribute to an understanding of mission that is broader than the conversion of individuals. David Bosch[23] reflects on the nineteenth-century pattern of mission where "for Protestants as others, mission came primarily to mean the planting of churches. This development was an important deviation from the pietistic view of mission as being first and foremost concerned with the saving of individual souls." The incorporation of converts into communities was recognized as important, not only for pragmatic reasons, to nurture and teach new believers, but because the gospel was seen to have communal implications. Living under the rule of God is not a solitary calling but an invitation to join a movement cooperating with God in the advance of his kingdom throughout the world. Church planting underscores this communal dimension of mission more powerfully than many other forms of evangelism.

But church planting can also contribute to an inadequate understanding of mission, if the wider perspective of the kingdom is not kept in view. A further comment of David Bosch, quoted in the previous chapter, about the "wider eschatological horizon" often being ignored in church planting ventures, relates to this issue. He suggests that an assessment of Lutheran missions in the nineteenth century was typical of the approach of many denominations: "The kingdom of God was reduced to a strategy by which Lutheran mission agencies planted Lutheran churches around the world. Questions were seldom asked at this time about the relationship of these churches to the kingdom of God. Their very existence appeared to be its own justification, and no further discussion of mission goals was required."[24]

The eschatological horizon, rather than the success of a church planting initiative or movement, is our true perspective. When church planting fills the horizon of those who advocate or practice this, this obscures the vision of the kingdom that alone is adequate to motivate and guide effective mission. The institutional church has lost this eschatological dimension quite often in the past twenty centuries and has replaced it with an ecclesiological focus: church instead of kingdom. The result has been a retreat from mission into maintenance. Church planting movements have frequently been energized by a renewed interest in eschatology,[25] but once church planting becomes the goal rather than one of the means of moving toward this vision, ecclesiastical developments have become dominant and the eschatological impetus has been lost once more. Setting church planting within the theological framework of the kingdom of God is crucial if the contemporary church planting movement is to escape this temptation.

Church planting may then be significant in the advance of the kingdom if it provides a channel for God to accomplish his mission purposes. If the new community that is established lives in ways that are consistent with the kingdom and incarnate the good news, church planting can be thoroughly integrated with the mission of God. But this is true also of existing churches. The point is that church planting is valuable only insofar as the purposes of the kingdom of God are served by such a strategy. Church planting is not an end in itself or self-authenticating. In common with every activity of the church, church planting must be assessed in the light of missiological and eschatological objectives.

These three concepts (missio Dei, incarnation and the kingdom of God) are key components of a theological foundation for church planting and also provide a basis for critical evaluation. Church planting initiatives are needed which are motivated by the privilege of participating in the mission of God, which are patterned on the incarnational way in which God has acted in mission, and which are energized by a vision of the coming kingdom of God as the goal of this mission.

Theological Reflections on Church Planting

In the first part of this chapter, we have suggested that it is helpful to set church planting in a theological framework. This framework does not provide clear-cut solutions to every practical problem faced by church planters, nor prescribe the adoption of certain methods or practices. But it does establish some parameters for church planting, within which issues encountered by church planters can be addressed. In this section, we are interested in working from practice to principle. We want to reflect on church planting and to ask what issues church planting might raise for theological investigation.

We have argued that church planting can be located theologically at the interface between ecclesiology and missiology. Since both ecclesiology and missiology have frequently been marginalized in theological reflection, it is not surprising that a topic on the borders of both has received little theological attention. This is unfortunate, given the significance of this practice throughout the history and global expansion of the church.

Church planting is not the only interface between these two disciplines: whenever consideration is given to the role of the church in the world, missiological questions arise, and whenever mission is perceived as more than individual action in the world, ecclesiological issues demand attention. Timothy Yates, in his survey of Christian mission in the twentieth century, relates how ecclesiological discussion became increasingly central to missiological debates during the second half of the century and insists that "it is impossible to avoid ecclesiology in the communication of the gospel, for the gospel does not come as pure message but issues from, and gives rise to, specific communities; and such communities will adopt certain characteristics which they believe express the gospel in churchly form"[26]

But some forms of church planting have the potential to bring into especially sharp focus the relationship between missiology and ecclesiology. Not all church planting does this. Replicating existing churches raises few ecclesiological issues. Church plants that represent no more than redistribution of church members into different premises pose few missiological questions. But where church planting is motivated by concern for effective mission and embraces the possibility of developing new forms of Christian community, fresh initiatives emerge that provide fruitful resources for theological reflection.

Church and Mission

The practice of church planting may serve to strengthen cross-fertilization between ecclesiology and missiology.

Church planting reminds missiologists that the church plays a pivotal role in mission. It is possible for mission strategists, enthusiastic evangelists, and academic mission theologians to concentrate on other dimensions of mission—such as the conversion of individuals, the transformation of society or relationships with other faith communities—but to ignore or marginalize the church in relation to these dimensions.

Church planting reminds ecclesiologists that mission is the primary task of the church. It is possible for local church leaders, denominational representatives, and ecclesiastical commissions to concentrate on other aspects of church life—doctrinal, sacramental, relational, and institutional—but to fail to relate these to the calling of the church to be a missionary community.

The conviction that mission is the primary task and calling of the church is now widely, though not universally, accepted. Not all have expressed this conviction as memorably as Emil Brunner's famous dictum: "The Church exists by mission as fire exists by burning." But, in various ways, missiologists and theologians have affirmed that mission cannot be detached from the church without fundamentally distorting the nature of both.

Edward Dayton and David Fraser see the church as "inherently missionary" and warn that "unless the missionary nature of the church is understood, the meaning and significance of the church is completely obscured."[27] Carl Braaten insists that "the very being of the church is shaped by its missionary calling," and that "because church and mission belong together from the beginning, a church without mission or a mission without the church are both contradictions."[28] Gerrit Berkouwer similarly thinks "the essence of the church cannot be thought of apart from that peculiar movement toward the outside."[29] And Orlando Costas writes: "The church is basically a missionary community . . . her fundamental character can only be understood from the perspective of God's mission to the world."[30]

Statements from international consultations representing diverse sections of the world church in recent years have endorsed this understanding of the interaction between missiology and ecclesiology. Documents emerging from various consultations held under the aegis of the evangelical Lausanne movement have, predictably, endorsed mission as the primary task of the church. There has been debate about the components of this mission, especially the relationship between evangelism and social action, but affirmation that the purpose of the church is to engage in mission. The opening paragraph of the "Lausanne Covenant" declared in 1974 that God "has been calling out from the world a people for himself, and sending his people back into the world to be his servants and witnesses, for the extension of his kingdom, the building up of Christ's body, and the glory of his name."[31]

The "Manila Manifesto," in 1989, endorsed this understanding of the church but recognized it was not always realized in evangelical churches: "We deeply regret that many of our congregations are inward-looking, organized for maintenance rather than mission, or pre-occupied with church-based activities at the expense of witness."[32] In terminology that seems surprisingly deficient in relation to the wholistic model of mission endorsed by many within the Lausanne movement in recent years, but which is unmistakably mission-oriented, participants expressed their renewed commitment: "We determine to turn our churches inside out, so that they may engage in continuous outreach, until the Lord adds to them daily those who are being saved" (par. 8).[33]

One aspect of "turning our churches inside out" might be a renewed commitment to church planting. This strategy was absent from the Lausanne Covenant, but appears in the Manila Manifesto in the same paragraph as this renewed commitment to mission-oriented churches. "Every congregation" is urged to "develop appropriate strategies for mission," one of which might be to "plant a new church in a neighboring district or village."[34] Church planting is a very minor theme in this document and in the many papers presented at the congress.[35] Church planting advocates do well to remember that the identification of church planting as a key component in evangelical strategies for global mission has emerged very recently, and its significance has yet to be evaluated. There is reason to hope that this practice may deeply impact the mentality of many congregations, turning them outward from their own concerns, and may play a crucial role in the world evangelization to which the Manila delegates dedicated themselves. But church planting needs to be set firmly within a mission perspective if it is in turn to help with the development of a more mission-oriented ecclesiology.

Recognition of mission as the primary task of the church is unsurprising in documents emerging from the Lausanne movement. But this ecclesiological prioritizing of mission is evident also in recent documents from other sections of the church. One of the major documents to emerge from the Second Vatican Council (1962-1965), the "Decree on the Church's Missionary Activity" (*Ad Gentes*) states that by its very nature the church on earth is missionary, participating in the mission of God in the world (pars. 1-3). The document ranges over various mission issues, including witness through presence, dialogue, social action and proclamation, the importance of unity, the missionary character of the Eucharist, and the aim of planting churches. It concludes that missionary activity is central to the life of the church and describes mission as "the greatest and holiest duty of the church" (par. 29).

Commenting on Vatican II, Lesslie Newbigin writes: "Fundamental to everything else that came forth from the Council were the reaffirmation of the missionary character of the church, the recognition of the unfinished task which that implies, the confession that the church is a pilgrim people on its way to the ends of the earth and the end of time, and the acknowledgement of the need for a new openness to the world into which the church is sent."[36] Ten years after Vatican II, the document *Evangelii Nuntiandi* reiterated this, using the terminology of evangelization rather than mission: evangelization is "inherent in the very nature of the church" and the "essential function" of the church (pars. 14-15).

In 1988, Recommendation 44 from the Lambeth Conference of bishops challenged the worldwide Anglican communion to recover the missionary dimension of church life: "This Conference calls for a shift to a dynamic missionary emphasis going beyond care and nurture to proclamation and service." An accompanying Lambeth pastoral letter acknowledged that Anglican churches in many places had marginalized mission in favor of pastoral ministry, but expressed the conviction that "the Holy Spirit is now leading us to become a movement for Mission."[37] It was this conference that called the Anglican communion "to make the closing years of the millennium a Decade of Evangelism; with a renewed and united emphasis on making

Christ known to the people of this world." Despite troubling memories that the 1980s had also been designated as a "Decade of Evangelism," with apparently insignificant results, this call was taken up by the Anglican communion and by many other denominations.

Renewed emphasis on mission as the task of the church can also be discovered in recent statements and documents from the World Council of Churches. Evangelicals have frequently expressed concern about the marginalization of mission in ecumenical circles, or at least its reinterpretation in terms of activities and emphases regarded as illegitimate or questionable. Evidence for this was not lacking. The merger between the WCC and the International Missionary Council, agreed at the Ghana Assembly in 1958, seemed to have resulted in mission concerns being swallowed up in internal structural discussions. Philip Potter, general secretary of the WCC, had expressed his distaste for the terms *witness* and *mission* and his preference for the idea of "Christian presence." The WCC meeting in Uppsala in 1968 had seemed both to reinterpret mission as "humanization" and to minimize the role of the church in mission. The call for a moratorium on missionaries, made by John Gatu in 1971 and endorsed by the All-African Council of Churches at Lusaka in 1974, seemed a logical further step in the same direction.

But the WCC meeting in Nairobi the following year has been recognized as the start of a process whereby the priority of the task of mission has gradually been recovered in the ecumenical movement. The contributions of the Evangelical Methodists, Emilio Castro from Uruguay and Mortimer Arias from Bolivia, emphasized the responsibility of the churches for world evangelization and mission as proclamation as well as action for social justice. Although differences remain, there has been continuing convergence between evangelical and ecumenical positions on mission. Evangelicals have endorsed a more holistic understanding of mission, although many continue to insist on the priority of evangelism within the mission responsibilities of the church. Ecumenicals have built on the stance adopted at Nairobi in such documents as "Mission and Evangelism—An Ecumenical Affirmation," in 1983. Here, not only is there renewed emphasis on evangelism, but church planting is identified as being central to mission:

> "It is at the heart of Christian mission to foster the multiplication
> of local congregations in every human community. The planting
> of the seed of the gospel will bring forward a people gathered

around the word and sacraments and called to announce God's revealed purpose....This task of sowing the seed needs to be continued until there is, in every human community, a cell of the kingdom, a church confessing Jesus Christ. . . ."[8]

The subsequent WCC world conference on mission and evangelism at San Antonio, Texas, in 1989, continued to explore this interrelationship between the church and mission. The writings of Lesslie Newbigin have been an important bridge between the evangelical and ecumenical camps, calling for a "missionary encounter" with the culture of modernity, which has dominated Western societies and has been exported to become arguably the first truly global culture. Evangelical churches have been challenged to develop a less privatized approach to mission; many other churches have been challenged to recover a mission perspective within society. The debate continues on how the mission of the church should be defined, but the conviction that the task of the church is mission is now widespread.

Separating Church and Mission?

But this conviction is not universal. Not all are convinced that it is legitimate or helpful to see mission as the primary task of the church. This may be because another aspect of the church is regarded as primary; or because mission is understood as the responsibility of others rather than the church; or because mission is regarded as inappropriate in a pluralistic environment.

The main contender alongside mission for primacy among the tasks of the church is worship. The first duty of all Christians, it is argued, whether as individuals or as churches, is to "love the Lord your God with all your heart and with all your soul and with all your strength and with all your mind" (Luke 10:27). The accompanying duty, to "love your neighbor as yourself," which calls the church into mission, follows from this. Mission is of vital importance but, in the famous words of the Westminster Confession, "The chief end of man is to glorify God and to enjoy him forever." The important concern that underlies this objection to according primacy to mission is that mission undertaken in isolation from worship can easily slip into humanistic activity or religious propaganda. Church planting, in common with other aspects of mission, can become divorced from spirituality and doxology, and degenerate into an ecclesiastical equivalent of business expansion.

One response to this objection is to argue that the chief task of the church *on earth* is mission, since all eternity will be given to worship. However, this response seems to imply both a static and monochrome vision of eternity (in its crudest forms, never-ending chorus singing), and the legitimacy of postponing until eternity that which is most central to the church's calling.

A better response is to reject as untenable any distinction between worship and mission. If the church worships a missionary God, then participating in his mission is an expression of worship. Any dichotomy between worship and mission reveals an inadequately limited vision of both, where "worship has ceased to describe the whole of life and has become restricted to cultic acts" and "mission has been regarded as an extra activity independent of worship."[39] Where church planting is accepted as one of the means by which this mission is fulfilled, the multiplication of worshipping communities completes the circle: the church, as an expression of its worship, establishes a new community of worshippers.

A second challenge to the idea that mission is the primary task of the church is posed by those who marginalize the church (perceived as an institution) and leave mission to God, to individual Christians, or to other agencies. To some, the church is so flawed that it is a hindrance to mission. Individual Christians can engage in mission, but they will frequently need to apologize for and distance themselves from the church. Or it may be that God's mission advances outside of and despite the church, through liberation movements and other agencies who unwittingly further the causes of the kingdom of God. Or perhaps the church should concentrate on nurture and edification, leaving specialist agencies to engage in mission.

The separation between the church and mission agencies evident in many periods of history, and the contemporary proliferation of mission agencies, demonstrate this tendency for mission and church to become disconnected. As we will see in a subsequent chapter, church planting movements have frequently reconnected these elements and recovered the link between missiology and ecclesiology. Church planting does not negate the significance of individual witness nor the freedom of God to accomplish his missionary purposes through other agencies, but it does represent a renewed commitment to the communal dimension of mission.

The third area of resistance to the identification of mission as the primary focus of the church concerns the status of the gospel in relation to other faiths and ideologies. This is a familiar issue within missiological discussions, but many churches in the West are still quite unfamiliar with theological and practical issues involved in mission within a pluralistic environment. Despite the presence of diverse faith communities in Western societies, some of them as evangelistic as any Christian denomination, the extent of contact between local churches and these faith communities is often not great, even in areas where those communities are strongly present. There is also uncertainty about how the religious convictions and experiences of members of other faith communities should be perceived in relation to mission.

Some have suggested that mission is inappropriate in a multifaith society, and that initiatives such as a Decade of Evangelism should be understood as applying only to nominal Christians. For others, the presence of other faiths in what are still regarded as "Christian" nations is seen as an affront and mission is distorted by the kind of imperialistic attitudes that plagued Western missionary work in other parts of the world in previous generations. Between these extremes many churches are unsure how to respond to what is perceived as both a challenge and an opportunity. How can churches engage in mission in a multifaith society in such a way as to affirm the unique significance of Jesus Christ, and yet value the religious and cultural heritage of other communities? How can pluralism be exposed as theologically untenable, but pluralization be endorsed as a process which has created a healthier environment for mission than a culture dominated by a single ideology?[40]

Clarifying the relationship of Christian mission to other faiths is one of the crucial challenges facing Western churches at the beginning of the twenty-first century. There are rich resources within the world church to help, both theologically and practically, and it is vital that hard-won lessons are remembered, so that mistakes are not repeated and wrong attitudes are not perpetuated. There is a better way for the churches to engage in mission in a pluralistic environment than either reinventing imperialistic evangelism or abdicating responsibility for mission.

It is important for Western churches to listen carefully to those with relevant experience, either as cross-cultural missionaries or as people who have lived in different cultures. One helpful recent book on this subject by a Sri Lankan evangelical, Vinoth Ramachandra, is entitled *The Recovery of Mission*[41] and presents a cogent and persuasive argument for the recovery of mission as the responsibility of the church in a post-Christian and pluralistic society.

The experience of church planting can help or hinder engagement with such issues. As the church planting movement matures, and more initiatives are taken to establish new congregations in areas where other faith communities are present, opportunities will arise to engage in theological reflection and develop appropriate missiological responses. The experience and perspectives of leaders of some of the ethnic churches planted in recent years will be invaluable. The growing familiarity among church planters with questions of inculturation and contextualization will provide a framework within which these important issues can be considered. Church planting could be a catalyst to help churches address the question of how the Christian community relates to other faith communities.

Reproduction

Vibrant church planting initiatives provide opportunities, then, for those concerned with the church and its mission to recover dimensions of missiology and ecclesiology that can easily become swallowed up by other institutional and programmatic demands. But does church planting offer any *new* insights in the areas of missiology or ecclesiology? Some forms of church planting, which do not merely replicate existing structures and practices, raise important issues for theological reflection. In chapter 6, we will examine a number of new models of church, with a view not only to evaluating these sociologically and pragmatically, but exploring the implications for missiology and ecclesiology.

But there is at least one aspect of church planting that may have more general significance. At a British Anglican church planting conference in 1994, George Lings (who has recently been appointed as the first Director of Church Army's Institute of Evangelism and Church Planting) suggested that one ecclesiological implication of church planting is that churches are by nature and by definition reproductive. The influence of the planting church on the new church will be substantial, just as children inherit characteristics from their parents and learn from them through nurturing in the early years of life, but the children may turn out very different from their parents in personality and lifestyle. Reproductive churches can impart much to the churches they bring to birth, but church planting is also an opportunity for their own renewal. The practice of church planting may encourage the conclusion that reproduction is a fundamental feature of the church as it is of biological organisms. A healthy church does not just develop internally and expand in size and social impact, but naturally expresses its life in new forms and structures.

Others have reached a similar conclusion. Stuart Christine, citing Genesis 1 as pointing to the Spirit's original and unchanging desire to engender fruitfulness and multiplication, writes that "The parenting of new congregations . . . is a natural instinct of those born again by this Spirit and gathered by him into local Christian families."[42] Howard Snyder argued in his paper for the Lausanne Congress that multiplication of congregations rather than indefinite growth of existing churches was crucial for effective evangelism and for a significant church impact on society. Normal church growth, like normal biological growth, involves division rather than unlimited expansion; indeed, "the growth of individual cells beyond a certain point without division is pathological," whereas "reproduction . . . feeds into a continuous cycle which, empowered by the Holy Spirit, makes the Christian church a dynamic, living organism."[43]

Church planting is not an unusual development, but a normal stage in the maturation of a Christian community. Indeed, Ellis and Mitchell argue that "if a church exists which never thinks about reproducing itself . . . never expects or anticipates that this is the natural business of growing up, then it is actually sterile."[44] Churches that do not engage in some form of church planting,[45] and so remain in their institutional form for generations, should perhaps be regarded as abnormal. They are liable to be inflexible and unresponsive to their context, especially in a rapidly changing social and cultural environment.

Where church planting does not occur, ecclesiastical traditions may take precedence over the needs of a new generation of church members. Ecclesiastical structures may stifle the creativity of those church members. Ecclesiastical priorities may lead to the neglect of the church's primary task of mission. In such situations, the church will either cease to exist, become a cultural ghetto, or be rescued through a process of renewal and reformation. The story of the church in Europe over many centuries can be understood as successive waves of ecclesiastical renewal, followed by periods of ossification and inertia. Church planting movements were frequently the catalysts of renewal, but church planting was generally resisted by existing churches, or regarded as extraordinary. Perhaps it would be better to regard reproduction through church planting as normal, and the survival of ecclesiastical structures for more than a couple of generations as abnormal and problematic.

It may be argued that this constant process of reproduction would make it difficult for the church to fulfill a role that many people, both within and outside the churches, expect from the church, that of being a stable institution in a shifting society. Clearly there is a psychological need for such institutions in periods of rapid change, and there is no doubt that churches are well placed to provide this rootedness. But it is not easy to equate this role with biblical images of the church, where the people of God are seen as a pioneering people, anticipating the coming kingdom, rather than a bastion of the status quo, pointing back nostalgically to a vanishing past. Furthermore, unless there is some degree of ecclesiological renewal, the cultural gap between the churches and surrounding society will be too large for this stabilizing role to be effective. Those outside the churches will be too alienated from them to benefit from it, while those inside the churches will enjoy cocoon-like stability at the cost of alienation from the culture into which they are called in mission.

Neither must church planting necessarily undermine the stabilizing role of the church, if such planting is integrated into normal church practice rather than perceived as an unsettling and exotic activity. Reproduction through various forms of church planting can draw on strengths of ecclesiastical traditions while introducing innovations that will enable emerging churches to relate more creatively and effectively to the surrounding culture. Church planting offers a middle way between ossification and revolution, enabling churches to evolve and renew themselves. Where church planting is only a minority practice, the benefits are minimized, as many churches resist change and become progressively less flexible, and as church planters react against this by rejecting traditions and retreating into innovations. Where reproduction is understood as a normal aspect of church life, the way is open for mutual enrichment between what Robert Warren has referred to as the "inherited" and "emerging" modes of the church.[46]

Adding "reproductive" to the list of epithets normally associated with ecclesiology, such as "one," "holy," "catholic" and "apostolic," might be a significant component in the integration of missiology and ecclesiology that is important for the health of both disciplines. Missiologists have been familiar for many years with the concept of self-propagating churches, and mission strategies have been de-signed to enable churches to escape dependence on outside agencies. But this concept has not generally been accorded the status that is being suggested here. Self-propagation, or reproduction, is not just an admirable quality of some churches, but integral to the definition of the church.

Church Planting and Theology

Church planting offers considerable scope for theological reflection. And church planting will need the stimulus of theological debate and the protection of a theological framework if it is to reach its potential. At its best, church planting has the capacity both to recall the church to its primary task of mission and to remind mission strategists of the significant role of the church. The former contribution is of particular significance in those regions where the church has been established for generations and has allowed maintenance to displace mission in its list of priorities, or where the arrival of other faith communities has unnerved churches and left them unsure how to respond. The latter perspective challenges mission strategies that assume that God's work in the world can be accomplished without the church.

Organizations that concentrate on encouraging individual conversions are challenged to acknowledge the weaknesses inherent in evangelistic activities that are not integrated with existing or developing churches. They also need to take more seriously the need for Christian communities both to nurture these converts and to deploy them effectively. Programs that anticipate the coming of the kingdom of God through social transformation are urged to consider how such transformation can occur, or be sustained, without communities of the kingdom to model alternative ways of living.

But church planting could also be a distraction. It is crucial that church planting strategies and other evangelistic initiatives do not monopolize the attention of churches and hinder them from facing missiological issues of this kind. One of the criticisms of the Church Growth movement[47] concerns the danger that preoccupation with numerical growth may obscure the extent to which growing churches are becoming socially and culturally isolated within contemporary society and distract attention from the major missiological challenges posed by this society. Church planting that is interested only in the number of churches that can be planted risks being afflicted by a similar myopia. Church planting that fails to engage in theological reflection on the many aspects of the mission in which the church is invited by God to participate may serve only to multiply the number of churches which are ill-prepared for the challenges of the twenty-first century.

3. CHURCH PLANTING: A NEW TESTAMENT PRACTICE

We turn now from theological reflection on church plant-ing to consider the relevance of biblical teaching for the practice of church planting. Proponents of church planting advocate, explain, and defend this practice in various ways, as we saw in chapter 1. There are many reasons for planting new churches at the beginning of the twenty-first century, and for including church planting policies in national, regional, and local strategy documents. Most proponents and practitioners, however, wish to undergird these strategic and contextual arguments with biblical foundations.

Arguably, there is no need for such a foundation. Church plant-ing can be valued as a sensible, even God-inspired, contemporary expression of mission, whether or not it has biblical precedent. Many other aspects of evangelism and church life flourish without explicit biblical endorsement (for example, evangelistic guest services held in church buildings, television and radio evangelism, the use of evan-gelistic tracts, thirty-minute monologue sermons, church secretaries). Mission strategies and methods certainly need to demonstrate con-gruity with biblical revelation, in terms of their ethos, motives, and goals. But their appropriateness to the contemporary context is of greater significance than the extent to which parallels can be found in the practices of first-century eastern Mediterranean congregations. Church planting has much to commend it without recourse to bibli-cal precedents.

Nevertheless, many involved in church planting who advocate this as an effective mission strategy draw inspiration and support from the New Testament. There is, of course, much church planting to be found there. A smaller number of advocates attempt to estab-lish their biblical foundations through key Old Testament passages and themes. Fewer still argue more systematically for church plant-ing to be undergirded by certain theological principles, such as those considered in the previous chapter. In this chapter, we will concentrate on ways in which the New Testament has been, and should be, used to provide a foundation for contemporary church planting.[1]

It may be helpful at the outset to distinguish two different uses of the New Testament in relation to church planting. Some are concerned to find a biblical *rationale* for church planting. Should we plant churches today? Is there New Testament warrant for this? Can we argue for the adoption of church planting policies on the basis of biblical revelation? Within some churches, those advocating such policies feel obliged to establish biblical foundations for the strategies under discussion. Others are interested in finding biblical *guidelines* for church planting. How should we plant churches today? Are there New Testament principles for this? Can contemporary models and practices be evaluated on the basis of biblical precedents?

These issues are frequently confused, but need to be kept separate if we are to interpret the New Testament responsibly and make legitimate claims for our church planting strategies and methodologies. The position we will consider in this chapter is that the New Testament provides a wealth of resources for contemporary church planters, albeit perhaps better understood as perspectives rather than guidelines, but that it cannot provide an adequate rationale for church planting today.

A New Testament Basis for Church Planting

Attempts to provide a New Testament rationale for contemporary church planting often employ one or more of the following three arguments.

Some focus on the great commission (usually Matthew's version) and the importance of evangelism throughout the New Testament, and subsume church planting under this argument, as if establishing a New Testament basis for evangelism automatically established a similar basis for contemporary church planting.

Others focus on the centrality of the church (especially the local church) in the purposes of God and argue that this requires church planting as a normal expression of the church's mission, as if establishing a New Testament basis for the church automatically established a similar basis for contemporary church planting.

A third line of argument is the simple assertion that because church planting was the primary method of evangelism in the New Testament, it should be so today.

These arguments are often employed with passion and conviction, but they have inherent weaknesses. These need to be recognized if church planters and proponents of church planting are not to be justifiably accused of naive biblical interpretation and drawing illegitimate conclusions. Put bluntly, one can be totally committed to evangelism, without necessarily being involved in church planting or advocating it in a given situation. One can be passionately committed to the church, local and universal, without endorsing the planting of new churches in contemporary society. And one can be fully persuaded that church planting was normative in the first century, without agreeing it should be normative or even prominent today.

The basic problem is the issue of context. The New Testament informs us about the mission of the earliest churches into a world without churches. Pioneer evangelism into virgin territory has, throughout history and in every area of the world, involved the planting of new churches. Where mission takes the gospel into regions where there are no churches, there is a reasonably close parallel to the situation described in the New Testament (although cultural differences may require different methods from those used in the first century). Though occasionally missionaries have resisted the establishing of new congregations and concentrated on winning individual converts, most mission agencies have recognized that church planting is at least a vital part of their calling, if not their primary concern.

But in most Western nations, our context is very different from pioneer mission elsewhere in the world, or in the New Testament. The need for continuing evangelism in a nation where a significant proportion of the population have little or no connection with the Christian community is evident, and planting new churches may be an effective way to engage in such evangelism, but the context is undeniably different from the New Testament. Attempts to find a New Testament basis for contemporary church planting must acknowledge this.[2] The fact that Paul planted churches in the first century does not require us to adopt his strategy or copy his methodology, any more than we should feel obliged to circumcise members of our church planting teams simply because Paul did this on one occasion!

Attempts to derive a biblical basis for church planting from the great commission are disadvantaged by the fact that there is no explicit mention of the church in this famous passage. The commission of the risen Lord to those who would plant the first churches was to "go and make disciples of all nations, baptizing them in the name of the Father and of the Son and of the Holy Spirit and teaching them to obey everything that I have commanded you."[3] This would certainly require the formation and multiplication of Christian communities, but the emphasis is on making disciples, baptizing them, and teaching them to obey Jesus.

Reliance on the great commission as motivation for evangelism has been popular for many years, but there is little evidence that the early Christians responded to it in this way. Nor did most missionary endeavors throughout church history derive from the great commission. Many theologians from the fourth to the eighteenth centuries considered it to have already been fulfilled and so to have no contemporary significance. Much church planting, therefore, has taken place with little or no reference to the great commission and has been motivated by other considerations.

Also lacking legitimacy is deriving a biblical basis for church planting from more general New Testament teaching on evangelism, by subsuming church planting under the heading of evangelism. In some church planting literature, this appears to be the logic of the argument in sections devoted to establishing a biblical basis for church planting. Not only is mission reduced to the evangelistic component of missio Dei, but church planting is presented as simply one means of evangelism. Since there is an extensive and familiar New Testament basis for evangelism, if church planting is perceived as an expression of evangelism, a biblical basis for church planting appears to be secure.

Attractive though this simplistic argument may appear to be, it is unconvincing for two main reasons. First, church planting is not simply a branch of evangelism: it is both narrower than evangelism (as a particular evangelistic strategy) and broader than evangelism (in that churches may be planted for other reasons than evangelism). Second, the argument appears to provide biblical support for contemporary church planting policies, whereas all that can legitimately be established is that evangelism has New Testament warrant and that church planting is a possible means of engaging in evangelism.

The focus on the church that is evident in church planting literature and practice is also problematic. The argument appears to be that the New Testament teaches that the church is God's agent in the world, and so church planting is vital to advance God's work in the world. But this appears once more to be claiming too much. Undoubtedly the church is crucial to the mission and purposes of God, but the primary concern of the New Testament, as we saw in chapter 2, appears to be with the kingdom of God, rather than the church. The kingdom cannot be separated from the church, but neither can it be confined to the church, for God is at work throughout all creation to advance his rule of love. The planting of new churches may contribute to some aspects of the coming of the kingdom, but it may also distract attention from other aspects of this kingdom. Although, as we have noted, "kingdom" language is not infrequently used in church planting literature, the implications of this are rarely explored in any depth. The dominant impression is that the kingdom will advance as long as churches are planted. This unduly ecclesiocentric approach is neither biblically warranted nor helpful in assessing contemporary church planting policies.

Then is there *no* New Testament rationale for contemporary church planting? As we have argued above, such a conclusion would not be disastrous, provided church planting is at least consistent with general biblical principles. But, in fact, we would contend that there is a New Testament basis for church planting, albeit one that is rather more tentative than is often claimed. The three lines of argument referred to above—concerning the great commission, the centrality of the church, and New Testament church planting practice—are far from irrelevant, but they cannot bear the weight often placed on them. What follows is an attempt to reformulate them and to include some other considerations. This is not intended to provide an exhaustive New Testament basis for church planting, but to be indicative of the nature and status of what can be claimed.

First, church planting is *one* means of evangelism and advancing the kingdom of God that has significant New Testament parallels and may be appropriate in certain situations. There are sufficient biblical precedents for mission strategists and local church leaders to regard church planting as an option that should be seriously considered. It should neither be regarded as a foregone conclusion nor dismissed out of hand. Church planting is not the only possible evangelistic strategy. Each situation will need to be assessed carefully.

In pioneer evangelism, church planting is almost certainly required, both strategically and biblically, unless converts are to be uprooted and transported to churches in other locations. Here the parallel with the New Testament context is very close. In other situations, there may be alternative means available that are contextually preferable, such as incorporating converts into existing churches. But there is a secure biblical foundation for including church planting among the options.

Second, church planting is congruent with the fact that the church in the New Testament is perceived as a mission agency. It also fits well with the assumption evident throughout the New Testament that an important goal of evangelism is the incorporation of new believers into church communities. The New Testament does not offer much support to evangelistic strategies that concentrate merely on the converting of individuals. Nor does it present the church as a static community, concerned only about its internal health or even about its local surroundings. The church is a mission agency with a worldwide vision that by definition is always looking to break new ground.

Undoubtedly churches can be involved in mission in various ways, locally and internationally, without church planting. And new believers can often be effectively incorporated into existing churches. But church planting is a particularly effective strategy for incorporating new believers into Christian communities where they can be discipled, especially when these new believers would find it less easy to join existing churches.

Church planting demonstrates a strong commitment to corporate aspects of evangelism. And church planting offers local churches opportunities to become sending churches and to be involved in mission beyond their own locality. Church planting combines "mission" and "community" in a way that the New Testament seems to endorse but which few other church activities or evangelistic methods do as effectively.

Third, the New Testament is concerned with communities as well as with territories. The existence of a local church in a geographical area that only provides a relevant incarnation of the gospel for a segment of the local community does not preclude the planting of churches that will be good news to other segments of that community. Territory is an inadequate frame of reference for churches. This argument raises difficult issues about the validity of homogeneous churches, to which we will return in chapter 5. But the reality of the situation is that in practice many churches are homogeneous, by default rather than by design. They are effective in mission, if at all, only within a narrow band of society.

The proposal made by some church growth writers[4] that the phrase *panta ta ethne* in the great commission, normally translated as "all nations," should be translated as "all people groups" and used to justify the adoption of the "homogeneous unit principle" is not persuasive on linguistic grounds. But the emphasis within the church growth movement on people groups and community networks is not only crucial strategically, but appears to be founded on a much broader biblical concern for communities than a dubious translation of one phrase in Matthew's Gospel.

Jesus does not just deal with people on an individual basis. He also refers to and relates to people groups such as tax collectors, prostitutes, the poor, the Pharisees, and children. His approach and message varies from group to group. In the book of Acts, the advance of the gospel and growth of the church is measured not only territorially but in terms of new groups of people receiving the message (e.g. priests Acts 6:7; God-fearers Acts 10:2; Greeks Acts 11:20, 17:12; Gentiles Acts 13:46). When Paul and the Jerusalem-based apostles met to discuss their mission strategy (see Paul's account of this in Galatians 2:8-10), their division of labor was not territorial but in terms of people groups—Peter would concentrate on the Jews, Paul on the Gentiles. Furthermore, both apostles were concerned that another people group, the poor, were not marginalized.

Although this reference may be primarily to the poor Christians in the Jerusalem church, it is consistent with a broader New Testament emphasis, rooted in the teaching and example of Jesus, on the priority to be accorded to poor people generally. Church planting is not the only way for churches to relate to such people groups, but it provides one response to the challenge of incarnating the gospel within diverse people groups in a pluralistic society.

Fourth, the New Testament envisages situations where new structures are needed because of the developing work and mission of God, and the inability of existing structures to adapt. The familiar image of new wine requiring new wineskins, and the warning about the destructive effect of trying to patch old garments with new cloth,[5] though not related to ecclesiological issues in their context, both have relevance for church planting. The mission of God and the advance of his kingdom are primary. Ecclesiastical structures, like the structures to which Jesus was referring when he used this powerful imagery, are of secondary importance. If the existing structures are effective, there is no need to jettison them; but if they are ineffective, new ones are needed. The question to be asked when considering church planting is not how many churches are needed, but whether existing church structures are facilitating or hindering God's purposes.

This may seem to open the door to judgmental attitudes and sectarianism, but the alternative appears to be the ruination of both the new wine and the old wineskins. There are situations where churches are no longer fulfilling their God-ordained purposes. A New Testament example is the church in Ephesus, which is warned that, unless there is repentance, Jesus will close it down. The issue here appears to be neither doctrinal error nor moral corruption, but spiritual lethargy: "You have forsaken your first love."[6] The threat to "remove your lampstand from its place" surely indicates that the church is in danger of losing its mandate to incarnate the gospel and to advance the mission of God in that city.

Is it not possible that contemporary churches have closed for similar reasons, or may be under the same impending judgment, or in fact (depending on our understanding of what removal of the lampstand means) may already have had the lampstand removed, even if the services continue as normal? Where repentance occurs, renewal is possible, but what happens when this does not occur? Presumably God still intended to carry out his mission into Ephesus, so if repentance was not forthcoming, the planting of a new church to help this would appear to be required.

It may seem strange for an advocate of church planting to argue in this way for a more limited biblical basis for church planting, but it is important for several reasons. First, claiming unwarranted biblical authority for our policy and practice damages our own integrity and risks alienating those unimpressed by our hermeneutical naiveté. A justifiable, though limited, biblical foundation is more helpful in the long run than an expansive claim that is indefensible. Second, claiming too extensive a biblical foundation risks encouraging a preoccupation with church planting at the expense of other valid evangelistic methods. If church planting is presented as *the* New Testament approach to evangelism, it may be adopted without due consideration being given to other, and perhaps more appropriate, ways of reaching a community.

Third, excessive claims about the biblical basis for church planting may lead to inadequate attention being given to other biblical principles and priorities, such as the unity of the church, making disciples, the kingdom of God, and prophetic involvement in society. Fourth, claiming too much risks assumptions being made about the correctness of embarking on church planting without proper attention being given to strategic, tactical, and locational issues. The stronger the claim that church planting is biblical, the greater the danger of failing to ascertain the viability of this approach in a given situation.

There is a New Testament basis for church planting, but it is more modest than is sometimes assumed. Acceptance of this does not undercut the contemporary practice of church planting, but rather undergirds it with a more responsible hermeneutical foundation. It may also encourage those considering church planting to explore contextual issues more thoroughly, rather than succumbing to the temptation to evade these, on the pretext that church planting is "biblical" and thus appropriate in their situation.

New Testament Perspectives on Church Planting

The second way in which the New Testament is used in relation to church planting is to provide perspectives on church planting, or guidelines for establishing new churches. Here, we have a wealth of material. If, as argued in this chapter, the biblical rationale for church planting is less extensive than is often suggested, biblical perspectives on church planting are much more extensive than is often supposed. The contextual differences between first century and twenty-first century church planting must be taken into account, but there are throughout the New Testament extensive resources for church planters and recently planted churches.

Several writers have attempted to summarize biblical guidelines for church planting,[7] most of whom wisely insist that the New Testament contains insights and principles rather than blueprints. Not all those involved locally in church planting are careful to make this distinction, which sometimes leads to the employment of methods which are "biblical" but quite inappropriate. For this reason, it may be preferable to speak about "New Testament perspectives" rather than "New Testament guidelines."

The obvious and popular starting place for those searching for New Testament perspectives is the book of Acts, which has sometimes been treated as a church planting manual, an account of the establishment of the first church in Jerusalem and its reproduction throughout the Roman Empire through various kinds of church planting. Acts has been mined by many writers and speakers for missiological principles and lessons for contemporary church planters.[8]

Some concentrate on questions of *strategy*: how church planting initiatives were planned and organized, where churches were planted, the role of the church planter, the operation of planting teams, how long church planters spent in various situations, the role of the mother church, and the relationship between the church planter and the recently planted church.

Some look for help with *methodology*: how evangelism took place, the use of apologetics, cross-cultural perspectives, guidelines for contextualization, and the discovery of church growth principles.

Some explore issues of *personnel*: who was involved in church planting, the gifts and experience needed, the selection of team members, guidelines for team ministry, and the provision of accountability structures.

Some are interested in *ecclesiology*: what kinds of churches were planted, the appointment and training of new church leaders, the difficulties encountered by newly planted churches, the administration of finance, the interaction between local and translocal leaders, and the structure of first century churches.

Some focus on *spirituality*: the place of prayer and fasting, the role of spiritual warfare, principles of guidance, the work of the Holy Spirit, and the impact of signs and wonders.

Many of these issues are also relevant, of course, in other contexts than church planting. But their New Testament context is church planting, and they seem to have obvious relevance to contemporary church planting situations.

However, the legitimacy of this approach has been questioned. One problem is that the book of Acts is not just about church planting but addresses various topics of concern to the early churches. These include the extent to which the churches posed a threat to the state, theological debates regarding inclusion of Gentiles in a hitherto Jewish community, and the internal economics and leadership of the community. These interests are presented by Luke within the context of the expansion of the Christian movement and the church planting which accompanied this. Many of these interests, translated into different contexts, have very considerable contemporary relevance. And the establishment of new churches may offer opportunities to explore such dimensions of church life in fresh ways.

But to treat the book of Acts simply as a church planting manual fails to recognize the author's purposes, does not do justice to the breadth of its interests, and may lead to illegitimate conclusions being drawn. The result of such treatment might be that church planters, and the churches which they plant, do not engage in theological, missiological, and ecclesiological reflection which Luke appears to invite, and for which the book of Acts provides resources.

However, whether Acts is used as a church planting manual or as a resource for wider reflection, we need to take cognizance of another important issue of interpretation, concerning the extent to which narrative literature can be used as a foundation for theological, ethical, missiological, or ecclesiological principles. The fact that some action was taken in the book of Acts, or that some strategy was used, does not require us to assume that this was the *appropriate* action or strategy in that context, or that this is transferable to other contexts. There is a temptation to defer unduly and uncritically to early church practices, rather than evaluating these in the light of wider biblical revelation.

For example, it is usually assumed that the apostles were the pioneers, constantly pushing forward in the task of world evangelization. But it is possible to read Acts from a different perspective, which identifies unknown disciples or individuals who should have been serving at tables in Jerusalem[9] as the true pioneers, carrying the gospel into new regions and planting new churches. The apostles, by contrast, seem to have got bogged down in Jerusalem and to have taken on maintenance roles rather than acting as mission leaders. Their reason for appointing the Seven (Acts 6:1-7) was apparently not to release them for mission, but to give them more time for prayer and the ministry of the word. Even persecution (Acts 8:1-3) cannot shift them out of Jerusalem.

When Philip evangelizes a Samaritan city (Acts 8:4-8), Peter and John, as representatives of the apostles in Jerusalem, come to inspect and validate this unexpected development. Although they not only participate in this mission but follow Philip's lead and evangelize other Samaritan villages on their way back to Jerusalem (Acts 8:15-25), they are not exactly at the cutting edge of the mission of the churches. Peter finally does seem to have become more mobile and mission-oriented (Acts 9:32), but he still requires the persuasion of a divine vision to respond to an opportunity at the house of Cornelius, an opportunity that he should arguably have welcomed as an opportunity to break new ground and advance the mission of God in line with the parting commands of Jesus.

Luke's concentration in the second half of Acts on Paul's ministry might indicate his judgment that the Jerusalem apostles were not engaged wholeheartedly in this mission. Antioch (Acts 13:1-3; 14:26-28) is presented as a missionary congregation, with the Jerusalem church functioning more as an arbiter of orthodoxy and brake on radical progress (Acts 11:1-18; 15:1-29).

It is not necessary to accept this rather jaundiced view of the apostles to appreciate the point, that narrative is open to different interpretations. Acts is a significant resource for contemporary church planting, but as a source of inspiration, encouragement, warning, and reflection, rather than of blueprints and unwarranted conclusions.

Whereas Acts is commonly recognized as directly and immediately relevant to church planting, the contribution of other books of the New Testament needs further investigation. An appreciation of the context within which these documents were written may help us appreciate their significance for church planting. Many of the epistles are letters sent from church planters to the young churches they had planted. They address vital doctrinal, ethical and pastoral issues that had arisen in the early months and years of the life of these churches.

Many of these issues are relevant also for recently planted contemporary churches. These include questions about structure versus freedom, the recognition of gifts and leadership roles, uncertainties about doctrine, pastoral issues concerning families with some members who are not Christians, issues of church discipline and establishing ethical norms, and warnings about those who would exploit the vulnerability of young churches and inexperienced leaders. In fact, it is arguably within church planting situations, rather than within academic faculties, or even within long-established churches, that the teachings of the epistles come alive. Attempts to interpret the epistles without reference to their original church planting context may distort their meaning, by exploiting them for proof-texts for systematized theological treatises, or by attempting to apply them, without adaptation, to a more settled ecclesiastical context for which they were not originally intended.

Perhaps the classic example of this tendency is in relation to Paul's letter to the church in Rome. This letter, from a church planter to a church he did not plant himself but which he longs to visit, is often interpreted, in theological commentaries and popular preaching, as if it were a doctrinal thesis.[10] Undoubtedly, it contains much foundational doctrinal teaching on such issues as law and grace, justification by faith, and the ministry of the Spirit. But, as Martin Robinson has noted, Romans is "not just a treatise on justification by faith, it is first and foremost an explanation of Paul's ministry in establishing churches among the Gentiles."[11]

The long section on God's purposes for Israel (Rom. 9-11), which seems rather tenuously connected to the earlier doctrinal section, is crucial in explaining Paul's church planting strategy. He is working among the Gentiles, not because he has lost hope for Israel, but because he sees a future harvest of Israelites as a result of the establishing of Gentile churches. The climax of the letter, which precedes various personal greetings, refers to Paul's ministry as a church planter and his motivation to preach Christ in unreached areas (Rom. 15:17-20), notifies his readers of his intention to visit Rome en route to a new church planting initiative in Spain (Rom. 15:23-24), and returns to the theme of how Gentile churches can begin to repay their debt to the Jews (Rom. 15:25-27).

The interpretation of other epistles requires a similar shift of focus. Their doctrinal and ethical teaching is applicable to a wide range of contexts, but the church planting context for which they were originally written needs to be recognized if illegitimate conclusions are not to be drawn and unwarranted applications made. Some of the teaching contained in the Epistles seems to be provisional rather than final, theology "on the run," vibrant and creative, but unsystematized. This is not to downgrade such teaching, or to dispute its authority as inspired Scripture, but to require that it is not interpreted without regard to its genre.

Three epistles (1 and 2 Tim. and Titus) are even more directly related to church planting strategies. It seems ironic that these epistles are often referred to as the "Pastorals." These are letters from the leader of a church planting team to team members he has left behind, in Ephesus and Crete respectively, to continue the planting work in which the team had been involved. They contain spiritual and practical guidance and encouragement for these young apostolic delegates, as they attend to the kinds of issues that contemporary church planters recognize without difficulty as common in the early stages of establishing new churches. These issues include the recognition and appointment of indigenous leaders; the essential doctrinal foundations that needed to be laid in the churches; the development of appropriate styles of worship, teaching, and pastoral care; the need to confront troublemakers and guard against division and wrong teaching. The cultural context may be different, but the challenges facing church planters are remarkably similar. These epistles provide excellent resources for church planting teams to study together.

The Gospels, too, need to be understood in relation to the mission of the early churches and the establishing of new churches in diverse cultural and social contexts. For the Gospels are not just accounts of the life, death, and resurrection of Jesus. Nor do they only provide material for teaching and discipling new believers. They are also mission documents, resources for the developing churches, dealing with issues that were important to them in their own community life and in their concern to share their faith with others. Each Gospel represents a different perspective on the story, an attempt to contextualize it for different situations and communities.

Church planting into pioneer areas or relatively unchurched communities involves telling the story of Jesus in a way that makes sense locally and relates to the surrounding cultural context. Just as the Gospels tell the same story but in four different ways, so church planters are concerned to find appropriate ways in which to retell the story for the communities they are hoping to evangelize. Contextualization is a vital issue for church planters, and the four Gospels offer a very helpful New Testament paradigm for this.

Although I know of no research to confirm this, I am convinced that recently planted churches use the Gospels in their teaching programs much more than longer established churches, which tend to concentrate on the epistles. One obvious reason for this is the concern of new churches to provide basic Christian teaching for those whom they are trying to reach and who might attend their meetings.

This recovery of the Gospels may prove to be a helpful corrective influence, especially within evangelical circles where the bias toward the epistles is very marked (and where the mission context of these letters is not always recognized). However, this emphasis on the Gospels is less evident among those who write about and develop strategic approaches to church planting.[12] The relative paucity of engagement with the Gospels among contemporary church planters is an issue to which we return later in this chapter.

One New Testament document that deals explicitly[13] with second-generation church life, rather than the challenges facing newly planted churches, is the book of Revelation. Early chapters review the life and witness of the seven churches in Asia Minor, call for endurance under pressure and continuing focus on mission, and identify doctrinal and ethical issues that require attention. Twice (Rev. 2:5; 2:19) there are references to what the churches are doing now compared to what they did "at first" after they were planted. Different opportunities and problems now face these churches.

The call to the church in Sardis to "wake up" and "strengthen what remains" (Rev. 3:2) and the warning to the church at Laodicea that it has become lukewarm (Rev. 3:16) focus on issues that are more characteristic of established churches than newly planted churches. A comparison between the issues addressed here and in the epistles is revealing, indicating the particular challenges facing recently planted churches, and confirming the point made previously concerning the way in which those letters need to be interpreted, with their church planting context in view.

The book of Revelation also of course presents the mission and destiny of the church in a cosmic and eschatological dimension. The planting of churches is not just a strategy for evangelism and discipleship, but one aspect of the mission of God which embraces the whole created order. The identification of the church as the Bride of the Lamb invests church life and church planting with tremendous dignity. But the scope of God's mission as revealed in this book precludes us from separating this task from the advance of God's kingdom throughout society and the whole universe.

So, whereas the New Testament *basis* for church planting is less extensive than is often supposed, every strand of New Testament teaching, it seems, can be mined for *perspectives* on church planting. This breadth of material clarifies why it is difficult to find a succinct biblical rationale for church planting. Church planting may be peripheral theologically by comparison with a theme like the kingdom of God, but it is the primary context within which the New Testament was written, and by reference to which it should be understood. Church planters can draw on the resources of the entire New Testament. Many treatments of the New Testament and church planting claim both too little and too much.

The New Testament can and should be read as a mission document, written primarily to leaders and members of first-generation churches, and addressing issues arising within this church planting context. Theological, ethical and pastoral teaching is provided in relation to these pressing concerns, not to provide a systematic textbook of theology or ethics. David Bosch comments, with delightful understatement, that "the missionary character of the New Testament has not always been appreciated." He concludes that the New Testament writers "wrote in the context of an 'emergency situation,' of a church which, because of its missionary encounter with the world, was *forced* to theologize."[14] It is important to recapture this context if we are to interpret the New Testament properly.

The New Testament, as a mission document, is not designed for static and ingrown churches, for theologians wanting to debate abstruse points of doctrine, or for church leaders with a maintenance mentality. Movement, growth, a concern for practical discipleship, and the planting of new churches are presupposed. It is vital that we rescue New Testament interpretation from its academic and establishment captivity and recover this missiological framework. Contemporary church planting experience and biblical reflection on this could have a role here.

We indicated in the previous chapter that church planting might be a stimulus to further theological reflection, especially in the areas of ecclesiology and missiology. Perhaps this practice might also make a contribution to the interpretation of the New Testament. Rather than trying to establish a questionable New Testament rationale for church planting, advocates might concentrate on appropriating New Testament perspectives on church planting. In the process, others may recognize this practice, and the biblical reflection to which it is subjected, as a catalyst by means of which the New Testament can be rediscovered as a mission document.

The Quest for the "New Testament Church"

We need briefly to consider the legitimacy and implications of one way in which the New Testament has been used by some church planters. The "quest for the historical Jesus," on which some New Testament scholars have embarked in recent generations,[15] is paralleled by the quest to discover and restore the "New Testament church," a holy grail for church planting movements throughout the centuries. New churches have been planted that were supposedly closer to the New Testament pattern than any contemporary expressions of church life. This quest has been both instructive and elusive. What appeared to one generation as a restoration of New Testament church life has been rejected by the next as inadequate, and often as unduly influenced by the culture in which such churches were planted.

But this constant revision has not diminished the hope that one generation will finally accomplish the task. Whatever the prospect of reaching this goal, the quest itself has undoubtedly recovered aspects of New Testament teaching that have been neglected and has enabled the church as a whole (not just the church planting movements) to develop in new and creative ways.

The problem with this approach is that it tends toward uniformity and inflexibility. It does not take seriously enough the diversity of New Testament teaching and practice. Which is the authentic New Testament church? Corinth? Philippi? Thessalonica? On what basis do we decide this? Nor does it recognize the extent to which churches in the first century were facing similar issues of contextualization to those facing churches on the threshold of the twenty-first century. The churches known to us through the New Testament were young and far from perfect. They are presented, warts and all, struggling to be faithful to the gospel in their various social contexts. How do we distinguish fundamental principles from contextual adaptations? Nor does this approach adequately take into account the extent to which first century churches may have failed to embody the teachings of Jesus.

There is a tendency to idealize first century churches in a way that might astound, amuse, or outrage a time-traveling Peter or Paul. There are important principles and examples here, but faithful discipleship and biblical ecclesiology may look quite different in different contexts. If a search for the authentic New Testament church has energized church planting movements, it has also hindered the development of an ecclesiology that is flexible enough to survive cultural changes. Structures and practices regarded as authentic expressions of New Testament church life are difficult to criticize, challenge, or adapt.

A second problem associated with this quest has been the failure to delve deeply enough into the New Testament to discover what kinds of churches should be planted. Three perennial tendencies can be detected in church planting movements: concentration on structural issues, rather than relational or spiritual issues; concern about internal arrangements, rather than the role of the church in society; and interest in the attempts of the early churches to follow the teaching of Jesus, rather than in the teaching of Jesus himself. All of these may be subsumed under a search for New Testament church life.

Structural reform or innovation may be necessary, both for the internal health of a new church and to equip it for mission. Relational and spiritual growth may be helped or hindered by the structures developed. But there is a danger of confusing the scaffolding with the building. The New Testament says relatively little about these structural arrangements, and most of what it does contain are values and principles that can be encapsulated in various structural patterns. It is these values and principles which are crucial, and which need to be recovered in each generation, rather than a pattern which represents the attempt of a previous generation to embody them.

Time and energy are expended on ensuring that the new church is properly governed and administered, that might more usefully have been spent on developing friendships and enabling it to engage in caring and evangelistic action beyond its own boundaries. It is not only church plants that are prone to postpone mission until their own affairs are in order, but a disturbing number of new churches are lured away from their initial commitment to mission into ecclesiastical perfectionism. When it becomes evident, after a few months or years, that the radical new structure looks remarkably like the structure familiar in many older churches (except that bishops are called apostles and ministers are called leading elders), it is difficult to justify this preoccupation.

Concern about the internal structure and shape of the church may not only distract the church from mission. It may also hinder the church from addressing the important issue of its role in society. The New Testament seems quite relaxed about whether churches are to be run by elders and deacons (1 Tim. and Titus), by prophets and teachers (Acts 13, 1 Cor.) or by nondescript leaders (Heb.). However, there is considerable interest in the relationship between the church and the state (Luke-Acts, Rom., 1 Peter, Rev.); in how the churches deal with family and work relationships, with issues of race and class, with poverty and slavery (1 and 2 Cor., Eph., Col., 1 Tim., Phil., James); and in the struggle faced by the churches to be relevant to their culture, yet distinctive (the Synoptic Gospels; 1 and 2 Cor.).

The ethos of the church, its attitudes toward nonmembers, and its social involvement are at least as important as its shape and structure. Those concerned to plant New Testament churches might do well to give greater attention to these issues. It is not that the shape of the church is unimportant, but there are more fundamental matters which, if ignored, will consign any reshaping of the church to strategic insignificance.

The third tendency relates to the general bias, noted above, toward studying the epistles at the expense of the Gospels. This preference for systematic theology over narrative theology, and for the teachings of the apostles over the teachings of Jesus, has influenced Western Christianity in numerous ways: doctrinally, ethically and ecclesiologically. Although it may be thought unhelpful to characterize and polarize the Gospels and the epistles in this way, it does seem that, in practice, renewed emphasis on the Gospels results in fresh thinking about mission and discipleship. The problem is not that the Gospels and epistles are contradictory or incompatible, but that they are different in form and content. Both the epistles and the Gospels were intended to help various early church communities develop theologically, spiritually, morally and relationally, in ways consistent with the example and teaching of Jesus. Both contain (though in different proportions) memories of what Jesus had said and done, and indications of how the communities might respond to this.

Several church planting movements have given renewed attention to the Gospels, usually because they have suspected older churches of marginalizing the radical teachings of Jesus contained in the Gospels. The dominant interest in the epistles had led, they believed, both to a systematized approach to Christianity and to the frequent marginalization of elements of Jesus' teaching and incidents in his ministry that are hard to systematize in this way. The provocative nonconformity of Jesus' life and the so-called "hard sayings" the Gospels faithfully record have been explained away or simply ignored.

Christocentric biblical interpretation, that takes Jesus seriously and interprets the rest of the Bible in light of his teaching and example, rather than trying to fit him into systems and convictions already established, has been a minority position in church history. It is of interest to see that it has been within certain church planting movements, notably the Waldensians and the Anabaptists,[16] that this Christocentric approach has been recovered. New churches have been planted, at least in part, to allow Christians to rediscover the subversive memory of Jesus and to explore the implications of his teachings in their communal life.

But not all church planting movements have been energized by this concern. They have searched the New Testament for guidance, but have concentrated on Acts or the epistles, rather than on the Gospels. Church planting, consequently, has frequently been ecclesiocentric rather than Christocentric. The fact that there are only two recorded instances when Jesus spoke about the church[17] has perhaps discouraged church planters from engaging in the search for Jesus' view of the church, but this has arguably resulted in distorted emphases and unexplored issues. In particular, it has allowed church planting to become detached from the central theme of Jesus' teaching: the kingdom of God.

On what issues related to church planting might the Gospels make a contribution?

The fact that Jesus did not refer often to the church might in itself be significant. His emphasis on the kingdom of God, as a divine initiative that, in mysterious ways, is at work to transform the created order, warns us against ascribing to the church any more than penultimate significance. The church is a sign, an instrument, an agent of the kingdom, but no more than this. Deeper engagement with the Gospels might help church planters avoid excessive interest in the church.

Jesus' teaching about wealth, violence, and power are also of fundamental importance in church planting. Changing terminology, structures, and styles of worship are of far less significance than creating communities where new patterns of economic sharing, peacemaking, and servant leadership are developing, communities that are rooted in the teachings of Jesus and contextualized into diverse social contexts. The epistles introduce us to communities struggling to work out the implications of these values in their social contexts. How should their finances be administered and distributed? How should peaceful relationships be maintained? To what extent should the roles of men and women mirror or challenge their roles in contemporary society?

We use the epistles wisely if we enter into dialogue with these communities and learn from their experience, as we reflect on the similar challenges we face in a different context. We misuse them if we fail to discern the contextual elements, and especially if we do not push back beyond them to the teachings of Jesus from which they derive their inspiration.

One passage (Matt. 18:15-20) where Jesus does speak about the church community contains profound implications for church planters. He describes a community which is serious about discipleship; a community characterized by open and loving relationships; a community that recognizes it is comprised of imperfect people, and develops a style of life that remains faithful to the highest standards but realistic about failure; a community that balances individual responsibility and corporate action; a community in which there is no hint of clericalism; and, arguably, a community small enough to operate in such a way. This passage has frequently been regarded as relevant only to the question of how to exercise church discipline. It has been poorly interpreted, unwisely applied, and widely ignored. It has not received much attention from church planters.

It does not answer all the questions we might ask about structures and strategies. But it contains fundamental principles and values that might challenge and inform contemporary church planting, if we can only reach back beyond the epistles. Once we have encountered this passage, we may discover similar teachings in almost all the epistles, as the early churches attempted to apply Jesus' vision of church life in their own communities.[18]

These are no more than a sample of the issues that the Gospels might raise for church planters. There are many others, which are, of course, relevant also to existing churches. But the planting of new churches offers opportunities to establish new ways of being the church that would be difficult to introduce into established churches. It would be disappointing if the failure of church planters to grapple with the teachings of Jesus resulted in only superficial or even inappropriate changes. The quest for the restoration of New Testament churches has been underway for many centuries, and we turn in the next chapter to consider some historical examples of church planting. But the challenge to contemporary church planters who search the New Testament for guidance and inspiration is to engage above all with the great Church Planter, who gave Peter the "keys of the kingdom" but promised, "*I* will build *my* church."[19]

4. CHURCH PLANTING: A HISTORICAL PERSPECTIVE

Church planting has been taking place for nearly twenty centuries. The rate of planting has slowed and quickened; different kinds of churches have been planted; the motivating factors have been various; and the strategies and methodologies adopted have ranged from the cumbersome to the audacious. Church history provides further resources alongside the New Testament (or more accurately a continuation of the story), from which much can be learned by contemporary church planters.

But tapping into these resources is not easy. Church planting has not, until quite recently, been regarded as a distinct subject. There are many fascinating accounts and instructive models, but these tend to be hidden within general historical or missiological studies. This may in itself be significant, warning us once more against ascribing to church planting an unwarranted status. A historical perspective confirms what we discovered in the New Testament. Church planting is one component in a much broader mission agenda, that includes evangelism, discipleship, social action, cultural engagement, political involvement, environmental concern, and much else. Located within this broader agenda, church planting has been throughout history of crucial importance, but extracted from this setting, it has been a distraction from wholistic mission.

Our interest in this chapter is not to provide an exhaustive survey of two millennia of church planting, but to set the contemporary church planting movement in historical perspective. One of the difficulties faced by advocates of church planting is the apparent newness of this practice. Very many church members have no experience of church planting or recollection of the story of how even their own church came into being. Church planting is not recognized as a normal activity, alongside practices like prayer, preaching, youth ministry, and evangelism. Even the terminology was not familiar within local churches as recently as a decade ago. A historical perspective may, therefore, be important. Those inclined to be suspicious of anything new may find this perspective helps them appreciate the potential of church planting. Those inclined to be equally suspicious of anything older than the past decade, if they can be persuaded to explore earlier experiences of church planting, may find some surprisingly useful parallels and be saved from reinventing wheels and repeating mistakes.

As with our use of the New Testament, however, lessons derived from church history must be extracted with care if they are to be applicable to different contexts. It is as easy to establish from church history as it is from the New Testament that, in the context of pioneer evangelism in pre-Christian societies, most missionaries planted churches. But the relevance of this to church planting strategies for post-Christian Western societies needs to be assessed before contemporary church planters adopt uncritically methods or expectations that were legitimate in very different contexts. Even where we can identify church planting movements in situations comparable to our own, care will be needed to distinguish between transferable principles and cultural or situational peculiarities.

Categorizing always risks oversimplification, but it may help us to attain a historical perspective on church planting if we consider four main kinds of planting.

Pioneer planting refers to the practice of establishing churches in areas previously unreached by the gospel, but now being evangelized and discipled. Wherever missionaries have advanced geographically, this form of church planting has been undertaken.

Replacement planting has to do with to the practice of establishing churches in areas where churches had previously been planted, but no longer exist, due to factors such as persecution or decline. History contains many instances of regions which had been evangelized, and in which churches had flourished in previous generations, needing to be reevangelized.

Sectarian planting refers to the practice of establishing more churches in areas where churches already exist, to express and embody distinctive doctrinal or ecclesiological convictions. This terminology sounds pejorative, but has been used descriptively by sociologists since Ernst Troeltsch,1 and is not intended here to imply that this practice is illegitimate.

Saturation planting refers to the practice of establishing more churches in areas where churches already exist, to enhance the ability of these churches to engage in mission within these areas. The new churches may differ in certain ways from the existing churches, but these differences tend to be pragmatic rather than ideological.

Pioneer Planting

Many examples could be given of each form of church planting. The New Testament, as noted in the previous chapter, tells the story of the pioneer planting movement that carried the gospel from Jerusalem to Rome and beyond in the first century. During the next 300 years, this movement continued to establish churches throughout the disintegrating Roman Empire and beyond its boundaries.

The pace quickened in the fourth century, as churches emerged from sporadic persecution to face the challenge of being invited by the recently converted emperor, Constantine, to construct a new imperial religion. Imperial support and resources made possible the proliferation of churches all over the empire, although the methods used and the kinds of churches established would no doubt have surprised earlier church planters. The pace slowed again in subsequent centuries, as the churches shifted from mission mode into pastoral mode, assuming that the great commission had been fulfilled, and as their leaders became immured in doctrinal controversies.

But followers of one of the casualties of these controversies, Nestorius, probably banished without just cause, saw in their expulsion from the empire a missionary opportunity and embarked on a remarkable but poorly documented evangelistic and church planting campaign that carried the gospel across Asia, as far as China. As European Christianity slipped into the maintenance mode that persisted with few interruptions throughout the medieval era, a battle for the heart of Asia was raging between Islam, Buddhism, and the Nestorian churches. Despite facing sustained competition of a kind European Christians had never experienced, Nestorian missionaries made disciples and established churches in such numbers that it has been estimated that, in the eleventh and twelfth centuries, there were more Nestorian Christians in Asia than Catholic Christians in Europe.[2] Wolfgang Hage has described this movement as "the missionary church *par excellence* in the overall context of medieval Christianity."[3]

Pioneer planting continued as European Christians seized the opportunity of the discovery of the Americas to evangelize new territories, although the use of bribery and force (sometimes referred to as evangelism by "flattery and battery") that characterized their missionary methods would not find favor among contemporary church planters. Nor would contemporary church planters wish to adopt some of the attitudes and assumptions of subsequent generations of missionaries who engaged in pioneer evangelism and church planting in Africa, Asia, and the Pacific. These missionaries were dedicated and frequently heroic individuals, and their endeavors have significantly reduced the scope for contemporary pioneer church planting, but many of the churches they planted were debilitated by cultural imperialism and inadequate indigenization. The focus was on individual conversions.

Church planting was often little more than a consequence or by-product of evangelism. Establishing new churches for converts was recognized as necessary for the progress of mission in these pioneer regions, but little ecclesiological thought was given to how such churches might differ from the sending churches of the missionaries.

Lessons have been learned; sensitivity to these issues has increased; and more appropriate forms of pioneer evangelism and church planting have been developed. Indeed, the change of emphasis during the nineteenth century, from the earlier Pietist concern for individual conversions, to efforts to plant churches that would be self-governing, self-supporting and self-propagating, significantly advanced the cause of indigenization. The more ecclesiocentric approach to mission that had been advocated by missionary strategists such as Henry Venn, Rufus Anderson, and Karl Graul, required missionaries to become more aware of ecclesiological issues and to treat church planting as an integral part of mission.[4]

The influential writings of Roland Allen, early in the twentieth century, renewed the challenge: "Are we actually planting new churches, or merely perpetuating a mission?"[5] Questions about the kinds of churches to be planted in different contexts, and the status of church planting—a necessary means to an end, an end in itself, or an integral part of a wider mission strategy—will recur as we continue to explore its contemporary practice.

Pioneer planting will continue until every community on earth has been evangelized. Those who participate in this form of church planting have rich resources within church history to inspire their commitment, to guide their activities, and to sound some important warnings. But most contemporary church planting does not fall within the category of pioneer planting. The inspiration, guidance, and warnings are still relevant, but the different context cannot be ignored.

Replacement Planting

Replacement planting has occurred both locally and regionally. In a number of pioneer situations, attempts have been made to establish new churches, but these have subsequently ceased to operate. This may be due to opposition from the local community, a lack of local converts, poor indigenization, inadequate spiritual foundations, or other factors. Fresh ventures to evangelize the region will require the replacement of these churches by new ones, but this is likely to be successful only if the reasons for past failure are understood and addressed. Replacement planting may appear to be planting on unclaimed territory, but it differs from pioneer planting in that there is a legacy from the past that may still be influential.

This legacy may contain both positive and negative elements: residual Christian faith within the community, familiarity with biblical teaching, resistance to outside influences, or bad memories of previous efforts to establish churches. Simply trying to repeat the church planting efforts of earlier missionaries may be ineffective.

A fascinating historical example of replacement church planting occurred during the reevangelization of England in the fifth and sixth centuries. The Roman Empire was collapsing, and pagan tribes were overrunning a supposedly Christian empire. Throughout Western Europe as well as in England, churches that had looked to Rome for political and ecclesiastical support were disappearing. The extent of nominality was becoming evident, as were the effects of the failure to develop indigenous churches that could survive the withdrawal of this support.

But Christianity had also penetrated beyond the boundaries of the Empire. In Ireland especially, through the apostolic ministry of Patrick and others, churches had been established that were rooted in the culture and clan structure of the Irish people. In Wales and Scotland also were Christian communities—churches and monastic centers—that owed much to Roman Christians for their foundation, but relied little on continuing patronage. Celtic Christianity had taken deep root, and within it were spiritual resources to survive the resurgent paganism and political upheavals of the fifth century.

There were two different responses to this situation from the Celtic churches:[6] spiritual renewal and church planting. The typical Welsh approach, which was shared by some from the other regions, was to dig deep, to preserve their heritage, to nurture spirituality, and to wait for better times. Their churches and monasteries became centers of learning, havens of peace, and providers of spiritual sustenance for those who sought such resources. This was not ineffective, and some today opt for a similar strategy of spiritual renewal and pastoral nurturing within the existing Christian community, as their response to the pressures of twenty-first century political upheaval, religious pluralism, and resurgent paganism. But, by itself, this response did not constitute an adequate strategy.

The second response was the Celtic missionary movement that emerged from Ireland and Scotland, a very different kind of monasticism, consisting of teams of church planting and evangelizing monks, who traveled all over England and on into Western Europe and beyond. The mission work seems to have involved a self-replicating model, whereby teams of men and women established new churches and new monasteries, missionary communities, and training centers from which further teams were sent out to continue the work. Team members became team leaders. All over England, the demise of the Roman churches gave way to the replacement planting achieved by this vibrant missionary movement. Although there were set-backs, many of their churches took root, survived, and flourished in these difficult times.

Why did they flourish? Certainly a primary factor was the spiritual vitality of the Celtic missionaries and the churches they planted. Evangelism and social action were rooted in a deep spirituality and often accompanied by signs and wonders.[7] This was a wholistic church planting movement. But a significant further factor was the extent to which these churches were contextualized. By comparison with the Roman churches that had been established in previous generations, they seemed quite unimpressive, characterized by simplicity and flexibility, and dependent on local leadership without much external support. They seemed vulnerable, but proved to be more enduring because of their rootedness in the culture. Undoubtedly they tapped into the residual Christian faith still to be found in many communities. But it was their ability to rekindle this and establish appropriate forms of church life that made this such an effective replacement planting movement.

The Celtic missionary movement was, in fact, only one aspect of the reevangelization of England. While Celtic missionaries moved south from their bases in Scotland and Northumbria, Roman missionaries were moving north and west from Kent, as papal delegates responded to the challenge of recovering England for Christendom. For a while, these two systems co-existed, but in the seventh century the need was felt for a unified English church structure, and the Celtic churches were co-opted into the Roman church system at the Synod of Whitby in 664. It is difficult to assess how the Roman mission would have fared without this Celtic movement, but the movement had played a crucial role for over two hundred years and left an enduring mark on British Christianity.

The contemporary interest in Celtic Christianity has tended to focus on aspects other than its church planting exploits, but there is much to learn here.[8] Among interesting features of this replacement planting movement were its reliance upon minimal resources, its self-replicating strategy that ensured that training centers as well as churches were established and that new church planters were constantly emerging. Also notable were its use of ordinary men—and women—in evangelism and pastoral leadership, the simplicity and flexibility of its structures, and the role of signs and wonders.

Replacement planting continues to be an important component within church planting strategies, whether to replace abortive previous attempts in pioneering environments, or to replace churches that have closed after decades or even centuries of life and witness and a long struggle against decline. Such planting may be initiated locally, as awareness develops of a de-churched community, or it may be undertaken by a denominational body or a mission agency. Whenever a local church that is linked with others through a national or international ecclesiastical system or a denominational network ceases to operate, those with translocal responsibility are faced with a decision regarding its possible replacement. The decision not to replace this church may be based on various factors: the existence of sufficient churches in the vicinity to provide alternative means of fulfilling the mission of the church in that area; decline in population to the extent that fewer churches are needed; or lack of resources to effect a replacement.

In a situation of overall decline in church attendance, the tendency is for denominational leaders to be wary of stretching limited resources too far. Churches that close may not, therefore, be replaced. Remaining members of the congregation may be encouraged to relocate to a nearby alternative. But in many situations, it is arguable that a failure to engage in replacement planting may exacerbate the decline or at least not reverse it. Strategic decisions are needed regarding the best use of resources, and it may be that some judicial church pruning is necessary to release these resources, rather than waiting for churches to wither and die. Perhaps replacement planting needs to be more proactive than it has sometimes been.

Where there are resources for replacement planting, an important lesson from history is the need to consider carefully what kind of church might be planted. Also how should any church planting initiative respond to positive or negative aspects of the legacy of previous churches in this area?

Sectarian Planting

Historical examples of sectarian planting are plentiful in the past 450 years. Sectarian planting, in fact, characterizes the early years of most contemporary denominations. Many Lutheran, Methodist, Baptist and Pentecostal churches were not planted in pioneer territory, nor to replace churches that had closed, but to provide opportunities for the congregational expression of deeply held convictions about doctrinal and ecclesiological matters. Sometimes this motivation was combined with the opportunity presented by population growth or demographic changes, so that planting new churches could be accomplished without overtly invading the territory or challenging the legitimacy of existing churches. But the intention was to establish different kinds of churches.

The planting in Western societies of thousands of house churches over the past thirty years is another example of this form of church planting. Contemporary discussions about the validity or otherwise of this strategy are reruns of disputes about earlier sectarian church planting. For example, Baptists who bewail the emergence of a house church in their vicinity may find it instructive to discover that similar feelings were expressed decades ago or longer by those who found the planting of their own Baptist church equally threatening, divisive, and unjustifiable.

The Anabaptist movement of the sixteenth century,[9] which predates and had at least an indirect influence on the emergence of these denominations, provides a challenging and relevant historical example of sectarian church planting. Europe was in political and religious ferment: the peasants were protesting about the social injustices associated with the feudal system; the invention of printing meant that radical ideas could now be disseminated more quickly and widely than previously; the monopolistic position of Catholic Christendom was being destroyed; and the Protestant Reformation had begun. The Reformers, outraged by what they regarded as the serious doctrinal errors and gross moral corruption of the Catholic churches, persuaded the political authorities in various European cities and states to embark on a process of reformation. Within territories influenced by the Reformers, Catholic churches became Protestant churches overnight.

But for Protestant leaders such as Luther, Zwingli, Calvin and their many lesser-known colleagues, church planting was rarely on the agenda. The system of Christendom had been transmuted, but not abolished. Europe was still regarded as essentially Christian, in need of doctrinally sound preaching and effective pastoral care, rather than evangelizing. There were churches in every parish, so no further churches were needed. What was needed was the reformation and renewal of these churches. Where they had state support, the Reformers relied on state sanctions to coerce church attendance and achieve ecclesiastical reform.

There are occasional examples of evangelism and church planting in situations where coercion was not possible, such as missions by Calvinists in Catholic France, but these were exceptions rather than the rule. This stance may encourage those who are convinced that a similar emphasis is needed today, and that planting new churches is a distraction from this crucial task. Few, though, are likely to assume, as did most of the Reformers, that Europe is Christian, or that evangelism is unnecessary and evangelists are obsolete.

But not everyone in sixteenth-century Europe accepted the Christendom framework. Some were less sanguine than the Reformers about the prospects for reformation within existing churches. In Zürich, erstwhile supporters of Ulrich Zwingli lost patience with the pace of reform and opted for a more radical approach that involved the planting of believers churches. In these churches membership was voluntary, believers baptism (attacked by their opponents as rebaptism or "anabaptism," a capital offense) was practiced, church discipline was exercised, and many other features of what was regarded as New Testament Christianity were adopted. From Zürich and several other centers where similar convictions were being expressed, Anabaptism spread across Switzerland, Austria, Moravia, much of Germany and the Netherlands.

Unlike most of the Reformers, the Anabaptists believed that the great commission had not yet been fulfilled in Europe, so evangelism was vital. They were also convinced that the Reformers had stopped short of the reformation that was really required by failing to deal with ecclesiological issues. Most Anabaptists felt that contemporary churches were beyond mere reformation and that new kinds of churches were needed. Through the work of their recognized apostles and evangelists, and through the efforts of unknown church members, they launched a church planting movement across central Europe that resulted in the formation of thousands of new congregations.

The movement was drowned in blood, regarded by Catholics and Protestants alike as subversive, heretical, and sectarian. Thousands were exiled or executed; many migrated to safer areas; and soon only remnants survived in central Europe. But the myth of Christian Europe had been exploded. Evangelism and church planting were now firmly on the agenda, and questions about the nature of the church had been raised that would exercise subsequent generations. The Anabaptist movement is a classic example of the search for a restoration of New Testament church life which has motivated many church planting movements and led to the emergence of many denominations. This search continues to inspire many contemporary examples of sectarian planting.

Sectarian planting is more liable to attract criticism than the other forms of church planting under consideration here. Those who engage in it must defend its legitimacy on the grounds that the distinctives that are expressed in the newly planted churches are sufficiently important to further divide the church, or that failing to plant will seriously impair the church's ability to fulfill its mission. One common concern about sectarian planting is that it merely rearranges the Christian community, rather than making further disciples, and that it may actually diminish the church's impact and witness. Some apparently successful examples of contemporary church planting are open to criticism on this issue.

For a sectarian movement to continue growing after the initial period of growth through the transfer of members of other churches, however, growth through conversion is required. The extent to which such movements are effective in mission cannot generally be assessed until this initial period has passed. Historical examples of sectarian planting offer resources for reflection on the arguments for and against planting new churches, rather than attempting to reform and revitalize existing churches.

Saturation Planting

The term *saturation planting* has become familiar within contemporary church planting circles. It describes a motivation and methodology that is different from the three forms of planting that have been used in this chapter to categorize historical examples of church planting.

The purpose of saturation planting is not to impact new areas, nor to recover lost ground, nor to develop new kinds of churches, but to plant more churches in already churched areas. This terminology has become familiar especially through the advocacy of the AD 2000 and Beyond movement,[10] whose motto has been "A church for every people and the gospel for every person by AD 2000." Its Saturation Church Planting Resource Network contends that fulfillment of the great commission will require strategies to enable "Christ to become incarnate in the life of a vital, witnessing congregation among *every* group of 500 to 1000 people of *every* class, kind, and condition of mankind."[11] Although the movement emphasizes evangelism among unreached people groups, and church planting in pioneer areas and underchurched regions is also envisaged, the concern is to saturate all nations with churches.

Increasing the number of active churches in a locality is regarded as likely to soften the area toward the gospel and promote church growth. Contrary to the fears of many that more churches will lead to greater competition for the allegiance of those who are open to the gospel, advocates of saturation church planting argue that more churches per head of population will benefit all the churches. Sandy Millar, vicar of Holy Trinity Brompton in London, from where several churches have been planted, acknowledges that this is contrary to accepted Anglican views. But he argues that "the more churches there are in an area (given a sufficient population), the easier and more successful the total effect of those churches will be."[12]

Not all church leaders would agree, as was evident from a recent conversation with a church leader whose congregation had been substantially reduced through church members leaving to join a church planted from Holy Trinity. Furthermore, unless it is applied regionally rather than locally, this approach, which is based on insights from the church growth movement, can result in the increasing saturation of already well-churched areas at the expense of substantially less churched areas.

Historical examples of this kind of church planting can be found in the aftermath of many pioneer planting movements. Once an area has been evangelized, and churches have been planted in strategic locations, further planting can be undertaken to ensure that there are churches within easy reach of local communities throughout the region. This second stage planting may be regarded as a further responsibility of the pioneer planters, or handed over to the churches that have already been established.

Paul's strategy, as described in the New Testament, seems to have been to concentrate on the main urban centers and then to move on, leaving these urban churches to plant further churches in the rural areas. His extraordinary claim that "there is no more place for me to work in these regions" (Rom. 15:23), so that he is now free to visit Rome and head for Spain, can only be justified if he regards saturation planting as the responsibility of local Christians, rather than part of the ministry of his church planting team.

Harder to identify are historical examples of saturation planting in areas that experienced pioneer planting decades or even centuries earlier. It is this feature of the contemporary church planting movement that distinguishes it from most earlier examples of saturation planting. The movement advocates further planting in towns or regions where, for years or even for generations, existing churches have assumed that there were sufficient churches to engage effectively in mission and to meet the pastoral needs of those who wished to be church members.

The DAWN (Disciple A Whole Nation) strategy is a contemporary expression of such a saturation planting policy. This strategy, designed and implemented originally by Jim Montgomery, an American missionary in the Philippines, has been influential in the development of similar strategies in at least seventy other nations. Its assumptions, values, and principles have been regarded as transferable and have informed and guided saturation church planting in contexts very different from the Philippines. Our intention here is not to examine the DAWN strategy in detail, nor to repeat the story told elsewhere of the effects of implementing this strategy in the Philippines.[13] Our interest is rather in identifying certain features of this strategy that have impacted the contemporary church planting movement and have encouraged it to develop in ways that distinguish it from earlier church planting movements. It is arguable that these developments might have taken place without the influence of the DAWN strategy, but this strategy has played at least an inspirational and reinforcing role.

Jim Montgomery has defined the strategy as follows:

"DAWN aims at mobilizing the whole Body of Christ in whole countries in a determined effort to complete the great commission by working toward the goal of providing an evangelical congregation for every village and neighborhood of every class, kind and condition of people in the whole country."[14]

This definition indicates certain characteristics of saturation planting, as understood within the DAWN framework.

First, it is avowedly nonsectarian. It aims to mobilize the whole church within a nation to participate in a national church planting strategy. The number of churches, their location, and their accessibility, geographically and culturally, to every person within the nation are the crucial factors. The DAWN strategy has emerged from the church growth school of missiology, which emphasizes the need to identify "people groups" within nations and to design evangelistic and church planting strategies to reach these groups. Saturation planting is concerned, not merely with replicating churches, but with ensuring that each identifiable people group has access to a church which is contextually relevant.

New kinds of churches may therefore be planted, but for cultural rather than sectarian reasons. Some of these new churches may be regarded by critics as inauthentic because of their homogeneity (an issue to which we will return in a later chapter), or for other reasons. But the motivation behind their planting is not sectarian in the sense that characterized many earlier church planting movements.

However, despite this apparent ecumenicity, it is clear from the above definition, and from the ethos of the movement, that the DAWN strategy is interested primarily in establishing evangelical churches. Whether this is regarded as inherently sectarian will depend upon the perspective of any asking this question. But it is important to recognize that church planting is not, and historically has not been, the exclusive preserve of evangelical churches. Some advocates of the DAWN strategy have chosen to express their objective in different language. *Challenge 2000*, the vehicle for the DAWN strategy in the United Kingdom, for example, has expressed its hope that there will be "a living, growing Christ-centered congregation in every distinct community and neighborhood." This appears to leave open the question of where any boundary lines are drawn regarding participation.

While it is true that some contemporary church planting is still at least partly motivated by sectarian interests, one of the distinctive features of the contemporary movement, as noted in chapter 1, is its attempt to foster cooperation and partnership. The influence of the DAWN strategy has helped in this, both through its capacity as an international movement to provide a framework that transcends denominational loyalty, and through its advocacy of cooperation. The "10 DAWN Principles for Responsible Church Planting"[15] provide a helpful basis for this. Although many of these principles seem self-evident, it is important to recognize how few previous church planting movements would have subscribed to such principles. The spirit of cooperation engendered within the contemporary church planting movement is impressive and may have long term benefits whatever the success of the movement in planting new churches.

Second, the DAWN strategy is not concerned primarily with pioneer planting or replacement planting, but with saturation planting. The assumptions on which this strategy is based are that there are already many churches to be mobilized, that the task of fulfilling the great commission is already under way, and that planting more churches will advance this cause and even bring the mission to completion. Pioneer planting will be needed in new housing developments, but in most areas this is not relevant. Replacement planting may be a minor component, but a significant net increase in the number of churches in the nation is the goal.

The identification of this goal is an important issue where saturation church planting is presented as the strategy and where such church planting is undertaken in contexts of overall church decline and accompanying closures. Any goals set to achieve saturation must be concerned with the *net* increase, rather than simply recording new church plants. So, for example, between 1980 and 1990, about 3000 churches were planted and about 3100 churches were closed in the United Kingdom. The planting of 3000 new churches in a context where 3100 are simultaneously closed is a valid and relatively successful example of replacement planting, but clearly it represents no progress toward saturation planting. Numerical church planting targets need to specify the purpose for which new churches are being planted—replacement or saturation—and measure progress accordingly.

Third, this is essentially a long-term strategy that requires, according to its designer, "a determined effort" and "working toward" agreed goals. Many evangelistic and church planting ventures are set within a short time frame, but this strategy envisages the planning and implementation of policies which will require decades to complete. Montgomery has warned against assumptions that the task can be quickly accomplished: "All talk of 'the end of the mission era' is tragically mistaken. We stand today at midday in missions. Much has been done: but by far the greater part remains."[16]

This aspect of the strategy was often obscured by linking of the DAWN strategy with projects associated with the year 2000.[17] In the United Kingdom, a target of 20,000 new churches by the end of the 1990s had been suggested by *Challenge 2000*, although this figure has received no official support from denominational bodies. Coming from a church growth perspective, it is no surprise that the DAWN strategy should encourage the setting of goals, but the time frame imposed by the nearness of the end of the millennium prompted the setting of goals to be achieved within a decade or less.

This approach carries with it dangers now becoming evident within the church planting movement. The adoption of short-term church planting goals is acceptable within an overall strategy that is more concerned with long-term aims, but if these goals become the focus of the movement they may, even if achieved, distract from what is needed to accomplish the long-term aims. Attempting to plant churches quickly to achieve these short-term goals may result in the planting of weak churches, with inadequately trained leaders, the shortcomings of which may discourage further church planting. Churches may be planted in areas where there are already strong churches, because it is easier to plant quickly in such areas, rather than in areas that are more strategic to fulfill the aims of achieving saturation and providing churches within reach of every community.

Such church planting, as we argued in chapter 1, may have the potential actually to set back the fulfillment of the great commission by increasing the alienation of certain sectors of society from a church that appears to be ever more firmly wedded to sectors with which they find it hard to identify. There may not be enough time given to engaging in the creativity required to develop new kinds of churches, with the result that existing churches are replicated in ways that do not significantly increase their mission effectiveness and merely spread existing resources for mission more thinly. Perhaps most important, the determination to plant so many churches so quickly may be at the expense of seemingly less exciting, but potentially more fruitful, attempts to transform the mentality of churches and denominations, so that church planting is recovered as a natural activity of all churches, rather than the hobby of enthusiasts.

These are dangers that will be faced even if the short-term goals *are* achieved. If, as is now obvious, they will not be achieved or even approached, there will be the additional problem of energizing again those who have become discouraged and who wonder whether church planting might after all not be the way forward. This is an issue that advocates of church planting, and especially those responsible for setting goals, need to address honestly and sensitively. This will need careful handling if revision of the goals, or adjustment of the time frame within which they are to be achieved, is not to become a deterrent to those considering church planting. But failing to tackle this issue carries greater risks.

The DAWN strategy has encouraged contemporary church planters and has influenced the development of a church planting movement in many nations. It is possible to criticize the DAWN strategy along similar lines to those suggested in chapter 1, but the concerns raised here relate more to the ways in which this strategy has been interpreted than to the strategy itself. Lack of contextualization and inadequate awareness of what is and is not transferable in the DAWN strategy are perhaps the most significant concerns.

The DAWN strategy was developed and tested in a predominantly Catholic nation in the Two-Thirds World. Montgomery himself suggested various other nations or regions where DAWN strategies would be appropriate, all of these in the Two-Thirds World. The strategy has now been adopted in many other nations, including post-Christian European nations, but it is questionable whether the differences between these contexts have been adequately recognized or the implications explored.

Certainly the DAWN strategy itself requires that national leaders take responsibility for adapting the strategy to the needs of each nation, and those who have adopted the strategy have undoubtedly given attention to this. But it is possible that these adjustments have been inadequate and have failed to engage with the contextual differences at a deep enough level. Attempts to apply church growth insights developed in the Two-Thirds World to North American or European contexts have foundered before because of such inadequate contextual examination.

Montgomery has insisted[18] that "the discipling of each nation is a unique task, each presents a different combination of circumstances . . . the fullness of time comes in different decades or different centuries." This appears to suggest not only that care is needed in applying the DAWN strategy in various contexts, but that in some contexts a DAWN strategy may not be appropriate. Saturation church planting assumes either the existence of a responsive population and rapid current church growth, or the imminent arrival of these conditions. It is a method for "reaping the harvest" (to use church growth terminology) rather than sowing the seed. In some contexts, different strategies and methods may be required because "the fullness of time" has not arrived. Pioneer planting may be necessary; replacement planting may be required; sectarian planting may be justified; but there is no prospect of successful saturation planting.

A question facing church planters in Western societies is whether a DAWN strategy is appropriate and timely at the beginning of the twenty-first century. The effectiveness of DAWN strategies elsewhere does not provide an adequate basis for adopting such a strategy here. There may be many factors contributing toward this effectiveness that do not apply in our post-Christian and pluralistic society. Acknowledging this need not lead to pessimism or defeatism, but to the development of appropriate policies and strategies that might result in significant progress toward a situation within which a DAWN strategy *would* be effective.

Asking this question and concluding that a DAWN strategy is appropriate—either because the signs of such a harvest time are evident, or because there is a conviction that it is imminent—would undergird contemporary church planting. Failing to ask or answer this question risks encouraging unrealistic expectations that are likely not only to damage contemporary church planting efforts, but to hinder the development of strategies that will foster effective and sustainable church planting into the next century.

Have such questions been asked and answered? The more recent advocacy of DAWN strategies for all nations has replaced the earlier tendency to suggest that not all are ripe for such an approach. But patient sowing may be needed in pre-Christian contexts, or where there is strong opposition from other religions or philosophies. Strategies for recovery or renewal may be required in post-Christian contexts, where there are many churches, but these do not seem to be engaging effectively with their society and culture. Perhaps the caution expressed in the early years of the DAWN movement should be restored, to help advocates of DAWN strategies examine their contexts more thoroughly and consider how appropriate such a strategy may be. It is possible that some kind of DAWN strategy could be developed for such contexts, but expectations, methodology, and time frame would need to be significantly adjusted.

If this does not happen, far fewer churches are likely to be planted than advocates anticipate, resulting in disillusionment and the demise of the church planting movement before its potential is realized. And even if thousands of churches are planted, unless these are contextualized for the challenges of the next century, they may not significantly contribute toward the fulfillment of the church's mission. The church planting movement may even come to be viewed as a significant distraction from the creative missiological and ecclesiological developments that are needed.

Contemporary Church Planting

Martin Robinson writes that "church planting in the twentieth century has been markedly different from that which has gone before."[19] If he is correct, there are clearly limits to what can be gleaned from historical examples of church planting. In most contexts today, there is little pioneer planting; in some, sectarian motives continue to operate, although often in conjunction with replacement or saturation strategies; and replacement planting continues to be a significant component in a context where the closure of churches continues to affect most denominations. Some of the distinctive features of contemporary church planting have been indicated above: for example, its cooperative ethos, its saturation strategy, and its greater awareness of neglected communities.

Church planting is not new. History contains much to guide, instruct, and encourage church planters. A historical perspective is helpful if we are to keep contemporary ventures and goals in proportion. But contemporary church planting does contain some new elements, and it is being advocated and practiced in a context that presents different challenges from those faced by previous generations of church planters. There are instructive parallels and transferable principles, but historical precedents are no substitute for contextual analysis, spiritual sensitivity, and faithful but realistic strategic planning. We turn now, therefore, to examine in greater detail the task of the church and the context within which this task must be carried out.

5. CHURCH PLANTING AND THE TASK OF THE CHURCH

One of the tensions evident in many periods of church history is that of *maintenance* versus *mission*. The church is both a community and a missionary organization, an institution and a movement. It is required to give attention both to its internal health and development, and to its external responsibilities of proclamation and service.

This balance is not easy to maintain. In general, first generation movements have tended to emphasize mission and to develop only rudimentary structures for maintenance. In the second or third generations, internal developments have predominated. This process of institutionalization can be observed in all human societies and is necessary if progress is to be maintained and gains consolidated. However, unless this process leads on to renewed mission, the institution that has been created will dwindle, and new forms of mission will be needed, either to replace it or to revive it.

It is not that maintenance is unnecessary. Unless the church develops effective structures for teaching, training, pastoring, and deploying those it reaches in mission, it will become progressively less able to continue to engage in mission. Furthermore, unless the church becomes a community of loving relationships and meaningful interaction, there is little to call others to join. Robert Warren has commented: "A church wholly given to 'mission work' is not a sustainable model."[1] The result is exhausting activism and a "sales-addicted organization." This is not what becoming a missionary congregation implies. But when maintenance becomes central or all-consuming, as it frequently has in European church history, for reasons we will explore below, mission has been marginalized, and the church has forgotten its *raison d'être*.

A frequent response to the perceived need to engage both in mission and maintenance has been to develop specialist groups to engage in mission with the support of the church. The church in its congregational and institutional form is thereby freed to concentrate on maintenance, and church members who are able and willing to engage in mission activities can be loaned to these groups. Some of these specialist agencies have been involved in church planting. Others have studiously avoided such activities, at least in those regions where there were already churches, to retain the confidence and support of the churches. From the Celtic mission bands and the medieval monastic orders, to the plethora of contemporary missionary societies, there is a long and honorable history of such organizations. The globalization of the church, and its evangelistic and social impact on human society, would not have been achieved without them.

Missiologists have identified these two structures within the church as examples of what sociologists have termed *modalities* and *sodalities*, or, in less esoteric language, as congregational structures and mission structures. The existence and influence of such structures is not in doubt, but some have questioned their legitimacy, especially if they do not interact effectively with each other.

Mennonite missiologist George Peters, for example, argues that the history of Protestant missions is predominantly the history of missionary societies and individual pioneers, rather than the church in mission. He attributes this development among Protestants to four features of the sixteenth century Reformation: the absence of a coherent missiology among the Reformers; their failure to establish churches free from state control; the teaching of some Reformers that mission was the responsibility of individuals rather than the churches; and their inability, due to the low spiritual state of their churches, to engage in mission. He describes this as "an unfortunate and abnormal historic development which has produced autonomous, missionless churches on the one hand and autonomous churchless missionary societies on the other hand."[2]

Others have argued that this diversification is not just a pragmatic solution to persistent institutional moribundity, but a theologically sound and biblically justified strategy. Ralph Winter does not accept that sodalities are unfortunate and abnormal, describing them instead as one of the "two structures of God's redemptive mission."[3] He explores the role of modalities and sodalities in the New Testament, and argues that from New Testament times both structures have been crucial for the church to fulfill its calling. Although he acknowledges that, at times, the symbiosis necessary for both structures to operate effectively has been lacking, Winter insists that this division of labor is appropriate and divinely ordained.

Some church planting movements have challenged the legitimacy of this dichotomy. They have functioned as renewal movements, calling the institution back to its missionary roots, and redressing the balance between maintenance and mission. The Waldensians, the Moravians, and many other such movements operated as missionary churches, holding together mission and community, refusing to leave mission to specialist agencies. They have reminded the church that its primary task is to engage in mission to the world beyond the church, and that this is the responsibility of the whole church. This task may be fulfilled through diverse structures, but it may not be delegated to a minority of enthusiasts.

Other church planting movements have strongly endorsed the dual approach identified by Winter, but have ensured that there is effective symbiosis between these. A vibrant church planting movement associated with Nee To-sheng (Watchman Nee) laid foundations in the earlier part of this century for the remarkable church growth which has taken place in China in the past forty years. Nee taught that there was a clear distinction between "the work" and "the churches,"[4] but this distinction in no way diminished the missionary task of the churches. Travelling apostles and evangelists brought strategic leadership and support to the churches, but mission and church planting depended on the mobilization of church members. Churches were sometimes planted by sending extended family units hundreds of miles away to form new congregations in unreached regions of the country.

Commenting on the debate between Peters and Winter, Peter Wagner accepts Winter's conclusion that the two structures are necessary, but insists (as does Winter) that there should be dynamic interaction between them. Both structures are expressions of church, and undue separation of church and mission is unhelpful. In particular, the common use of *parachurch* terminology to describe sodalities should be avoided. In this context, he refers to the sixteenth-century Anabaptist church planting movement as a historical example of such dynamic interaction. This movement grew, not through the work of mission agencies, but through the proliferation of local churches and the mobilization of most of its members as missionaries. Wagner concludes that "the nature of the Anabaptist movement was a sodality-type structure."[5]

The planting of new churches has the potential to recall local churches to their essential task of mission. Whether this task is performed through two structures or one, mission is no longer a subsidiary point on the agenda, or something that can be delegated to a subsection of the church; it *is* the agenda, and the whole church shares the responsibility for fulfilling this task. The contemporary church planting movement provides another opportunity to recover this wholistic model of church and mission. Church planting will not in itself achieve this recovery, but the fresh ecclesiological thinking that often accompanies church planting, if this is nurtured and encouraged, may help to restore mission to the heart of the church. Various changes will be needed.

Following Wagner's suggestion, one simple but influential conceptual change would be to abolish the popular but very unhelpful *parachurch* terminology. If any separation between the church and its mission is untenable, as we have argued, and if the primary calling of the church is to engage in mission, it does seem ridiculous to describe parts of the church that are most actively involved in mission as "parachurch," as if they were secondary or peripheral. The use of this terminology stems from the long-standing dominance of maintenance thinking. If the terminology is to be used at all, perhaps it would be more accurate to describe maintenance-oriented congregations as parachurch organizations! They may look like churches and perform certain church-like functions. But they are not really proper churches, because they are not demonstrating a commitment to the real task of the church.

We are not arguing for disbanding specialist agencies or missionary organizations, as some have urged who have challenged this "parachurch" terminology. The idea that local congregations should take over the tasks of these specialist agencies stretches credulity. It reflects also a restrictive understanding of the nature of the church and an unrealistic appraisal of how its mission can be fulfilled in contemporary society.[6] There is scope for local congregations to develop as missionary communities, but the church is not limited to functioning only in neighborhood units. Now, perhaps more than ever, flexible and specialized forms of church life are necessary.

We are not arguing that specialist agencies should be denigrated or abolished. Rather, we should wholeheartedly endorse their ministry and refuse any longer to denominate them as "parachurch." We can then work toward a symbiosis that would benefit both modality and sodality structures, and might lead to new structures emerging that are as delightfully difficult to classify as the sixteenth-century Anabaptist communities. These specialist mission agencies are not "parachurch," they are "church."[7] Indeed, they may be much closer to the New Testament understanding of the church than many local congregations, for whom mission has become optional.

The Church in a Post-Christian Context

Changes in terminology may at first glance appear unimportant, but can have surprising impact as they challenge familiar assumptions and practices. Further changes will be needed, though, if mission is to be recovered as the task and focus of the church. To appreciate what changes may be required, we will need to examine in greater detail the reasons why mission has so often been marginal, rather than central, to the church. Institutional development (or degeneration) alone is an inadequate explanation. There have been times of renewal and reformation in the history of the church when all kinds of new structures and emphases were introduced, but the church remained entrenched in a maintenance orientation.

Perhaps the classic European example is the Reformation of the sixteenth century, to which we referred briefly in chapter 4. Protesting against widespread abuses, challenging doctrinal errors and superstitions, the Reformers were a first-generation movement of reform and renewal that profoundly affected church and society. But they did not often engage in mission. Some taught that the great commission had been fulfilled centuries earlier and was not applicable in their generation.[8] They insisted that the office of evangelist had died out with the apostles and prophets, leaving pastors and teachers to lead the churches.

They turned Catholic churches into Reformed churches wherever they had liberty and governmental support to achieve this, but they did not generally plant new churches. They did not subject contemporary ecclesiology to the same radical critique that they used to reform contemporary soteriology, nor did they challenge the maintenance orientation of the church. Why?

Fundamentally, the Reformers accepted the presupposition of the previous millennium that Europe was Christian. Ever since the Roman Emperor Constantine's early fourth-century adoption of Christianity as the state religion and the subsequent decision at the end of that century by the emperor Theodosius to outlaw all other religions, the church had been operating in maintenance mode, at least within the boundaries of what became known as "Christendom." The imperial invitation to the church to become, in effect, the religious department of the empire revolutionized the idea of mission and the practice of evangelism, along with many other aspects of Christian faith and practice. Church and state were now the pillars of a sacral society, where dissent was suppressed and where almost everyone was assumed to be Christian. Infant baptism marked entry into this Christian society.

From being a powerless and sometimes persecuted minority that nevertheless could not refrain from talking about their faith in Jesus and his impact on their lives, Christians had organized themselves into a powerful institution that could impose its beliefs and practices on society. Evangelism was no longer a winsome invitation to choose a deviant and dangerous way of living and join a community that was puzzling yet strangely attractive. The church's mission now involved ensuring doctrinal conformity, enforcing church attendance, enshrining moral standards in the criminal law, and eradicating choice in the area of religion. David Bosch concludes that "it is only in recent decades that the full significance of those events at the beginning of the fourth century has begun to dawn on us. For mission and the understanding of mission the events of those fateful years had equally drastic implications."[9]

Mission in a New Testament sense became irrelevant. If the whole empire (with the awkward exception of the Jews) was now Christian, evangelism was obsolete. The role of the church was to teach and provide pastoral care and to ensure that church members were loyal citizens. Church leadership was essentially maintenance-oriented. Pastors and teachers were needed, but evangelists were redundant and prophets rather a nuisance. The great commission was declared to have been fulfilled, at least within Christian Europe.

For over a thousand years this remained the orthodox view, with only marginalized radical groups, like the Waldensians, dissenting. Among these groups, the ministries of apostles, prophets, and evangelists were sometimes rediscovered; maintenance was set firmly in a mission context; and something closer to New Testament evangelism was restored.

The Protestant Reformation challenged neither the Christendom framework nor the demise of mission. But their church-planting contemporaries, the Anabaptists, rejected Christendom as a delusion, engaged in serious ecclesiological reflection, and designated Europe as a mission field. To the Reformers, as to their Catholic opponents, this was an affront, and dangerous to both church and society. One of the few subjects on which Catholics and Protestants agreed in this era was that Anabaptism was subversive and needed to be eradicated. The Catholics tended to burn them; the Protestants normally beheaded them; but both operated on similar Christendom assumptions and applied similar Christendom methods.

Christendom survived the challenge represented by Anabaptism. The monolithic medieval Christendom was fractured into competing Catholic, Lutheran, and Reformed mini-Christendoms; the seeds of the "free churches" had been sown. But for centuries yet the Christendom (or Constantinian) mentality would dominate European Christianity and ensure that the church was oriented toward maintenance over mission. Ecclesiology and missiology were disconnected. David Bosch writes: "The Reformation definitions of the Church were silent on its missionary dimensions. Ecclesiological definitions were almost exclusively preoccupied with matters concerning the purity of doctrine, the sacraments and church discipline. Mission had to content itself with a position on the church's periphery."[10]

Eventually, mission perspectives gained ground, and Protestant churches responded, as medieval Catholicism had, by setting up missionary organizations to engage in mission on their behalf. But the Christendom mentality ensured that mission would remain a peripheral concern for most denominations. It also meant that imperialistic attitudes and unchallenged cultural compromises would infect the spread of the gospel and the planting of churches in other parts of the world. The legitimacy and influence of Christendom has gradually waned, but its legacy remains.

Opinions are sharply divided as to whether Christendom was a positive or negative development. Some, following the lead given by Constantine's biographer, Eusebius, have argued that this was a God-given opportunity to assert the lordship of Christ over all areas of life and society.[11] Others have concluded that it was the worst thing that could have happened and represented the triumph of ideology over faith, the domestication and perversion of Christianity, the "fall" of the church.[12] Others again have asked what else the church could have done in the fourth century, when asked to refashion European culture.[13]

However we evaluate this long period of European church history, Western Europe is now widely regarded as post-Christian. Although many countries still have a state church, this arrangement is thoroughly anachronistic. Christendom survived the challenges of the Renaissance and the Reformation, but was fatally weakened by the eighteenth-century movement known as the Enlightenment. This began to erode the authority of the church, as reason replaced revelation as the accepted source of knowledge. The steady advance of secularization has effectively demolished the sacral society, marginalized the churches, and privatized religious issues. Secularism[14] has proved unsatisfactory, and spirituality made something of a come back during the twentieth century, but religious plurality rather than religious uniformity characterizes modern Europe.

However, even though Christendom as a political arrangement may be defunct, many vestiges of Christendom remain. These include prayers on state occasions and daily at the start of business in Parliament, the presence of bishops in the House of Lords, the use of oaths in the law courts and in a surprising number of other situations, the survival of blasphemy laws and other legal provisions that are biased toward Christianity, and residual restrictions relating to Sunday observance. But these vestiges are inappropriate and unjust in a pluralist society. The stance taken by some sections of the church when the legitimacy of these vestiges is challenged betrays continuing enslavement to Constantinian assumptions.

Although constitutional separation of church and state has ensured that North American society has never experienced an official version of Christendom, its Christendom mindset is probably more pervasive and more strongly established than in European nations where official Christendom is waning. The perennial tendency to conflate the American dream with expectations of the coming of God's kingdom and to identify American values and interests as Christian are evidence of the ability of Christendom to flourish in contexts where theoretically it should not survive. Many Christians in Europe look back to Christendom with nostalgia and argue for a return to a "Christian nation." Many North American Christians still regard their nation as Christian and resist any move toward pluralization. "Constantinianism," concludes Stanley Hauerwas, "is a hard habit to break."[15]

Indeed, in some parts of Eastern Europe, a renewed form of Christendom is threatening to emerge after the collapse of communism, as some established churches demand a monopoly position. Bosch comments: "Whereas the dismantling of Constantinianism began in parts of Western Europe as long ago as the Renaissance, there are even to this day regions and communities where for all practical purposes the population still thinks and acts in Constantinian categories."[16] Constantinian attitudes and assumptions have also resurfaced in movements as disparate as Latin American Liberation Theology and North American Christian Reconstructionism. John Howard Yoder has identified this phenomenon as "neo-Constantinianism," a transmuted version of Christendom that may look quite different politically, but shares basic assumptions about the role of the church in society.[17] The demise of Christendom appears to be neither total nor rapid. The Christendom mentality has outlasted Christendom as a political entity.

Nevertheless, it does now seem valid to describe most of Europe as a post-Christian society, to anticipate a similar movement away from Christendom in North America, and to explore the implications of this context for the church and its mission. What now is the task of the church? What aspects of missiology and ecclesiology that have been inherited from Christendom must be jettisoned, or at least adapted to respond creatively to the new challenges and opportunities? What kinds of churches are needed in a post-Christian society? Models that are effective in a pre-Christian society or were suitable for a Christendom context may be quite inappropriate now.

It is tempting either to retreat from the challenges of a post-Christian context, taking refuge in familiar forms and structures, or to persuade ourselves that we are now back in a context analogous to that of the early Christians and attempt once more to establish "New Testament churches." There may be some parallels with the early pre-Christendom centuries, and some instructive examples of church life and mission on which to reflect, but there is a fundamental difference between a pre-Christian society and a post-Christian society, as various missiologists have recognized.

Robert Warren accepts that we are living in the "end times of Christendom" and agrees that "a post-Christendom culture is not the same as a pre-Christendom culture."[18] We can no longer continue as if living under Christendom. But he argues that mission in this culture does not mean abandoning the past but drawing on the experiences we bring from the past into this new situation. This is a legacy not available to the church in pre-Christendom times.

Valuable though this legacy may be, it may also constitute a mission liability, confirming the views of those who have concluded that Christianity is not the answer to their spiritual quest, and hindering the churches from developing more appropriate models of mission. Other missiologists are more wary. David Bosch asks: "Is a secularized and dechristianized European . . . a not-yet-Christian or a no-more Christian?" He concludes: "Such a person is a post-Christian rather than a pre-Christian. This calls for a special approach in communicating the gospel."[19] There are both advantages and disadvantages in this situation.

Lesslie Newbigin insists that contemporary society is a pagan society, and its paganism, having been born out of the rejection of Christianity, is far more resistant to the gospel than the pre-Christian paganism with which cross-cultural missions have been familiar. "We are in a radically new situation and cannot dream either of a Constantinian authority or of a pre-Constantinian innocence."[20]

Mission in a post-Christian society is not easy. Unrealistic goals and expectations hinder the careful and prayerful reflection needed to exegete this context and develop appropriate strategies. There are many aspects to consider, but the fundamental issue is the recalling of the church to its primary task. This may have been obscured under Christendom, but it is inescapable in a post-Christian society, that the task of the church is mission. Church planting may be a crucial element in mission to post-Christendom, but only *creative* church planting will do.

In a society where those with spiritual questions naturally assume that the church is not the place to find answers, since Christianity has been tried and found wanting, why should planting more churches be a sensible strategy—unless new kinds of churches are planted that are able to connect with those who have spiritual interests? Renewed commitment to the missionary task of the church will require, through both church renewal and church planting, creativity in developing new forms and shapes through which the gospel can be expressed in contemporary society.

Beyond the Parish Church

The traditional European shape is the *neighborhood* church, where most members live locally and are drawn to the church by its proximity to their homes. The neighborhood church model, whether the official parish church or the unofficial free church with its defined territory, has a long history and may remain a popular model for generations to come. But it is not the only model, nor necessarily the most effective model for the missionary task of the church, especially in a post-Christian culture. Three important social and ecclesiastical changes require us to reassess the suitability of this model.

First, the parish structure was developed under Christendom, was based on certain assumptions about the role of churches in society, and functioned well in a sacral culture where the established church had a monopoly. But in a post-Christian culture, churches can no longer make these assumptions or play this role. Missionary congregations are needed. But can parish churches, which for generations have been operating with a pastoral paradigm, operate with, or even understand the implications of, the very different paradigm required for this? Despite the efforts of advocates of missionary congregations to work slowly through parish structures, experience may show that new models are needed for this new mission mentality.

Second, the proliferation of denominations in the last three centuries has destroyed the monopoly position of the established church, and undermined attempts to present one neighborhood church as the church to which all local believers belong.[21] With the important exception of some rural areas, most would-be church members can choose between various churches in the same neighborhood. Belonging to a local church is still seen by many as a significant factor in the choice of a church, but locality is not the only issue. Many church members walk or drive past a number of churches that are nearer to their homes, to belong to a particular church. This tendency is much further advanced in North America, where the neighborhood church has been less deeply rooted and has faced competition from eclectic churches for many years.

Third, contemporary society, especially in urban areas, is more complex than this neighborhood model allows for. No longer do people live, work, relax, and worship in one community or location, but in several. Networks of relationships are formed, that may not intersect at any other point than the individual. The recent Anglican report on church planting notes that "human life is lived in a complex array of networks . . . the neighborhoods where people reside may hold only a very minor loyalty."[22] Relationships are based on shared interests rather than a shared neighborhood. Freedom to travel radically affects the building of relationships and the choice of activities. Belonging to the church nearest to one's home may also mean belonging to a church at a considerable distance from the homes of friends, colleagues, and the wider family. This has obvious implications for mission (especially given the widespread recognition that friendship evangelism is of crucial important importance), but serious consequences also for the level of commitment felt by such members to their local church, especially if they appear to have little in common with other members.

It is tempting to respond to this challenge by working harder, or by tinkering with the neighborhood church model. But this response may accord to the parish structure a status that is undeserved. Sandy Millar has noted that "every recent church report has recognized that the parish is no longer the appropriate geographical area with which to work."[23] The WCC Report, *The Church for Others,* in a section entitled "The Relative Importance of the Parish," explains both how the parish developed and why it is now inadequate for contemporary society:

> Its form was determined by the shape of a society characterized by its division into small, closely co-ordinated, comparatively isolated communities.... It represented the whole Church face to face with what was, to all intents and purposes, for most people, the whole of life. It continued as a virile missionary structure throughout the early stages of the industrial revolution, and its missionary response to it was the creation of new local congregations [church planting] in the new concentrations of population. But social change has now gathered such momentum that it threatens to sweep away all the old landmarks. As long as churches persist in regarding the parish of the local congregation as their normative structure they will not confront life at its most significant points. The local congregation can still minister to certain of the various areas of life . . . but we must go on to say that, while they are important, they still represent a small sector of life.

The report urges local congregations to accept that new ecclesial structures "designed to serve society in all its complexity are also the Church carrying out the original intention of the 'parish' church."[24]

But is there no way to rescue this neighborhood model and transform it into a missionary congregation? The parish was originally a mission structure, and it has been argued that it could become again an effective mission structure, if the church were to understand the parish missiologically rather than pastorally. For centuries, in a society considered to be at least nominally Christian, the parish was regarded as the pastoral responsibility of the parish church and its ministers. Previous generations of church planters challenged this pastoral model and attempted to plant new churches among those whom they regarded as unevangelized, but they found that the parish system was a hindrance to mission. Anglican church planting today is still inhibited by this parish structure,[25] and there have been calls for its abolition or suspension. But attempts to circumvent or ignore the parish structure have usually been met with consternation and hostility,[26] much to the dismay of those who see church planting as an opportunity to ask more radical questions about the parish system and other aspects of Anglican ecclesiology.[27]

However, in European societies where only a fraction of the population attends any church, and an even tinier percentage attends the parish church, the only possible justification for retaining a parish structure is as one component in a more complex mission strategy. Careful analysis of a local community, strategic planning to determine how many churches (and what kinds of churches) are needed to engage in mission to this community, and cooperation between existing churches to achieve what is needed, *might* make use of existing parish structures. The territorial division the parish system provides may offer a useful starting point for planning a mission strategy, but flexibility is needed in areas where parish boundaries no longer represent community boundaries, particularly in large cities. In nations where the parish structure is less well-established, it is doubtful whether it is worth concentrating on this when developing mission strategies.

Provided there is a readiness to think flexibly, strategically, and cooperatively, some form of parish structure, or at least the continued use of the neighborhood church model, may be appropriate in many nations.[28] But it is unlikely that this alone will be adequate for the mission of the churches in contemporary society. Ecclesiological reflection and renewal will be needed, leading to the development of new forms of church life. Creative church planting may be crucially important for mission in a post-Christian culture.

Planting or Cloning?

I suspect that the creativity needed to engage in such ecclesiological renewal is already present among contemporary church planters, but that this is frequently stifled by inadequate training in the process of theological reflection and contextualization, and such pressures as time-related goals and denominational expectations. The result is all too often that churches are *cloned* rather than being planted. Cloning, the exact duplication of an organism, is a technique once associated primarily with science fiction, and the scary notion of producing human beings through replication rather than reproduction. In recent years, however, it has moved into the realm of science fact, as plants and more recently animals have been cloned. Cloning has attained respectability, although the term is still loaded with rather negative connotations, and the ethical implications of the process remain disputed.

Following publication of an article on church planting using the language of cloning,[29] I was urged not to use this apparently pejorative terminology in relation to church planting. I am not a scientist and did not pretend to understand the technicalities of the language of cloning or the processes involved, and I was informed that I was not using the term accurately. Concerns were expressed also that the negative connotations of cloning might be a deterrent in contexts where church planting is still striving for acceptance. Advocates of church planting, who are struggling to persuade their denomination or local church that church planting is legitimate and vital, are understandably not keen to grapple with the issues and emotions raised by the use of such language.

My initial response was to respect these concerns, to avoid this terminology, and to look for other ways of addressing the issues raised in this chapter. It is possible to contrast "church planting" with "church extension," or "new church planting" with "old church planting."[30] I have reverted to the language of cloning for four reasons. A friend with a doctorate in biochemistry has assured me that I am using the terminology and the concept appropriately. I have discovered that others are also using the language of cloning.[31] I have been unable to find any other terminology that adequately expresses the issues involved. And I have become convinced that the practice I am designating as cloning needs to be recognized and clearly differentiated from other forms of church planting. I am *not* arguing that cloning is illegitimate, but that it should be recognized as only one aspect of church planting. If the church planting movement becomes dominated by this methodology, it will have missed its way and squandered an opportunity, however many clones are produced.

In the context of church planting, then, cloning describes the process of replicating the structures, style, ethos, activities, and focus of one congregation in another. The location of the church may change, but its shape remains the same. There are obvious advantages in this approach, not least in drawing on the experience of the planting church and developing a new church with which core members, at least, will feel comfortable. Much can be taken for granted, enabling church members to concentrate on the task of recruiting new members for this church and engaging in its missionary task.

Several factors increase the likelihood of churches being cloned rather than planted. Such factors include location, motivation, personnel, and structure. If the new church is planted *near the planting church*, or in a similar community, little thought may be given to developing a different kind of church. The assumption may well be that another congregation of the same kind will be as effective as the planting church in reaching this community. If the new church is planted *for logistical reasons*, because the church building is full, there may be little incentive to think radically about the style of this new church. All that is required is another base to cope with the numbers already attracted to this kind of church. If *those involved in planting the new church* are inexperienced, untrained or dependent on the leaders of the planting church, they are less likely to be ecclesiologically creative.

Often those involved in church planting are strong in the areas of evangelism, interpersonal skills and enthusiasm, but ill-equipped for theological and sociological reflection required to develop new forms of church life. If *the relationship between the new church and the planting church or agency is strong*, and denominational or doctrinal convictions are expected to be reflected in the new church, then the freedom for maneuver may be slight.

It is arguable that in some situations cloning is perfectly acceptable, and that there is no need to ask searching questions about the shape of the church. Where a church in a monochrome suburban area is dividing its membership into two or three congregations, because it can no longer fit into its buildings, and where this church has been successfully reaching out into the local community, and where the new congregations will meet in a very similar social context, the need to ask questions about the shape of the church may not be immediately obvious. It is when the same suburban church attempts to plant a new congregation on a local council housing estate, or a few miles away in an inner city community, that the importance of such questions becomes very evident.

However, this distinction may be overdrawn. Some research into this supposedly monochrome suburban area, that the church appears to be reaching successfully, may well show that there are significant sections of the community for whom the church is not an appropriate or attractive mission agency. Thus, it would seem reasonable to encourage all churches that are considering planting new churches, wherever they are doing this and for whatever reasons, to ask questions about the shape of the church and the relation of this shape to its mission.

Starting a new church is a glorious opportunity to ask questions and to experiment. The familiar response to new ideas—"we've never done it this way before"—is even less relevant than usual. In a new church, nothing has been "done this way before." Everything is open for debate. The founding members can make fresh choices and set new priorities. They can dream dreams, take risks, experiment with new patterns, and enjoy the refreshing, but sometimes frightening, liberty of pioneering a new church. Of course, this does not happen in a vacuum. Church planting is not creation *ex nihilo!* These founding members bring with them their own convictions, cultural baggage, prejudices, preferences, fears and traditions. Their previous experience of church life will inevitably be a major influence upon their thinking. But this influence can be recognized, and valued, without being allowed to predetermine the future. Elements which are negotiable can be distinguished from those which are non-negotiable.

Asking questions and experimenting does not imply a humanistic approach to church planting. If church planting is set within the context of missio Dei, our overriding concern will be to listen to what God is saying to us about the kind of church needed to participate in his mission. Captivity to traditional patterns is no more likely to ensure faithfulness to God than openness to new possibilities. Nor does asking radical questions imply that radical changes will always be made. Consideration of various options may result in these being discarded and something quite similar to the planting church being planted.

Many traditions developed for good reasons. Some church plants try various alternatives before reverting to tried and tested methods with renewed appreciation of their worth. The crucial element is the

122 • *Church Planting*

awareness that questions need to be asked and the freedom to ask these questions. Prayerfully asking questions, experimenting prayerfully with possible answers, reflecting prayerfully on the missionary task of the church in a post-Christian culture, prayerfully developing new forms of church life that may equip the church to fulfill this task: these are some of the components of creative church planting.

Missionary Communities

In the next chapter, we will examine some recent attempts to develop new forms of church life, some of which result both from reflection on the shape church life might assume in contemporary society and from a recovery of a mission perspective. As we conclude our discussion of the task of the church, the fundamental point is that, whatever diverse shapes the church assumes, church planters and church leaders in a post-Christian context are required to operate according to principles which have been common among cross-cultural missionaries for many years. The paradigm shift that underlies this requirement is the recognition that all church leadership in Western society is missionary and cross-cultural, and that the shape of the church must reflect this. Church planting requires the same missionary encounter with surrounding culture and the same concern about developing appropriate forms and structures as is evident in areas of the world that have been regarded as the "mission field." Complex issues of indigenization, inculturation, and contextualization need to be addressed. The local community is now the "mission field," and missiological perspectives and skills are required.

For the missionary task of the church is not only to preach good news but to be good news, to incarnate good news. Lesslie Newbigin has argued that "the *only* hermeneutic of the gospel is a congregation of men and women who believe it and live by it."[32] This may be overstated (and Newbigin does in fact attempt to qualify it), downgrading the impact of the witness of individual Christians in society, and of groups involved in mission through noncongregational structures. But, undoubtedly, the congregation is a primary "hermeneutic of the gospel," interpreting the meaning and implications of the gospel in its life together as a Christian community. So its shape and ethos are of huge importance. Ecclesiology and missiology are inextricably related. Churches involved in mission need to understand themselves as missionary communities.

The concept of "missionary congregations" has become familiar in recent years. This term has been traced to a report published by the World Council of Churches in 1967, entitled *The Church for Others: A Quest for Structures for Missionary Congregations.*[33] This report (and the subsequent WCC meeting in Uppsala the following year) attracted considerable criticism for its understanding of mission. Phrases such as "secularization, a fruit of the gospel" and "the world provides the agenda," the apparent marginalization of the church in *missio Dei* (as defined in this document), and the redefinition of mission as "humanization," rang warning bells, especially in evangelical circles. It is perhaps a surprising source of a concept that has challenged and energized many who would profoundly disagree with the main thrust of the document. Much of this report now appears very dated (especially its interpretation of secularization), but it contains some little known but interesting perspectives and ideas that we will draw on in subsequent chapters.

The idea of "missionary congregations" or "the missionary structure of the congregation" continued to be explored in various contexts. A report adopted by the Methodist Conference in 1987, for example, referred to the attention given in recent years to "the missionary shape of the congregation."[34] But it was the stimulus of the 1988 Lambeth conference twenty years later, calling for "a shift to a dynamic missionary emphasis," that resulted in the concept of missionary congregations being extensively explored and increasingly popularized. If this concept escapes the trap into which similar missiological perspectives have fallen, of becoming "flavor of the month" and the subject of numerous conferences, then slipping back into obscurity without achieving its potential, there is much here to help churches refashion themselves for a post-Christian culture.

Robert Warren, in his books, *Being Human, Being Church,* and *Building Missionary Congregations,* has begun to explore the implications of this shift and to make recommendations for its achievement.[35] He defines the concept in these words: "A missionary congregation is a church which takes its identity, priorities, and agenda, from participation in God's mission in the world."[36] The church under Christendom operated in "pastoral mode, but in a post-Christendom culture it must operate in "mission mode." This will require a paradigm shift, whereby mission is not bolted on to church programs but is recovered as the purpose of the church. Since many others are talking and writing about missionary congregations, we will not explore in any detail the practical implications of this model, although some of these will inform our discussion in later chapters.

Among the marks of a missionary congregation will be a commitment to what Warren calls "whole-life issues," equipping people for witness in the world, rather than in-house activities; a balance between distinctiveness and engagement; and an emphasis on being as well as doing, on stillness rather than frenetic activity, on streamlining and focus. Pastoral care remains vital, but this is set within the context of mission, rather than being the focal point with mission as an extra activity.

The development of missionary congregations does not necessarily require the planting of new churches. Indeed, although this option appears in Warren's book as one of the more radical options, it is given little attention. The focus is on the renewal and reformation of existing churches, even though it is acknowledged that this may be a slow process and that not all churches will be able to make this transition.[37] Advocates of church planting may be rather less sanguine about the prospects of achieving such fundamental transformation through reformation. However, church planters need to ensure that the churches they are planting are missionary congregations, rather than additional examples of churches that are oriented toward maintenance and pastoral care.

Of particular significance for church planters is Warren's helpful distinction between missionary congregations and churches in "activist pastoral mode."[38] Church plants are often busy churches. Their members are highly committed and enthusiastic, and the temptation to develop a wide range of church activities is strong. But activism does not equate with effective mission and may in fact betray an inadequate missionary engagement with the community the new church is hoping to reach.

Among other things, a commitment to planting missionary congregations means that church planters will not be interested primarily in designing new churches to suit the preferences of church members, but to serve the purposes of God's mission to those who are outside the churches. The needs of church members are important, and a wise church planter will attempt to strike a balance between the legitimate demands of mission and maintenance. But the current situation in most churches is so lopsided toward maintenance, and has been thus for so long, that achieving a proper balance will require significant reorientation. There may be an uncomfortable period during which many will feel the balance has been tipped too far toward mission.[39] But in a mission context, the task of mission and the efficacy of church structures and activities to engage with those the church is concerned to reach take precedence over the preferences of church members.

Church planting is an opportunity for the church to recover its challenging commission to be a "church for others," a community that exists to serve others before itself. Although strangely reminiscent of the Founder, this way of ordering church life is not popular either among traditional churches or the younger denominations. We tend to run our churches to suit our preferences, denominational policies, convenience, and diaries. Churches that have tried to introduce changes designed to make them more mission-oriented or accessible to the local community have discovered, even in young and supposedly very flexible congregations, entrenched attitudes and a great reluctance to put mission before maintenance. As soon as mission is restored to its central position in ecclesiology and in local church priorities, many other aspects of church life require fresh thinking. Practices and assumptions that seemed acceptable for the church in "maintenance mode" can no longer go unchallenged as the church moves into "mission mode."

Where there is sufficient flexibility to achieve the reorientation necessary, church planting may be unnecessary. But often only creative church planting can enable sufficiently radical steps to be taken. That is why cloning will not suffice, and why some of the church planting currently taking place is contributing less than it might to the missionary task of the church. It may even be distracting us from addressing this task with the rigor and courage that is required.

6. CHURCH PLANTING AND THE SHAPE OF THE CHURCH

One of the most popular quotations from church planting literature is Peter Wagner's assertion that "the single most effective evangelistic methodology under heaven is planting new churches."[1] Evidence is collected and arguments are marshaled to support this assertion, and church planting is advocated as the primary method of evangelizing this or any other generation. Although some attention is given to the *nature* of these new churches, interest appears to focus mainly on the *number* of churches that may be required to saturate a city or nation. Thus, the aim of *Challenge 2000* that "there will be a living, growing, Christ-centered congregation in every distinct community and neighborhood" indicated that the churches needed should be "living" and "Christ-centered," but no attempt was made to define further these characteristics.

Indeed, within such a denominationally diverse movement, any attempt to be prescriptive regarding the kinds of churches to be planted would endanger the level of cooperation that has been a crucial achievement of the movement. The movement has researched and publicized the number of churches needed to achieve the penetration of society envisaged in its stated aim. Discussion about the kinds of churches required has been less evident, or at least has not been accorded the same public profile.

As indicated in chapter 4, this is a characteristic of saturation planting that differentiates it from sectarian planting. Sectarian planting has weaknesses, but among its strengths are the ecclesiological debate that it engenders and the new forms of church which emerge. With saturation planting, sectarian motives may be less evident, but the impetus to plant as many churches as possible may discourage such debate and stifle such creativity.

Concentrating on the question "how many?" is understandable given the range of churches and denominations involved. It reflects also the influence of church growth teaching on the church planting movement.[2] But this may prove to be a serious weakness that could undermine the practice and reputation of church planting. There are several related problems.

First, can we assume that simply establishing more churches will lead to effective mission? There is evidence to suggest that some newly planted churches may be attractive to those currently beyond the reach of existing churches. But there is also evidence to suggest that other new churches have been completely ineffective in reaching their surrounding community and have grown in numbers only through transfers from other churches. Indeed, there are situations where a new church has quickly become more introverted and less potent evangelistically than the church from which it was planted. Planting more churches will not necessarily increase evangelistic effectiveness. Nor will this automatically ensure that the mission agenda will include more than evangelism and growth in church membership. We need to ask questions about the kinds of churches that are being planted, about their understanding of the meaning of mission in a post-Christian society, and about their capacity to engage effectively in this task.

Second, why should we invest energy in planting thousands more churches of the kinds most people in our society do not want to attend or belong to? In a nation like Britain, where church attendance is declining, the expectation that replicating existing churches, and saturating local communities with such churches, will arrest this trend does not appear to be well-founded. This strategy does not appear to make any more sense than an evangelistic organization, discovering that its tent campaigns are attended by decreasing numbers, investing in acres of extra canvas and determining to hold more campaigns than ever before, to attract more people.

Fundamental questions about the relevance of such campaigns are thereby avoided. Such questions also need to be asked in nations, such as the United States, where church going is static. Planting more churches of the kind that are currently not making much impact on our society risks a similar release of energy into activities that avoid the strategic questions.

Some may argue that most church planting is carried out by the kinds of churches which *are* relevant and attractive, and that planting more of these kinds of churches is exactly what is required. The very fact that a church is able and willing to replicate itself indicates that it has something worth replicating. The churches to which people do not want to belong are not the kinds of churches that are planting new churches. There is, of course, some truth in this argument. But it may not adequately take into account the extent to which such churches appear to be confined to certain sectors within society, and their failure to make any impact on large unchurched communities. Replicating successful churches may be effective within these limited sectors, but it will not enable the churches to impact effectively sectors of society which for generations have found little good news in the churches. New kinds of churches will be needed for these communities.

Third, setting numerical targets and concentrating on achieving these may postpone consideration of issues that are crucial for the health and growth of *existing* churches. Many new churches are planted by local churches which are thriving and appear to be successful. The motivation for planting varies from concern to impact a different community, to logistical reasons such as premises which are inadequate for further growth, to providing opportunities for leadership development and the increased mobilization of church members. Where the planting church is thriving, there may seem little need to ask questions about what kind of church should be planted. The natural assumption will be to plant another church of a similar kind.

But what has been effective in the past may not be as effective in the future. Church cloning, by replicating existing patterns, may be successful in the short term, but this runs the risk of consigning both planting church and church plant to longer-term irrelevance. In a changing culture, reflection on the task and shape of the church is a constant necessity. Planting a new church is a wonderful opportunity to engage in this process of reflection. Simply to plant another church of the same kind represents a missed opportunity for ecclesiological renewal and missiological creativity. If this is true of churches planted by thriving local churches, how much more significant a factor is it for denominations who advocate church planting to redress decline. Policies and programs designed to increase the number of churches within that denomination may or may not succeed. But any success achieved may be at the expense of serious reflection about theological, ecclesiological, and spiritual renewal that is crucial if the denomination as a whole is to be healthy and effective.

The replication of existing churches in new locations is not necessarily good news. In some situations, planting another church of the same kind as the planting church may be appropriate; in other situations, it is less than ideal and may even be counterproductive. In most cases, this similarity is by accident rather than design, the result of unquestioned assumptions rather than mission strategy. The *unthinking* replication of existing churches betrays a misunderstanding both of the needs of our society and of the potential of church planting.

Church planting is *not* just about establishing more churches. It is not even primarily about establishing more churches. Allowing this to become the preoccupation of church planters or denominational strategists would be a serious mistake. Church planting is an opportunity for theological reflection and renewal, for asking radical questions about the nature of the church and its task in contemporary society, and for developing new kinds of churches. New churches are needed, not only to bring the Christian community closer to where people are geographically, but closer to where they are culturally, sociologically, and spiritually.

The loss of tens of thousands of people from British churches throughout the 1990s, for instance, was related less to where these churches met than to the kinds of communities they were and the kinds of subculture they represented. Planting more and more churches of the same kind will not reverse this trend.

Some advocates of church planting have called for such reflection and creativity. Rob Warner urges rejection of "the 'McDonald's mentality', which turns church planting into a franchise operation." He calls for "a fresh and creative enculturation of our church forms" and insists that "every church plant must have the freedom to respond in a unique way to the local community it seeks to serve and reach."[3] Martin Robinson and Stuart Christine emphasize this in the introduction to their handbook on church planting: "The challenge for church planters is therefore to give birth to new forms of the church rather than replicate the same structures that have already failed elsewhere."[4]

Stuart Christine adds later: "Creative church planting that discovers new ways of being the Body of Christ in a changing world will help keep the sinews of our denominations supple and more able to respond sensitively and vigorously to the as yet unforeseen challenges of tomorrow's world. . . . New churches, and the fresh theological insights that they generate, counter the tendency to ecclesiological ossification that turns structures into strictures."[5]

A recent Anglican publication, *Recovering the Ground,* urges similar ecclesiological reflection in relation to church planting. In his introduction to this collection of papers subtitled "Towards Radical Church Planting for the Church of England," editor Nigel Scotland welcomes the publication of the report on church planting in the Church of England, *Breaking New Ground.* He comments, however, that "much that the report contains is frustrating and reactionary" and suggests a more accurate title might have been "Entrenched in the Old Ground."[6] This collection of papers engages, within the context of Anglican structures, in just the kind of ecclesiological and missiological reflection that is vital for church planting movements in all denominations and networks.

It may not be as easy for groups with less ancient structures and traditions to appreciate how crucial such reflection is. The newer the denomination, the stronger may be the deference to traditions, and the more likely church members are to be oblivious to this. Furthermore, not all church planting advocates or practitioners, in their concern to plant as many churches as possible, as quickly as possible, seem prepared to engage in such a process. Reflection and creativity require time and energy. Fewer churches will be planted, at least in the early years. Where numerical growth is the primary concern, the replication of existing church structures will predominate. The result, however, may be that church planting flourishes only briefly, and fails to achieve the substantial ecclesiological renewal that might result if more attention were given to the *kinds* of churches being planted.

New Models of Church

Despite the concerns we have registered about the lack of ecclesiological reflection and renewal in the church planting movement as a whole, there are some interesting and instructive examples of new kinds of churches being planted. When future church historians look back on the Decade of Evangelism, and the resurgence of interest in church planting that accompanied this during the 1990s (presuming this period is regarded as sufficiently interesting to warrant their attention), it is possible they will regard as the most significant development, not the planting of thousands of churches, but the emergence of new forms of church life and new understandings of how Christian community may be expressed.

Most of these new models of Christian community are of recent origin (or even still on the drawing board), and attempts at this stage to evaluate their lasting significance would be premature. Each has its champions and critics. Some may be short-lived experiments that are found to be flawed. Others may become familiar or even dominant forms of church life in the twenty-first century. But even those which do not endure may pose important questions. We will not attempt here to provide an exhaustive list of such models, nor to explore all their ramifications, but to select some models which are becoming familiar, and which raise significant questions about the task and shape of the church. We will briefly describe these models, indicate the reactions they have provoked, and identify some of the issues that need to be addressed if they are to be implemented. Our main concern, however, is to explore theological and ecclesiological principles that undergird these models.

(1) Seeker-Targeted Churches

One such model is the *seeker-targeted*[7] church that draws inspiration from the Willow Creek Community Church in Chicago.[8] Those who have visited Willow Creek have been impressed by various aspects of this church, including its clear and uncompromising mission statement, its small-group structure, its gift-identification program and the size of its car park (!). But the distinctive feature of the church is its determination to provide those who are not Christians with a nonthreatening but challenging opportunity to consider the gospel.

Making use of music, drama, audiovisual media, testimonies, and "issue-based" preaching, "seeker services" are presentations to audiences rather than participatory events. These have been lauded as examples of a church breaking out of a Christian subculture and engaging with the concerns of the wider community. They have also been accused of being "market-driven," "consumer-oriented," and comprising "entertainment rather than evangelism."

These seeker services are not in themselves very different from traditional "guest services." But the quality of presentation is outstanding; the sensitivity to what is and is not appropriate for the target audience is highly developed; the diminution of worship elements in these events is radical; the attention to detail in the design and use of church premises is creative; and the attention given to contextualization is exemplary. What is also unusual—and threatening to churches considering such a model—is that these services for "unchurched people" are the main activity on Sundays, with services and activities for nurture taking place midweek.

Currently, many churches in North America and Europe are adapting their existing programs to include "seeker-sensitive" approaches or seeker services. Some have reported encouraging responses. Some have been appalled at the time and resources needed to put on such events. Some have been disappointed at the lack of interest from unchurched people. Churches that have tried to remodel themselves more thoroughly to be "seeker-targeted" have been surprised by the considerable resistance they have met from church members.

It may be that attempts to plant seeker-targeted churches from scratch, of which there are as yet fewer, may be more effective than trying to change the shape and ethos of existing churches. Some advocates of the Willow Creek model are critical of attempts to adopt only certain high-profile elements, such as the seeker-services, without understanding or engaging with the whole philosophy of the church, including its core values and seven-step strategy.[9] Eclectic methodology is attractive, but this may prove to be less effective than an integrated and locally contextualized ecclesiology.

Willow Creek's mission statement expresses its concern to be a "church for the unchurched." While appreciating this motivation and commitment, it is arguable that in fact this church predominantly reaches *semichurched* or *dechurched* North Americans. Attempts to replicate this in communities that have been unchurched for generations, such as some parts of Britain, may fail to appreciate this vital difference. North American church planters distinguish between the "boomer" generation, targeted successfully by the Willow Creek church, and the "buster" generation and the so-called "generation X," which are progressively less churched and likely to require different models of church and methods of evangelism. Some argue that Willow Creek does not reach such unchurched people: to reach unchurched communities may require a more radical model. For all its creativity, this model of church still relies on the readiness of nonmembers to "come to church."

What is ecclesiologically significant in this model is the priority given to nonmembers over church members, expressed in this key phrase in its mission statement: "A church for the unchurched." At the core of the philosophy of the church is a commitment to mission, with pastoral care and other crucial dimensions of internal growth deriving from this. The idea of the church as a society which exists for the benefit of nonmembers is not new, but the Willow Creek model is a thoroughgoing attempt to incarnate this. This model also has missiological significance in its recognition that effective evangelism in contemporary society does not assume much prior knowledge of the gospel or look for quick conversions. Rather it attempts to connect with contemporary issues, and allows people time to understand the gospel, reflect on its implications, and make considered commitments.

One of the core values endorsed by Willow Creek is "respect for the spiritual journey of the seeker." In an increasingly post-Christian environment, "process evangelism" rather than "crisis evangelism" will surely need to become the norm.[10] Willow Creek is an example of an evangelical church that is working creatively with the "journey to faith" paradigm, which has been familiar in other traditions, but is still regarded with a degree of suspicion by many evangelicals. Whether or not the seeker service method is found to be appropriate in other contexts, this paradigm shift is crucial if churches are to develop appropriate evangelistic strategies for post-Christendom and avoid unnecessary discouragement in evangelism.

(2) Network Churches

The neighborhood church, whether or not it is seeker-sensitive, is one model. An alternative model is the *Network* church, where geographical factors play only a secondary role. More important are networks of relationships and common cultural components. Those who belong to, and are reached by, these network churches have other things in common than the place where they live. They may be members of a particular ethnic group or youth culture. They may live in the same senior citizens' home, study in the same institution, or work for the same employer. Obviously there must be some degree of locality for them to meet together at all, but the determining factor is not the neighborhood in which they live, but the network to which they belong. Contemporary British examples are Ethnic churches[11] and Youth churches,[12] which have proliferated in recent years. Although ethnic churches and youth churches may seem quite different in style and ethos, both are expressions of this model of church.[13]

In a mobile society, it is possible to travel several miles to worship and learn together with others who belong to the same family or share a common culture. For young people, such journeys may be preferable to isolation within churches that are not sensitive to youth culture. For members of ethnic communities, ethnic churches may be regarded as crucial for the survival of their cultural identity, for evangelism within their community, and for discipleship. Ethnic and youth churches often draw people from a wider area than most local churches, although it is not this which constitutes them as network churches. City center churches, churches with famous preachers, and churches with particular doctrinal emphases have over many years drawn members from miles around. But these members are generally not connected to each other in any other way than through their church involvement. Members of network churches have other things in common than their church membership. Even where they operate very locally, ethnic and youth churches may not constitute neighborhood churches.

Other kinds of network churches may emerge, based on different common factors than age or ethnicity. Some may develop from existing Christian groups. Student Christian Unions, for example, rarely regard themselves as churches,[14] but in practice these often function as such for Christian students. Their development into campus churches might enable them to become more effective than they already are in mission within the student community, and ensure that evangelism is not separated from discipleship, nor witness from community life. The emergence of churches based on work relationships, interest groups, and recreational gatherings would be further expressions of this nongeographical church model.

The development of such network churches (especially ethnic churches) is regarded with dismay by some, who realize that they represent the failure of existing churches to incarnate the gospel within certain communities. Others are excited by the growing diversity of church life in a multicultural society. But network churches are regarded with suspicion for several reasons. First, the pattern of church life described in the New Testament seems to be based on locality rather than networks. Second, the church in the New Testament seems to be characterized by heterogeneity rather than the homogeneity that tends to characterize network churches. Third, critics question the impact of network churches on family life, if different family members attend different churches. Fourth, there are concerns about the danger of nominality, in situations where young people or members of ethnic minorities are drawn into churches where they feel at home culturally, but may not have been confronted by the claims of Christ.

The first issue is another example of the common tendency in ecclesiological debate[15] to "read off" patterns of church life from the New Testament, without considering the cultural and contextual factors. But in the first century the pattern of community life was not the same as the pattern of life in the twenty-first century. Today, as we have noted, many people live in one locality, work in another, and take recreation in a third. We may look back nostalgically to a neighborhood-based community life—though we might find this very restrictive if it were imposed on us—but we must not develop a mission strategy or ecclesiology based on nostalgia.

We may wish to argue for neighborhood churches rather than network churches on other grounds, such as a strategy to develop community life in neighborhoods threatened by atomized urban existence. But we cannot subscribe to a naive hermeneutical approach that attempts to legitimate a familiar pattern at the cost of ignoring vital contextual issues and responsible interpretative practice. The New Testament provides principles for church life, but leaves us free to adapt the shape of the church to the challenge of society. If society is structured increasingly along network lines, the development of network churches may be of crucial importance.

The second concern—about homogeneity—is not new. There has been for many years animated debate over the infamous Homogeneous Unit Principle (HUP). The principle is based on the observation of Donald McGavran, founder of the church growth movement, that people "like to become Christians without crossing racial, linguistic or class barriers,"[16] and the conclusion that mission strategies should be developed that do not require the crossing of such boundaries, at least at the point of conversion. Few doubt that the observation is accurate, but there is considerable debate about its implications.[17] This principle has been among the most controversial (and most misunderstood) of church growth principles.

The HUP has been used by some as the basis for mission strategies focused on "people groups" and the development of culturally sensitive ways of reaching such groups. Others have condemned the HUP as fostering apartheid churches and the watering down of an essential element in the gospel: the reconciliation achieved by the death of Jesus (Eph. 2:11-22), and the consequent challenge to followers of Jesus to transcend social and cultural barriers.

The HUP is susceptible to criticism on various grounds: sociological, missiological, theological, and ethical. It is often presented with scant regard for proper biblical interpretation. And it can undoubtedly be a dangerous ideological tool if used inappropriately. But a basic confusion is between use of the HUP as *one component* in a mission strategy and planting of homogeneous churches. Any neighborhood church which runs an evangelistic event for pensioners, a study group for young mothers, or a holiday club for children, is using the HUP. Use of the HUP in a mission strategy does not require *either* that only homogeneous methods will be used, *or* that homogeneous churches will result from this strategy. In some situations, the HUP may be of little use. In others, it may be a crucial perspective for effective mission, enabling churches to escape the captivity of their cultural assumptions and reach sensitively subcultures which have previously been neglected and marginalized. Such activities may or may not lead to the emergence of homogeneous churches.

But network churches do tend to be homogeneous, and so their development is viewed with suspicion. Even if the HUP is accepted as a component in a diversified mission strategy, the emergence of homogeneous churches is another matter. The prospect of hundreds or thousands of homogeneous churches being planted fills many observers with horror. Not even the rapid growth of network churches in areas where most neighborhood churches are struggling and closing is sufficient to justify this development.

The argument is that the development of more and more churches that simply mirror the divisions in society is not only questionable as a sustainable mission strategy, but is objectionable as a perversion of the gospel. The planting instead of multicultural churches would be an ecclesiological development with tremendous significance for mission. Especially in areas where communities are divided along racial lines, the witness of church communities that demonstrate the power of the gospel to bring reconciliation and to inspire action for justice is crucial and full of potential. Such churches point hopefully to the coming of the kingdom.

The validity of this concern and the attractiveness of the proposed alternative must be recognized. But very many churches are already quite homogeneous in terms of age, ethnicity, color, and income bracket. In some situations this simply reflects the surrounding community, but in others it represents a failure to reach out to or welcome into fellowship people from other social and ethnic groups. Those who object to the emergence of separate ethnic or youth churches may need first to consider the reasons for the prevalence of homogeneous white middle-class churches. If the planting of new homogeneous churches is illegitimate, perhaps steps should be taken to close down thousands of older homogeneous churches? Alternatively, we may prefer to recognize that we inherit an imperfect situation and work patiently, realistically, and generously toward the breaking down of barriers and the emergence of a mature and multicultural church community. Paradoxically, planting different kinds of homogeneous churches from those which already dominate the ecclesiastical landscape may be a step toward this goal. Without this diversity, attempts to achieve heterogeneity may simply represent cultural imperialism.

Perhaps a rather static ecclesiology is again causing difficulties. There is no doubt that the eschatological vision of the church is heterogeneous,[18] and that churches in every generation face the challenge of anticipating this heterogeneity and modeling it in a divided world. But it does not follow that this must be done by insisting that every expression of the church must contain a requisite variety of members. The planting and growth of homogeneous congregations does not necessarily threaten the unity of the church, or its progress toward the eschatological vision. It is possible for heterogeneous congregations to have homogeneous subgroups, or for homogeneous congregations to express their commitment to a heterogeneous vision by meeting with and engaging in mission alongside different homogeneous congregations.

Indeed, it is arguable that such homogeneous units are vital for the mission of the church and for the church to be able to draw on the diverse cultures from which its members come. With a more flexible ecclesiology, we can recognize the potential of homogeneous churches and address important concerns about divisions in the church. The key issue is the way in which homogeneous units relate to other groups and to the wider church community.

The third concern about network churches—that they threaten the integrity of families by encouraging family members to worship in different churches—applies less to ethnic churches than to youth churches (although this is relevant in some Asian churches, with younger members tending to prefer heterogeneous churches and older members enjoying more homogeneous settings). Youth churches are a recent development, and their impact on family life has yet to be assessed. But any assessment must be set in the context of alternative structures that are generally failing either to reach and keep young people,[19] or to provide forms of "all-age worship" that are appropriate for the majority of the congregation. Often the real choice is between encouraging youth churches or losing teenagers from the church. Many parents will prefer their children to worship in youth congregations than not to worship anywhere. Furthermore, in many traditional churches, different age groups have separate activities, so the reality of families worshipping together may apply to little more than sharing transport to and from the church building.

Nevertheless, this is an important issue, and there is no easy or fully satisfactory answer to it. As with other expressions of homogeneous churches, youth churches will benefit from an ecclesiology that discourages isolation and encourages the building of vital relationships between churches of various shapes. Members of youth churches may be encouraged to interact with members of other churches in appropriate ways (perhaps by participation in a shared social action project rather than by holding joint worship services). And, in due course, decisions will be needed regarding the future of youth churches. Do they feed members into intergenerational churches, or do they develop into monogenerational middle-aged churches? Will a new generation of youth churches emerge, in our rapidly changing culture, to reach those whom older "youth" churches are not reaching?[20]

The fourth concern—about nominality—similarly needs to be assessed by comparison with other forms of church life, where church membership may also comprise both highly committed and largely nominal components. It is not only the members of youth or ethnic churches who may be drawn into membership for cultural rather than spiritual reasons (if such a distinction is valid). Parishioners may belong to the parish church for cultural reasons. Second generation members of churches which emphasize the importance of personal faith and commitment may nevertheless have been inculturated into them.

The extent of nominality has been charted by Peter Brierley and described by Eddie Gibbs,[21] who analyzes the causes of this phenomenon and suggests some strategies to confront it. It is arguable that network churches, rather than encouraging nominality, may be one means of countering this. One cause of nominality Gibbs identifies—culturally inappropriate worship—is manifestly not applicable to most youth and ethnic churches, whose very existence may owe much to their concern to provide culturally appropriate worship for those alienated by its absence in other churches. Where cultural reasons have been significant in drawing people into churches, care is needed in nurture of these members. But network churches may be particularly effective in providing such nurture.

It is interesting that three of these four criticisms of network churches—homogeneity, dividing families, and nominality—are also applicable to neighborhood churches. The difference may be that many network churches recognize these issues and choose to work with them, aware of the dangers and ambiguities, but convinced that the traditional alternative is less effective. Network churches have strengths and weaknesses, as do neighborhood churches. In the contemporary context, it is likely that both forms of church life—and others—will be necessary if the church is to engage effectively in mission.

Some network churches are distinctive, not only because they are not constituted on the basis of geographical proximity, but because they are attempting to contextualize the gospel and church life in ways that are quite different from most neighborhood churches. Both youth and ethnic churches have developed styles of worship, models of learning, and patterns of meeting together which would be alien and uncongenial to traditional churches (and many neighborhood church plants). In African, Asian, or youth congregations, language, music, seating arrangements, theological emphases, and various other features may create a very different environment from that which is familiar in typical suburban congregations. Open dialogue and creative interaction between neighborhood churches and these network churches, as well as readiness to learn from one another, rather than dismissive attitudes, will benefit both. Distinguishing between gospel and culture remains an important and ongoing task for churches committed to a missionary engagement with their culture.

(3) Cell Churches

Another increasingly influential model, but one which seems to represent a move in the opposite direction, toward a more local form of church than the neighborhood church, is the *cell church*. This is a popular model in several non-Western nations, including Chile, Japan, Korea, China, Ethiopia, Thailand, and the Ivory Coast (where cell churches are sometimes huge). Cell churches can also be found in several Western nations: they are becoming familiar in Britain, and well-established examples are the Home Church movement in Australia, associated with Robert and Julia Banks,[22] and the house churches or cell churches of North America associated with Ralph Neighbor.[23] Some would regard as further examples the base ecclesial communities of Brazil and other nations associated with Latin American liberation theology,[24] although there are arguably as many differences as similarities between these and cell churches.

Some advocates claim that, although cell churches are as old as the first century, over the past thirty years Christians all over the world have introduced cell church structures independently, based solely on their study of the New Testament, and that this is a significant contemporary move of God. This development is referred to in revolutionary language: a "second Reformation," "building a church for the Last Days," or "a new way of being church." Some advocates dismiss traditional structures as unbiblical and a deviation from God's intention for the church.[25] Others regard cell churches as appropriate only in certain contexts.

Cell churches are not the same as *cell groups* or house groups, popular in many churches since the 1960s. Here the small groups are additional to the existing program and can be stopped without dismantling the church. Membership of the cell groups is secondary to membership of the church. These cell groups normally do not engage in the pastoral care or evangelism characteristic of cells in cell churches. Nor are cell churches the same as *house churches*, although in the United States they are sometimes known as house church movements.

Early house churches in the United Kingdom had many similarities to cell churches, but did not develop in the same way. Those which grew generally reverted to a traditional ecclesiology,[26] where small groups were subsidiary to congregational activities. Those which did not grow tended to stagnate as isolated independent house churches. The difference between these two expressions of the church can be summed up as follows: when house churches grow, they become larger house churches; when cells grow, they multiply into more groups. From the perspective of cell church advocates, the British house church movement looks like an aborted cell church movement. Recent interest in cell church ideas within some sections of the house church movement indicates a possible return to its roots.

Cell churches are communities of Christians where all the main activities of church life take place in small home-based groups, groups which are linked together within a larger network for certain purposes. Cell churches have two main components: the *cell* and the *celebration*. Some have a third intermediate level *congregation*. This structure is familiar in larger traditional churches with house groups and/or multiple congregations.

What differentiates cell churches is their focus: the small group is the center of the church, not a peripheral activity. A cell typically has between eight and fifteen members, meets weekly (the day and time are unimportant) and provides most of what traditional churches provide: ministry, teaching, celebration of communion, baptism, and pastoral care. The task of the cell leader is to facilitate meetings rather than dominating these (although guidelines for cell activities provided by advocates and consultants are, for a movement that emphasizes a "bottom-up" approach, surprisingly prescriptive).

There is strong emphasis on relational evangelism, and the cell splits to form new cells once it reaches fifteen members. The celebration, which takes place regularly but not necessarily weekly, is not the center of the church nor its focus, but a community event involving members from all the cells, primarily for praise and worship.

Advocates list as follows the main differences from traditional churches: a focus on the small group rather than the large; that is, an inverted model of church; a focus on homes rather than church buildings; a focus on people rather than programs; evangelism takes place locally through friendship; in other words, the entry point to the church is through small groups rather than large events; the small groups are expected to multiply, avoiding problems of stagnation and sterility associated with traditional house groups; leadership is widely shared and nothing is the exclusive preserve of professional ministers. In fact, these characteristics can be found in various combinations and to differing degrees in other churches, but cell churches represent attempts to follow through radically the implications of these commitments. It is the primacy of the commitment to the cell that distinguishes this model of church. Few other churches could survive as effectively if they were to lose their buildings, professional leaders, and opportunities to meet all together.

Because cell churches are not yet widespread in most Western nations, it is too early to know how culturally appropriate and evangelistically effective they may be. Some are attempting to plant cell churches from scratch, others are trying to transform (the term used in the literature is "transition") traditional churches into cell churches. The latter model is sometimes known as the "metachurch,"[27] a church that is changing into a cell church structure. Advocates recognize that this process may take several years to complete, because a change of mentality is needed as well as a structural change.

Some churches may choose not to become pure cell churches but to combine features of cell churches and traditional churches. Involvement in cell groups and in the larger celebrations may be regarded as equally important. As with the attempt to move toward a seeker-targeted model, it is doubtful whether many churches will be able to cope with the radical changes in ethos and structure required to develop fully into cell churches. If cell churches are to proliferate, they may need to emerge predominantly through church planting.

It may be helpful to consider some perspectives from those who have observed the development of cell churches in various parts of the world. Many are enthusiastic about this development, seeing it as evidence of a belated recognition that church members, in common with all human beings, need meaningful primary level relationships. Cell churches also fit well with contemporary sociological developments, where the emphasis is on networks rather than hierarchies, on grass roots rather than top-down initiatives. Similar developments are taking place in politics and the world of business, and in other religious contexts, such as the New Age movement, which mainly operates through small groups rather than large gatherings or organizations.[28] However, we should note various concerns and reservations.

Some argue that the differences between cell churches and traditional churches with cell groups are real, but limited. The effort and time required to transition a church into a cell church may not be compensated by the anticipated rewards, and may hinder the mission of the church for a decade or longer. The issue of motivation is important also, since the cell church model is sometimes presented as a means to church growth.

But many advocates of cell churches warn that making this transition to achieve church growth (or arrest decline) is unlikely to be effective. Ralph Neighbor has said that "cells that are developed to make a church grow will fail *every* time." Many successful large cell churches were in fact already large before adopting a cell format; the change in structure acted as a "turbocharge" mechanism to help further growth. This observation was made by Mikel Neumann of Wheaton College, who has researched into cell churches in several different cultures, and concluded that "growth has taken place before the cells came along. I've seen that in *every* single case." A typical successful cell church will have a dynamic leader and a "critical mass" of highly committed people in a growing situation. Changing to a cell structure will not transform a static, inward-looking church into a dynamic, growing church.

The alternative strategy of planting new cell churches promises faster progress, but research suggests that attempts to plant cell churches from scratch will falter, unless they achieve a critical mass of people and cells relatively quickly. Some cell churches which were hailed initially as successes have subsequently struggled and failed. To be successful, cell churches need to function within a network that is large enough to sustain and service the cells. Neumann suggests that cell churches operate best in urban areas and appeal primarily to people with a high level of education and socioeconomic status. It may also be that more private cultures will resist the intimacy implied by membership in cell groups (thus, cell churches flourish in the United States, but struggle in Canada).

So cell churches may be effective in situations of rapid growth. They may also be very effective in situations of persecution. Ethiopia offers a remarkable recent example. In 1974, a military coup overthrew the government, and the new communist regime confiscated church property, imprisoned church leaders, and forbade all church meetings. But many churches re-formed as underground cells and continued to meet. When the communists were overthrown in 1991, the underground church emerged, and Ethiopian church leaders discovered that there were now many times more Christians than in 1974. The Mennonite church, for example, had grown from 3000 to 90,000 members. Many churches continued to operate in small groups, since there were no public buildings large enough to hold the congregations.[29]

But how effective will cell churches be in post-Christian societies, where neither rapid growth nor persecution are presently the experience of most churches? Perhaps they may be a component in the evangelization of the nation and the renewal of the church, but they will probably be only one component. Many will not join such a structure.

Signs of Hope

The emergence of these models is an encouraging sign of ecclesiological reflection and creativity. There is common ground between them, such as the search for contextually relevant church life, expressed in different ways by the seeker-targeted model and by youth or ethnic churches; or the concern to be rooted in the wider community that characterizes both cell churches and ethnic churches. Cell churches and youth churches may be as committed to reaching unchurched people as churches running seeker events.

Some churches attempt to incorporate features of different models. Churches with seeker services may aim at a group that is as homogeneous as any ethnic church. Cell church structures may be built into youth churches or used to develop several ethnic congregations within a multicongregational church. They may also form a component within churches with seeker services. The Willow Creek church is not a pure cell church but places great emphasis on its small group structure and might be classified as a metachurch, where members' commitment to both cells and celebration events (here evangelistic in orientation) is equally important.

But there are also significant differences: the cell church model advocates small units, the seeker-targeted church generally requires larger numbers. Youth and ethnic churches are homogeneous, and churches running seeker events often target a specific section of the community, whereas cell churches may be intergenerational and more effective as heterogeneous groups. Some of these new churches have a centripetal understanding of mission, others a centrifugal ethos. Proponents of one model may be quite critical of others. For example, some cell church advocates question the seeker service approach, asking whether such churches grow as effectively as pure cell churches; whether they can avoid the focus of attention being on the seeker service, which is professional and large-scale; and whether they can really reach unchurched people, or only fringe people. They suggest that there is evidence that cell churches may be more effective in reaching unchurched people than churches with seeker services.

These models do not necessarily require planting extra churches. Cell churches can be developed from traditional churches through the restructuring process known as transitioning. Seeker services can be grafted onto existing churches. Ethnic and youth congregations can be parts of a multicongregational church. Each model can be seen not as a new kind of church but a radicalized version of traditional churches: seeker services as radicalized guest services; network churches as radical versions of churches with diverse activities for homogeneous units; cell churches as radical expressions of churches with home groups. However, the change required to establish these new models is greater than many existing churches can manage; thus often what emerges becomes in practice a new church.

Elsewhere, church planting has been regarded as preferable to introduce the radical changes envisaged. Such developments are generally examples of planting rather than cloning, although there is a danger of imposing structures or activities that have been developed elsewhere without adequately contextualizing these.

All the models we have considered have strengths and weaknesses. Some have been operating for several years. Others are recent innovations; time will be needed to assess whether they are appropriate and effective. Hopefully, those who advocate and experiment with these models will be willing honestly to evaluate their strengths and weaknesses, and especially whether they are more relevant in certain contexts than others.

Through such evaluation, significant lessons can be learned about the diverse shapes the church may need to assume in contemporary society, if it is to fulfill its mission. And if cross-pollination takes places between these models, the diversity of the models already available augers well for the refining of these models, and the development of further models.

Church Planting in a Postmodern Culture

Such diversity is a response to the pluralist nature of contemporary society, and to the influence of the much-vaunted and sometimes wearisome interpretation of our culture known as *postmodernity*. Not surprisingly, since this is an inherent feature of the concept itself, postmodernity means different things to different people. It is not easy to define, because of its scope and varied expressions; it is as much a mood as a set of beliefs and carries a range of meanings. All we intend to do here is indicate some aspects of postmodernity that are relevant to our discussion of the shape of the church.[30]

Some use the term to mean that modernity (the worldview that emerged from the Enlightenment and has dominated Western civilization) is moving into a new phase, and deny that this worldview is in terminal trouble. Barry Smart[31] argues that postmodernity represents "modernity coming of age." "Postmodernity offers us the possibility of a critical view of modernity. Not the end of modernity, but the possibility of a reconstituted modernity. Calling modernity to account, demanding that the costs as well as the benefits are acknowledged, the unintended consequences and the limits recognized."

Some use the term to signal the collapse of modernity, arguing that it has no distinctive content of its own but simply marks the end of an era. Graham Cray[32] defines it as a general term to describe the awareness of a changing era and writes: "One of the best descriptions of postmodern culture is that of 'shopping,' that the world and all of history is a vast supermarket, and you can just pick out the ingredients you like, and assemble them into your own version of something."

Some use the term with reference to various features of a new worldview that is coming into being, albeit not fully formed. Mike Featherstone[33] insists that "to speak of postmodernity is to suggest an epochal shift or break from modernity involving the emergence of a new social totality with its own organizing principles."

Common to these interpretations is a recognition that we live in a time of cultural uncertainty. What is unclear is whether this will lead to the emergence of a new and more diversified culture, or to a reassertion of the culture of modernity, either in a chastened and modified form, or with renewed vigor. The export and globalization of modernity over recent decades means that, whatever the impact of postmodernity in the West, modernity will remain a significant component in the culture of the global village, with every prospect of recapturing its erstwhile heartland.

The challenge facing churches, as they consider mission in a postmodern environment, is to remain flexible and alert, neither buying uncritically into an apparently emerging culture that may be short-lived, thereby leaving the church stranded in a cultural deadend; nor remaining "trapped in a modernist mode,"[34] ignoring or resisting cultural changes that require clear and creative thinking about the shape and role of the church in society.

David Bosch[35] describes this situation as a paradigm change similar to others faced by the church and society in previous centuries.

He urges: "Neither extreme reactionary nor excessively revolutionary approaches will help the Christian church and mission to arrive at greater clarity or serve God's cause in a better way. In the case of each paradigm change reviewed so far, there remained a creative tension between the new and the old. The agenda was always—consciously or unconsciously—one of reform, not of replacement."

Postmodernity is a challenge facing all churches. Some may see their role as the provision of security and unchanging patterns in a culture that is changing at a frightening rate and in unsettling ways. This might be a contemporary application of the Welsh monastic response (considered in chapter 4) to the collapse of Roman civilization in Britain. Others may choose to explore new ways of being the church tailored to this emerging culture. Church planting provides the church with opportunities to develop and assess diverse responses.

A brief summary of familiar features of postmodernity identifies some of the issues that church planters will need to consider as they design churches for a postmodern culture. These include commitment to relativism in relation to questions of truth; understanding meaning as subjective rather than objective; the significance of spiritual values without allowing claims to exclusivity; the importance of imagination as well as rationality; interpreting the world through a biological rather than a mechanistic model; concern for the environment and an understanding of humanity as part of this environment, rather than separate from it; a distrust of institutions, hierarchies, and structures and a preference for networks and grass-roots activities; a rejection of male domination; an iconoclastic refusal to respect established traditions, or to take anything, including itself, too seriously; an emphasis on the chaotic and fragmentary rather than order and harmony; a readiness to hold together contradictory beliefs; a commitment to choice at every level; and deep skepticism.

The challenge facing church planters in every generation is to plant churches which are "in the world but not of the world,"[36] culturally relevant and contextualized, but also distinctive and provocative. In a pluralist society, responses to this challenge are likely to be diverse—and prone to misinterpretation. Richard Niebuhr's classic categorization of the possible relationships between Christ and culture[37] was susceptible, even under modernity, to the criticism that a monolithic view of culture was presupposed that was simplistic and misleading.[38] In a postmodern culture, this model breaks down even further. The choice is not whether to be for or against culture, but which aspects of culture—indeed which aspects of which subculture—the church affirms or challenges.

There may be features of postmodernity which are perceived as liberating, which should be endorsed within the churches. There may be other features which are dehumanizing, to which churches should offer alternatives. The challenge is to move out of modernist mode and plant "postmodern churches." These are not churches that adopt uncritically the values of postmodernity or the philosophy of postmodernism, but churches which will be good news in a postmodern culture. Such churches will be both engaged and distinctive. Effective church planters will need to be familiar, both with the general features of our complex culture, and with the specific features of the sector of this society that their church is being planted to reach and serve.

Each of the models considered in this chapter may be seen as a response to some aspect of postmodernity.[39] Seeker services and youth churches employ a range of communication media rather than the linear monologue style of modernity. Network churches recognize the decentralized nature of a postmodern society and operate within this fragmented environment. Cell churches offer another grass-roots approach which may provide community in a society where individualism is rampant.

On some issues there may be widespread agreement among church planters; with regard to some of the features of postmodernity listed above, there may be room for different responses. What one may regard as essential, another may see as peripheral; what one introduces as a radical alternative may be criticized by another as accommodation to the spirit of the age. The ecumenicity and cooperation that has marked contemporary church planting will be tested as we move beyond cloning into creative and risky church planting.

Developing Further Models

The models we have examined in this chapter are indicative of the creativity necessary to engage effectively in mission in a postmodern society. Each, as we have seen, has strengths and weaknesses. All are recent developments, and some may be short-lived experiments rather than enduring patterns of congregational life.

But in a shifting culture, longevity may not be the primary test of validity. More important than the models themselves are the fresh insights these are generating and the permission to question accepted traditions that they represent. The questions remain valid whatever our evaluation of the answers.

Cloning more churches of the kind we already have will not do. Most church plants do not reach different sectors of society or new subcultures, even if they are effective in reaching more members of those sectors of society where the church is already quite well established. Indeed, some question whether current forms of church planting are even effective in reaching nominal Christians, let alone those who would not identify themselves in this way. Roy Williamson, Bishop of Southwark, London, suggests that "the majority of the 'believing but not belonging' fringe remain outside the institutional church, including those newly planted parts of it."[40] He urges the discovery of new models of church and mission which will enable the church to come alongside those for whom most expressions of church are too threatening.

Among encouraging signs, he notes the emergence in various places of grass roots communities patterned on the Latin American "base churches," the creativity of the "Nine O'clock Service" in Sheffield (despite its traumatic problems), and an initiative known as the "Picture Palace" in South London. These may not be the most helpful examples. The problems experienced by the Nine O'clock Service have been widely publicized, and this example may be more effective in alerting church planters to the dangers of inadequate safeguards and illegitimate forms of contextualization. Leaders of the "Picture Palace," contacted to find out more about this initiative, seemed rather embarrassed that their limited venture should be regarded as an example to emulate. And there is little evidence as yet that "base churches" have the capacity to take root in this country, although transmuted in some culturally sensitive way they may have considerable potential for urban mission.

Nevertheless, even limited, flawed, or short-lived initiatives can contribute toward an escape from what the WCC Report which coined the phrase "missionary congregations" calls "morphological fundamentalism," and defines as "a rigid and inflexible attitude toward the *morphe* or structure of the congregation similar to the attitude prevalent in biblical fundamentalism. Consciously, or more often unconsciously, the existing forms of the life of the Christian community are taken to have been fixed once and for all; their historical nature—and that means their relativity and changeability—is ignored."[41]

There are other examples of churches providing access points for those for whom most churches are culturally inaccessible. "Holy Joe's," meeting in a pub in Brixton, in South London, is one of the better known.[42] "Cornerstone," which meets in the "Odd One Out," a pub run by Christian landlords in Colchester, Essex, is introduced by one of its leaders as "open to all who are searching spiritually yet find conventional church services too daunting."[43] Such initiatives are emerging in various parts of the country. Are they in fact churches or outreach activities? We confront again the question raised in relation to "parachurch" organizations: what is a church? The borderline between church planting and mission initiatives may not be easy to locate. Eddie Gibbs made one of the most profound comments at the *Challenge 2000* congress in Nottingham in 1995: "Mission is messy." Neat and tidy church planting, using standard models and methods, will not suffice.

Further experimentation is needed. Many sectors of society are beyond the reach of most local churches. They will need what Martin Robinson calls "breakthrough congregations,"[44] able to reach communities who have not previously responded in significant numbers to the gospel. The multicultural and thoroughly unchurched[45] inner cities are desperately in need of new churches, but they do not need suburban church structures and cultural forms imposed from outside. New believers from the diverse Asian communities[46] that now constitute a significant sector of Western society will need churches that allow them to follow Jesus in ways that are relevant to their cultures, and that do not impose as "Christian" styles and structures that are merely European or North American.

Secularists, more open in a postmodern culture to consider the possibility of a spiritual dimension to life, but for whom most existing churches are completely irrelevant at best, and a hindrance at worst, will need new kinds of communities of faith if they are to find and follow Christ. Those influenced and attracted by New Age ideas are unlikely to be discipled in significant numbers, unless new churches are planted that incarnate principles and address concerns which have been neglected by most existing churches, but which New Age philosophies rightly endorse.[47] Shared interest in Celtic spirituality (though often eclectic and romanticized by both groups) may be a bridge between those influenced by New Age ideas and the churches.

But church planting that can respond creatively and courageously to the mission opportunities of contemporary society is hindered by various factors. Time pressures, denominational expectations, the concern for numerical success, and the temptation to clone rather than plant all militate against such innovation. A further problem is the tendency to marginalize or patronize creative alternatives, to regard these new forms of church life as interesting but peripheral experiments, and to continue to endorse as "normal" forms of church life with which we are more familiar.[48] Even those urging the development of missionary congregations, as a necessary response to the challenges of post-Christendom and a postmodern culture, seem locked into a model of church that is deeply rooted in Christendom and too monochrome to meet the challenges of a postmodern environment. Thus, Robert Warren prefaces a brief discussion of various alternative models with the proviso: "Stimulating though the creative alternatives to the parish church are, the primary work of building missionary congregations must lie in bringing about the renewal of the normal parish church."[49]

It might be more helpful to treat the parish model as one of several that will be needed for mission in contemporary society. The WCC report, The Church for Others, again urges radical rather than cautious action: "The churches' attitude toward experiments should not be one of silent toleration, especially toward experiments which are seeking to create new forms of Christian presence in terms of particular situations. A missionary church should welcome such attempts and encourage their multiplication."[50]

Another hindrance to creative church planting is poverty of *theological* reflection on the shape of the church. Church planting movements have often eschewed theological reflection and theological training. Enthusiasm, commitment, spirituality, giftedness, energy, and interpersonal skills have been regarded as the necessary qualifications. In this chapter, we have advocated that those engaged in church planting should give attention to the kinds of churches to be planted. The sociological and contextual reflection that is evident in some contemporary church planting is encouraging, and this has led to the emergence of some new models of church life. But often this reflection leads to pragmatic decisions that fail to engage deeply enough with underlying theological issues.

Dale Stoffer, a Mennonite church planter and trainer, warns that "in the modern church planting and church growth movements, there is too little attention to developing a theological rationale for new practices. Pragmatic considerations seem to be the litmus test for any new technique."[52] Such pragmatism needs to be accompanied and evaluated by theological reflection on the nature and task of the church and its role in society. Otherwise new models may become popular and new churches may be planted which promise much but deliver little. Some may be incompatible with fundamental aspects of the mission in which they are supposed to engage. Some may be so culturally attuned that they become indistinguishable from the culture.

The theological reflection required will not be achieved by attempts to find biblical proof texts for these new models. Of those models we have examined in this chapter, the cell church model is most prone to fall into this trap. Contextual and theological assessment of such churches will not be helped by claims that this is "the" New Testament model. The fact that Christians in the first century frequently met in homes is irrefutable, but this does not require us to do the same. Questions need to be asked before drawing such a conclusion: Why did they meet in homes? How comparable are the "households" of the New Testament with the suburban semidetached houses in which contemporary cell groups meet? Are meetings in homes perceived in our context in the same way as they were in the first century? What were the theological, missiological, and ecclesiological implications, if any, of home-based churches?

If churches are accorded the status of "New Testament churches," evaluation of their effectiveness in mission and ministry becomes more difficult, and resistance to the development of other forms of church life increases. We have argued that the contemporary context is increasingly post-Christian and postmodern. Churches in many shapes will be needed to engage in mission in such a context. The important questions that need to be asked about the shape of the church relate to its role in this kind of society, rather than its conformity to an often mythical New Testament structure. Theological reflection, drawing on biblical resources rather than reading back preferred models into the New Testament, is crucial if these questions are to be addressed at sufficient depth.

Resident Aliens

The shape of the church needs to be related to its task. Missionary communities do not structure themselves for maintenance, nor for cultural adaptation, but to engage in mission. Their form is determined *both* by the message they are wanting to incarnate, *and* by the context in which they are engaging in mission. Identification with those with whom they are wanting to communicate is vital, but this cannot be at the expense of losing their own identity. Salt must be spread around to have any effect, but it must remain salty. Victimizing members of a minority community to gain the trust of local racists may enable churches to identify with this subculture, but it is not an appropriate form of identification. Similarly, distinctive witness is vital, but not distinctiveness for its own sake. There is something distinctive to proclaim, and to demonstrate, but this distinctiveness is itself contextual. Proclaiming the gospel in New Testament Greek would make a church distinctive (and is certainly biblical!), but it would not be an appropriate form of distinctiveness.

Os Guinness, calling for "authentic contextualization," insists that "the principle of identification is basic to communication. . . . But Scripture and history are clear: Without maintaining critical tension, the principle of identification is a recipe for compromise and capitulation."[52] Contextualization is a vital but complex issue, on which there is an extensive literature in cross-cultural mission circles,[53] a resource that has not yet been adequately tapped into by many involved in church planting. All we can do here is note the significance of contextualization for contemporary church planters and suggest some principles and parameters.

Contextualization does not mean restricting our message to the questions being asked within contemporary culture, or responding only to the felt needs of a community (the popular, but mistaken notion of "letting the world set the agenda").[54] It does mean listening to our culture and finding appropriate theological images to engage with this culture. For example, if research indicates that many people do not feel guilty,[55] we may choose initially to present the challenge of Christ in other ways, not because guilt is no longer an issue, but because it is not the only issue confronting people, nor necessarily the starting point on a journey to faith.

Contextualization does not mean designing a church that is captive to the spirit of the age, that is indistinguishable from other organizations, or that embraces uncritically values, structures, and activities that are currently popular. It does mean prophetic engagement with contemporary culture, discerning what can be affirmed and what must be challenged, sometimes by living in the opposite spirit, by being a deviant community, or by living in ways that pose questions or suggest alternatives to popular wisdom. But this engagement is possible only if cultural sensitivity and theological reflection go hand in hand. We suggested in chapter 2 that the incarnation provides a basis for authentic contextualization. "True contextualization happens when there is a community which lives faithfully by the gospel and in that same costly identification with people in their real situations as we see in the earthly ministry of Jesus."[56]

Authentic contextualization is especially hard in a pluralist and rapidly changing culture. The "Gospel and our Culture" movement, associated with writings of Lesslie Newbigin, has attempted to engage at considerable depth with the culture of modernity. The movement offers helpful resources to churches in their missionary engagement with this culture, as they consider what aspects of modernity the gospel affirms and challenges. But it has been suggested that this culture is in fact waning, and that postmodernity will require a radically different missionary engagement. On the other hand, if churches attempt to become contextually distinctive in an emerging postmodern culture, what will they do if this cultural shift is short-lived and gives way to a different culture or resurgent modernity? And in a pluralist environment, what does it mean to be distinctive?

Attempts to be "countercultural" may simply identify churches with existing countercultural elements—and often just as these elements are becoming acceptable. Nigel Wright has warned[57] that attempts by churches to escape from conformity to the dominant culture by identifying themselves with new cultural trends or movements may result only in conformity to this "adversary culture." Neither kind of conformity is adequate for the mission of the church.

The only alternative is an approach to church planting that reflects theologically and prayerfully on the ecclesiological implications of mission in a diverse and changing context. Robert Warren concludes that "what the church can do is pray for the discernment to know how far we should welcome each trend, how far we should adjust to it, or how far this is a trend we should confront."[58] Such reflection and discernment are ongoing, open to challenge, informed by biblical teaching and narrative, provisional rather than final, stimulated by central theological concepts rather than proof texts, and concerned to maintain the critical tension of which Os Guinness speaks. The shape of the church is important, but this shape is theologically as well as culturally determined.

A New Testament term, which is used only occasionally but conveys powerfully this concept of authentic contextualization, is *paroikos*. Meaning literally "someone who dwells alongside," and referring to those who live in a country that is not their own, it is used by Luke to refer to the experience of Abraham's descendants in Canaan (Acts 7:6), in Ephesians 2:19 to refer to the inclusion in God's new community of those who had previously been strangers, and by Peter (1 Pet. 2:11) to encourage members of this new community to live distinctively. *Paroikoi* are "in the world," but "not of the world." They are at home in every culture, but fully at home in none. They know that their true home, their ultimate allegiance, their source of energy, and their perspective on every issue is the kingdom of God. But this knowledge is the basis, not for withdrawal into ghettos, but for renewed engagement with their temporary home. They have been converted from the world and to the world. Since they are citizens of a heavenly city,[59] they are neither entranced by nor despairing of their earthly city. Two possible translations of this term are "sojourners"[60] and "resident aliens."[61]

Paroikos is the word from which we derive the terms *parish* and *parochial*. The word parochial has become emasculated and perverted, so that parochial thinking now designates attitudes which are narrow-minded, selfish, and lacking in perspective. This mirrors the development of the parish as a subdivision of a so-called Christian society, where maintenance replaced mission and where those whose calling was to be "resident aliens" became comfortable and indistinct "residents."

Whether or not parish structures have any future in a post-Christian and postmodern culture, parochial attitudes must go if churches are to engage in mission. The *task* of the church requires it to be distinctive. The *shapes* it must assume to fulfill this task will vary. The churches that are planted in the coming years will need to be made up of resident aliens, thoroughly immersed in the surrounding culture, but radically distinct.

7. CHURCH PLANTING AND THE ETHOS OF THE CHURCH

Why Do People Leave Churches?

Although many churches today are experiencing overall numerical growth, many are also declining. This decline is partly due to the death of church members in aging congregations, but disaffection is also a significant factor. It is tempting for growing churches, and those involved in church planting, to dismiss this as an issue that does not concern them and to rejoice in their increasing numbers. But many of these growing churches are also losing members. Both the front door and the back door appear to be wide open.

To advocate or engage in church planting without addressing this question risks the establishment of more churches that people will leave. New churches frequently attract those who were previously members of other churches, but who left those churches and have been part of the extensive group in contemporary society who "believe but do not belong."[1] A new church offers the possibility of a fresh start. Perhaps their experience of church will be different this time? For some, this hope has been realized, and they have become highly committed members of new churches. But for others, involvement in this new church has been short-lived, and they have drifted away again. Furthermore, they have left the new church for the same reasons they left their previous church, but feeling even more disillusioned.

Those involved in church planting are often delightfully enthusiastic about this new venture, thrilled with the freedom they are enjoying, welcoming to newcomers, and deeply concerned that the new church should be good news in the community. This enthusiasm, welcome, and freshness are significant factors in attracting to the church those who have never been church members before, and some who are hoping that this church will be different from their previous experience. But the initial growth that many church plants experience sometimes stalls, and may give way to decline. Newcomers decide not to stay. Those hoping for a fresh start become discouraged. Even some of the church planting team return to the planting church, or opt out of church life altogether. The mood can swing quickly from enthusiasm to despair.

If despair can be avoided, in favor of prayerful and honest analysis of the factors involved, the church planting team may discover, albeit belatedly, why people have left the church. A better option would be for churches considering church planting to explore this question before planting a new church. This may require a longer period of planning and preparation, but it might result in the planting of churches which attract and retain those who are unwilling to belong to existing churches, or to the new congregations they clone.

One way to avoid the disturbing question of why people leave churches is to suggest this is a problem that *other* churches face. Another stratagem is to blame those who "fall away" or "backslide." People do leave churches because their faith has waned, because there are moral challenges that they prefer not to tackle, or because there are broken relationships they are unwilling to restore. But it will not do to suggest, or to imply by ignoring this issue, that church decline is always the fault of those leaving the church, rather than the fault of the church they are leaving. This is to indulge in self-deception, and the same kind of self-justification that blames those who are not healed through our prayers for their lack of faith. Recent research indicates that deficiencies within the churches are often responsible, and conversations with ex-members reveal issues that should cause us great concern.

Pastoral concern for those whom the churches are hurting should motivate us to examine these issues carefully. In addition, the demands of mission in a post-Christian society require us to discover the reasons why people leave our churches—and to avoid planting any more of these kinds of churches. We do not engage in this process of reflection as an exercise in navel-gazing, that threatens to postpone church planting and other mission initiatives until the church is perfect. Such reflection is crucial if we are to plant churches that will reach and keep those who are alienated from the expressions of church with which they are currently familiar.

A number of recent books have considered the reasons for such alienation. Some are based on extensive research and present a range of factors that those leaving churches have identified as significant. Two particularly helpful surveys of the British scene, which both appeared in 1993, are presented in The Sheep That Got Away by Michael Fanstone,[2] and in Peter Brierley's appendix to Winning Them Back by Eddie Gibbs.[3] Two years earlier, in The Irrelevant Church, Robin Gamble[4] analyzed the relationship between the churches and the British class structure, and highlighted the implications for mission of the captivity of the churches to a middle-class ethos and values. Other books have drawn heavily on the experiences of disillusioned ex-church members.

In 1992, Morris Stuart wrote passionately about the exodus from the churches of committed, gifted, yet deeply disillusioned Christians. His book, So Long, Farewell and Thanks for the Church?[5] contains several letters written by "refugees" from the churches, which make for painful but illuminating reading. In 1995, David Tomlinson wrote The Post-Evangelical,[6] drawing both on his own discontent with much contemporary church life and on conversations with many who had left evangelical and charismatic churches.

Various factors are identified: boredom, irrelevance, clerical dominance, sexism, racism, introversion, narrow-mindedness, fear of "the world," ghetto-mentality, overcommitment, judgmental attitudes, inflexibility, fundamentalism, the confusion of gospel and culture, reductionist approaches to mission, imperialistic and patronizing attitudes toward others, absorption with trivial issues and many others.

These books, and others like them, should be required reading for aspiring church planters. This is not because they contain many surprises: they mainly confirm what sensitive and discerning church members have known for years. Nor should they be read because they prescribe simple remedies or set out strategies that will transform the situation. There are pointers and challenges, but many questions remain unanswered. Nor do they all agree on the fundamental issues, although there are substantial areas of overlapping concern. Nor do they present a balanced picture, which recognizes the extraordinary ability of flawed churches to be beacons of hope and communities of loving acceptance, which continue to draw thousands into living relationships with Christ and his people. Outrage at the deficiencies of the churches, and amazement at the grace of God which continues to work through these churches, are both appropriate responses to the evidence.

But they should be read and pondered by those who want to plant new churches, so that at least we ask *some* of the questions that need to be asked about the kinds of churches we are planting. Expertise in church planting methodology is ultimately less important than sensitivity to the missiological and pastoral issues raised in such books. The planting of yet more churches which damage their most committed members, and further alienate those already beyond the reach of existing churches, will hinder rather than advancing God's mission.

We have already considered many ecclesiological issues as we have reflected on new models of church, and on the importance of the church taking relevant shapes for its mission in a postmodern and post-Christian context. We turn in this chapter to an underlying issue, which has surfaced already on several occasions—the less tangible, but crucially important matter of the *ethos* of the church. Relatively few people now leave their churches because of disputes over doctrinal formulations, discontent with sacramental understandings, or dismay at liturgical practices. Issues which have in the past divided churches into denominations are regarded by most church members (let alone those outside the churches) as almost irrelevant. In our postdenominational era, people more often leave churches because they do not feel at home in them. There may be a specific issue that prompts withdrawal, but what is really at stake is something more fundamental, a mixture of style, values, priorities, and mood.[7]

The intangibility and complexity of this matter of ethos makes this a difficult chapter to write. Any attempt to address the issues involved is bound to be selective, and risks being simplistic. It is tempting to identify this as a vital concern, then refer those who are interested in exploring the issues further to other books which deal with them at greater length and in greater depth. But to do this might imply that church planting can marginalize the question of ethos, or postpone consideration of this until later. In fact, almost everything we have explored in previous chapters (and will continue to explore in subsequent chapters) is secondary to this. Renewed commitment to the missionary task of the church and fresh thinking about the shape of the church are important, but failure to address issues of ethos risks jeopardizing any progress made in these areas. Examining the ethos of the church takes us to the heart of fundamental missiological and ecclesiological issues raised by church planting.

Evangelical, Charismatic, and Postmodern?

Perhaps a legitimate way of proceeding is to concentrate on a section of the church which is extensively involved in church planting and which has also experienced significant, though not always widely acknowledged, problems with disaffection.[8] Although church planting is by no means restricted to charismatic evangelical churches, such churches are heavily involved in the contemporary church planting movement. According to Archbishop George Carey, "the most successful types of church planting come from churches which have a clear cut identity; usually evangelical/charismatic."[9] Most books on the subject, most speakers at conferences and training events, and a large number of recently planted churches come from this constituency.

Lumping together "evangelical" and "charismatic" risks irritating those who belong to noncharismatic evangelical churches or to nonevangelical charismatic churches. There are three reasons for doing this: first, our concern here is with the ethos of churches rather than their theological distinctives; second, churches which are both evangelical and charismatic are at the forefront of the church planting movement; and third, as David Tomlinson has convincingly argued,[10] "it is now clear that the whole centre ground of evangelicalism has gradually become charismaticized, adopting the *style and ethos* of the charismatic movement."

Raising questions about ethos is of vital importance for this section of the church. But there are obstacles to be overcome if such questions are to be addressed. These include a tendency to activism rather than reflection; a culture of triumphalism rather than self-criticism;[11] and a dominant concern about numerical growth and concentration on short-term goals. The issues raised in the books listed above (all of which relate especially to this section of the church) are serious. Yet it is doubtful whether most evangelical charismatic churches have recognized the extent of the problem.

Perhaps new evangelistic programs, church planting goals, exciting experiences of renewal and expectations of revival, and other such distractions will make it difficult to address such issues. But it remains important to keep asking the questions, and to encourage church planters, especially, to consider the issues involved. To understand some of these issues in all their complexity will require us to reflect further on the postmodern context within which churches are being planted.

Postmodernity, for all its shortcomings, represents a necessary challenge to the overconfidence and reductionism of the culture of modernity. It is important for churches in a postmodern environment to learn from this cultural paradigm shift. We should be able to recognize areas of agreement between the postmodern critique and concerns about modernity which have been expressed by Christians over many years, and embrace aspects of the postmodern ethos.

These aspects are to be embraced, not because they are postmodern, but because they are consistent with theological principles and biblical teaching and recall us to dimensions of our heritage which have been lost. There are other features of postmodernity that are fundamentally inimical, not just to modernist expressions of Christianity but to the Christian faith itself. It is important for churches in a postmodern environment to discern these features, to recognize their implications for church and society, and to develop effective missionary responses. We will challenge these features, not because they are postmodern, but because they are inconsistent with theological principles and biblical teaching, dehumanizing, and socially destructive.

The challenge facing church planters and those wanting to develop missionary congregations is to determine which aspects of postmodernity are to be embraced, and which are to be challenged. It may be helpful here to distinguish between *postmodernity* as a temporal term, indicating that the era of modernity is over, or at least in apparently terminal decline, and *postmodernism* as an ideological term, indicating the philosophical, religious, and moral values that are emerging in this era. A missionary encounter with this complex culture will lead to the development of postmodern churches—not churches which have sold out to a philosophy of postmodernism, but churches which engage faithfully and creatively with the postmodern worldview and which are authentically contextualized in a postmodern environment.

Evangelical charismatic churches are potentially well placed for this missionary encounter. Contemporary evangelicalism owes much to a previous missionary encounter, with the worldview of modernity, which stemmed from the eighteenth-century cultural shift known as the Enlightenment. Evangelicalism began in the mid-eighteenth century and has interacted in diverse ways with modernity,[12] Although often (and understandably) confused with fundamentalism, evangelicalism developed a distinct stance vis à vis modernity.

Evangelicalism attempted to avoid both what it perceived as the dismissive hostility of fundamentalism and the accommodating syncretism of liberalism. How successful it has been in developing an authentic contextual response to modernity is open to question,[13] but within its history are resources on which it might draw to face the contemporary challenge. There are positive lessons to learn and some serious mistakes to avoid.

The charismatic movement, on the other hand, arose in the period during which postmodernity invaded popular culture.[14] Without diminishing the extent to which this movement may be regarded as an initiative of the Holy Spirit, it is legitimate also to interpret charismatic renewal as an ecclesiological development that has significant parallels in the emerging postmodern culture. The combination of evangelical and charismatic impulses and traditions could enable churches to develop effective responses to the postmodern environment.

This is by no means inevitable. Charismatic and evangelical churches also have the potential to become reactionary and to draw on the least attractive features of their shared heritage. Harvey Cox writes: "As both scientific modernity and conventional religion progressively lose their ability to provide a source of spiritual meaning, two new contenders are stepping forward—"fundamentalism" and, for lack of a more precise word, "experientialism."[15] Neither the resurgence of fundamentalism nor unbridled experientialism are prospects to relish, since neither will enable the church to engage at sufficient depth with contemporary culture. The possibility of these contenders joining forces to produce a "fundamentalist experientialism" cannot be discounted, however appalling this might seem. Indeed, within some charismatic evangelical churches such a development appears already to be well under way.

We return again to the conviction underlying this book—that the kinds of churches we plant are more important than the numbers. Since charismatic evangelical churches will be planting many of these, it is vital that such churches recognize the strategic significance of what they are doing and plant churches which are adapted for, and present a missionary challenge to, a postmodern environment.

What does all this mean for church planters? Starting a new church is an opportunity, not just to introduce a new style of music or a new evangelistic strategy, but to establish a new church culture or ethos. Postmodernity is not yet established as a new culture; its ability to replace or refine the fading culture of modernity is uncertain, and it may change shape in various ways in the years ahead. But church planting is now taking place in a postmodern context. Theological reflection on this context is crucial if churches are to be planted which will be missionary congregations in a postmodern culture, not only in terms of their shape, but in terms of their core values and ethos. In a changing and uncertain context, such reflection and any practical outworking of this reflection will need to be provisional rather than conclusive. But planting more churches in modernist mode is not the way forward.

Church Boundaries

An important aspect of the question of ethos is the way in which churches define their *boundaries*. Communities of all kinds establish boundaries, to include some and exclude others. Churches are no different.

A model that many have found helpful in understanding community boundaries was developed by anthropologist Paul Hiebert and has been adapted for a church planting context by David Shenk and Ervin Stutzman.[16] There are four basic approaches. The first is the *bounded set*, where there is a clear line between the church and the world outside the church, where church members are required to subscribe to these boundaries, and where violation of the boundaries leads to exclusion.

The second is the *fuzzy set*, where there is more room for ambivalence, where doctrinal and ethical issues are fudged rather than being resolved, where there are still boundaries which can be violated, but it is less clear where these are.

The third is *the open set*, where there are effectively no boundaries except those which are self-imposed, where belief and lifestyle are not matters of community concern.

The fourth is *the centered set*, a dynamic rather than static model, where the direction in which a person is facing is more important than their distance from the center. "It may be that someone who appears to be close to the center in terms of lifestyle is actually far from Christ because he or she is moving in a direction opposed to Christ."[17] Similarly, some whose beliefs or behavior do not conform to community norms, either because they are new to the community or because they are questioning their convictions, may actually be moving toward Christ.

Charismatic evangelical churches frequently operate with a bounded set mentality, so that new members are inducted into the doctrinal beliefs and ethical behavior expected of them. Teaching, pastoral care, and encouragement help church members to delve more deeply into these beliefs and conform more closely to a lifestyle that is consistent with these beliefs. For many, this process is very beneficial, and even those who later withdraw from such churches often look back with gratitude to this period, when important foundations were laid in their lives. In healthy churches, members are encouraged to develop at their own pace, to grow in their own relationship with God, and to participate in a community where there is mutual accountability.

But not all charismatic evangelical churches are so healthy. In *The Post-Evangelical*, David Tomlinson has voiced the concerns of those whose experience within such churches was marred by such attitudes as legalism, authoritarianism, judgmentalism, and sectarianism. Two problems are apparent: where the boundaries should be drawn and how the boundaries are perceived. If the boundaries are drawn so as to include a vast array of doctrinal, ethical, experiential, and cultural expectations, there is a danger that members will be excluded, or will exclude themselves, unnecessarily. Inability to differentiate between essentials and nonessentials can make bounded sets oppressive.

Even if less extensive boundaries are drawn, this kind of community may still operate oppressively in the way it perceives its boundaries. Discouraging honest questions and doubts, exalting conformity over integrity, standardizing spiritual experiences, and many other practices, can result in the marginalization and eventual loss from the community of its less compliant members—to the detriment of the individuals and of the community.

One response to these problems is transition to a fuzzy set mentality, where there is much greater flexibility with regard to belief and behavior. Although some critics have advocated this transition, it is unlikely to appeal to most charismatic evangelical churches. The dangers of relativism, compromise, and confusion loom. Attempts to define such transition in ways that do not produce such results have not been persuasive. The progressive decline in churches which have operated in this way does not offer much encouragement.

Might the centered set approach offer an alternative strategy? This is a community which has a core or center, rather than boundary lines. That center may be identified as "Christ," or defined in terms of doctrinal, experiential, or ethical norms, and it is this core that gives shape and focus to the church. Those who become part of the church community are free to move in and out; they can approach the core from different directions; they can explore freely the many dimensions of belief and practice that do not constitute the core; and they are not rejected by the community if they question elements of the core itself. Formal membership of the church may be limited to those who identify with the core convictions, but this is an open community where questions, doubts, nonconformity, and reservations do not preclude involvement.

Models and terminology are inevitably limited, and centered set communities may in time become as exclusive and inflexible as bounded set communities. But this model does at least emphasize two important aspects of ethos: first, that discipleship can be viewed dynamically, rather than in static terms; and second, that it may be possible to chart a course that avoids both the Scylla of narrow and inflexible absolutism and the Charybdis of slippery relativism.

One attempt to chart such a course is *The Radical Evangelical*, by Nigel Wright, the subtitle of which is *Seeking a Place to Stand*. This succinct and cogent argument attempts to identify the fundamental core around which evangelicals gather, by relegating to secondary status issues which have often functioned as shibboleths. It also advocates a more inclusive and generous spirit than is sometimes evident within evangelicalism, which recognizes what is of value in other traditions and welcomes ongoing conversation.

The Post-Evangelical identifies many problems endemic to charismatic evangelical churches, but fails to provide convincing solutions or a "place to stand." *The Radical Evangelical* lacks the sharp critique of contemporary evangelical churches, but offers a vision of a renewed evangelical community, characterized by a more modest but radical theological and ethical foundation, and by attitudes and reflexes that promote personal integrity and growth. These two books need to be read together.

The "centered set" concept relates well to the "journey" imagery and "process" model that have become increasingly popular in thinking about evangelism and discipleship. Charismatic evangelical churches have traditionally been more comfortable with crisis experiences of conversion, rather than seeing conversion as a process and spiritual growth as a journey into faith (with the Damascus Road

rather than Emmaus Road model, as John Finney helpfully characterizes these approaches[18]). But research suggests that, even in
charismatic evangelical churches where the expectation of crisis conversion is strong, nearly two-thirds come to faith gradually.[19]

This has important implications for evangelistic methodology
and expectations, but also for the way in which the church community is defined. Those who are searching for faith and those who are
growing in faith can walk together toward the center, without worrying unduly about boundary lines. The journey has a destination—
there is a center to the community—and the process may involve
periods of crisis, but there is freedom for people to walk or run,
choose alternative paths, and consider various routes.

In a postmodern and post-Christendom context, churches which
operate as "centered sets" may be contextually most appropriate.
This may not be immediately obvious. In a changing culture,
"bounded sets" with their comfortable certainties appear to offer a
refuge, as the rapid growth of ideological, political and religious fundamentalism demonstrates.[20] Those who find such an environment
stifling may be drawn toward the apparently liberating "fuzzy set"
and "open set" options. But in a relativistic culture, a community
that has nowhere to stand, and no way of identifying the destination
of the journey, may be found to have little to offer.

Graham Cray sees the journey imagery as important for mission
in a postmodern context, but explains this in terms of "rootedness"
and "core certainties" as well as movement. He writes:

> "The image of the journey has a number of other strengths. It is
> corporate; individuals are not being invited through a lonely jour-
> ney to self-realization but to join a people on a pilgrimage. The
> journey also speaks of rootedness. People on the journey of faith
> are the latest of many generations dating back to Christ. They
> have a sense of history, a sense of the past and some core cer-
> tainties which give them hope for the future and the final desti-
> nation."[21]

We face again the issue of "authentic contextualization," the challenge to be both distinctive and engaged. "Bounded sets" are certainly distinctive, but often churches operating in this way represent
withdrawal from cultural engagement. Churches operating as "fuzzy
sets" and "open sets" fit well within a culture which resists notions of
commitment, but can such churches really be missionary congrega-

tions? "Centered set" churches, churches which invite people to join them on a journey, rather than inviting them to join a club with strict rules of membership, may foster a liberating rather than restrictive ethos and be more effective in mission. They may also be acting in ways that are authentically biblical, recovering the New Testament designation of Christians as "people of the Way."[22]

Postmodern Churches

What features might characterize postmodern churches?

(1) Doubts and Dialogue

They will be communities where doubts can be expressed without fear of censure, where people are encouraged to explore their uncertainties, rather than towing a party line. Unbelief and unquestioned beliefs will be recognized as the enemies of faith, but doubt will be valued as a spur to growth. Thomas, famous for his doubts, was not rejected by his apostolic colleagues, but was present with them the next time Jesus appeared to his disciples, and doubt gave way to faith and worship.[23] Postmodern churches will be equally accepting and affirming. They will create space for their members to think, question, debate, wrestle with issues, and disagree without needing to disengage. Dishonesty, rather than honest argument, will be recognized as a threat to unity.

They will value opportunities to explore different views, will learn to listen to other perspectives, and will not be threatened if they cannot identify "the" answer to every question. This is not because these churches believe nothing, but because they are not afraid to subject their beliefs to scrutiny. Their core convictions are the basis for this free and generous spirit.

Such churches will make more use of dialogue than monologue. They will recognize that the lecture format represented by the traditional evangelistic address or teaching sermon is culturally rather than biblically determined, and a very ineffective tool in a postmodern culture.[24] Authoritative pronouncements from experts who do not allow opportunity for feedback or challenge are not conducive to sharing faith with those who are not Christians or to stimulating growth in understanding within the Christian community. They were of limited value in modern or premodern cultures, but in a postmodern culture, they can no longer be tolerated. Drawing on examples from the early church, who used dialogue extensively,[25] and recalling the methodology of Jesus, postmodern churches will rediscover this neglected mode of evangelism[26] and of learning together.

They will also realize that, if their teaching program is to connect with the world beyond the church rather than deal with esoteric and ecclesiocentric topics, this postmodern world is far too complex for one preacher (especially a preacher who spends most of the week in church activities) to address alone. The resources of the Christian community will need to be shared if "word" and "world" are to come together. The trained biblical scholar offers significant resources for this shared task, but so does the Christian businesswoman, the single parent, the detached youth worker, the retired civil servant, the unemployed miner, the poet, and the disabled teenager. A radical commitment to the priesthood of all believers[27] which breaks the interpretative monopoly of the preacher, will be needed to undergird such communities. They will develop the art of congregational hermeneutics[28] and the discipline of communal reflection.[29]

(2) Spirituality

Postmodern churches will embrace enthusiastically the renewed interest in spirituality evident in contemporary culture, and accept the challenge presented by the fact that many who are more open to a spiritual dimension are not turning to the churches. They will welcome this openness as confirmation of the inability of modernity to satisfy this dimension of the human psyche, and see it as an opportunity to review their own spiritual ethos. In a period when the surrounding culture is becoming more spiritually aware, the spirituality of the churches is of crucial importance.

Postmodern churches will recognize also that "postmodern people are more likely to come to faith in Christ through spiritual experience which leads to understanding of doctrine than through prior intellectual assent."[30] John Finney's research confirms this: most new converts defined their faith in terms of a relationship with God rather than in terms of theological beliefs.[31] This does not mean that doctrine is unimportant, but it does mean that the intellect is not the necessary starting point for faith, and that propositional approaches to evangelism may make little impact. The evangelistic methodology and forms of apologetics that were effective in a modernist culture may need to be jettisoned or substantially adapted for a postmodern culture.

Those who pray or who have had spiritual experiences, however little these seem to be connected to Christian faith, can be encouraged and nurtured in their quest for spiritual reality and helped toward a relationship with God. It will not be helpful to dismiss their experiences, interpret these negatively or confront them with doctrines to believe. Doctrinal foundations are crucial, but they need not be accorded temporal priority. Spirituality may be the bridge over which doctrinal truth can be carried. John Finney compares this approach to Paul introducing the Athenians to their Unknown God, and advises: "Christians should be more prepared to explain the spiritual life they have already begun to enjoy than to seek to persuade others of doctrinal truth."[32]

(3) Story

Another means of communicating truth is through the use of story. The art of storytelling has been damaged by modern media, although there are some signs of its recovery in a postmodern culture. Narrative theology has become increasingly popular in recent years, and it would be good to see this accompanied by the use of storytelling in evangelism and teaching within the churches. This may involve the encouragement of learning through testimony, reflecting together theologically on the experiences of individuals and communities. It may mean a fresh encounter with the teaching methods of Jesus, whose parables, questions, humor, and stories offer rich resources for churches to draw on. As with dialogue, the use of stories is not just contextually appropriate, but thoroughly biblical. Adapting to postmodernity does not mean becoming less biblical, but recovering neglected biblical practices.

If the use of story fits well within a postmodern culture, the claim that individual stories relate to a bigger story, a story which spans space and time and connects with an eternal story, presents a clear challenge to this culture. Postmodernism rejects this "big story" and any attempt to develop a "metanarrative," a foundational explanation of truth and purpose in the universe. At this point, Christianity stands squarely against postmodernism, insisting that there *is* a big story, that God has revealed himself in history as well as through individual mystical experiences, that history is not cyclical but moving toward a climax, that there is a cosmic and eternal dimension to the human story, and that Jesus Christ is the focus and interpreter of this story.

To engage with postmodernity on this issue, evangelical charismatic churches may need to ask to what extent they have helped their members to find their place in this bigger story, and whether the big story they have presented is big enough. Using the language of the kingdom of God, but interpreting this primarily in individual and ecclesial terms, turns an epic into a novelette. In their evangelism, postmodern churches invite others not only to join them on a journey, but also to participate with them in a story, to contribute their own story to the many other stories that together comprise the big story.[33]

And it is the story of Jesus, rather than doctrine about Jesus, that may prove to be our most potent evangelistic resource. Walter Wink suggests: "In the spiritual renaissance that I believe is coming to birth, it will not be the message of Paul that this time galvanizes hearts, as in the Reformation and the Wesleyan revival, but the human figure of Jesus."[34] Without wishing to downgrade Paul's teaching or the importance of theological concepts such as the holiness of God, human sinfulness, and justification by faith, it may be that the teaching, relationships, values, and character of the Jesus of the Gospels form the crucial points of contact with contemporary culture.

(4) Community

This story is the story of community. The Trinity, God in community, reaches out in creation and in redemption to form a human community to participate in the divine community. Missionary congregations invite people not just to make individual faith commitments, but to become participants in communities of faith. Church planting is about establishing new communities of faith. Postmodern churches will need to give careful attention to this issue of community. There is much about the postmodern context which tends toward fragmentation, disharmony, independence and multiple superficial relationships.

Should churches accept this and adapt their expectations or offer a distinctive alternative? Commenting that "one of the most significant shifts in contemporary society is that of non-participatory belonging," a recent report by the Anglican Mission Theological Advisory Group asks whether churches "might well have a need to allow people to relate in non-intense ways."[35] On the other hand, there has also been a proliferation of small groups and networks, evidence of the unchanging human need for community.

Postmodern churches will recognize that developing and sustaining community is not easy but vital, both for mission and for nurture. In a society where time pressures on working people are substantial, where individual freedom is highly valued, where leisure pursuits occupy more time, and where long-term and regular commitment to organizations is unpopular,[36] creativity and sensitivity will be needed. Churches which do not recognize the altered dynamics of social interaction, and which attempt to perpetuate community models that suited a previous era, will fail to engage with this new context. Community will not be achieved by the proliferation of church meetings, but by their reduction.[37] It will require diverse shapes and rhythms. It will involve interaction at many levels, and for various purposes. And it will function best if set in a mission context, so that community life is open and outward looking.

Churches will need to be creative and patient to achieve this kind of community life. But those which discover authentic community will be well-equipped to nurture their own members in a culture where corporate faithfulness rather than individual heroism is needed. They may also be able to respond to the need for lasting friendships in a society where relationships are often as "throwaway" as most commodities.

Post-Christendom Churches

We have argued that postmodernity is not the only feature of contemporary culture with which church planters need to grapple. We need to plant not only postmodern churches but also post-Christendom churches. The fact that we live also in a post-Christendom culture recalls us to our primary task of mission and to our self-perception as a missionary community. It also impacts the question of ethos.

Christendom as a political arrangement may be defunct, surviving only in the form of vestiges of the era when church and state presided over a European sacral society. But, as we indicated in chapter 5, unofficial Christendom has flourished in North America because it is a mindset as well as a political arrangement, and this mindset continues to pervade churches and hinder their engagement with a post-Christendom culture. It also continues to influence members of other faith communities and secular people, whose understanding of Christianity is distorted by the Christendom ethos.

The development of missionary congregations requires, among other things, a disavowal of Constantinian attitudes and reflexes, and the adoption of a different understanding of the role of the church in society. Post-Christendom need not be perceived as a threat, although mission and church planting in this context are hard work, but as an opportunity to recover ecclesiological and missiological perspectives which were lost or obscured under Christendom. Where this is recognized, churches will not be found desperately clinging on to their previous position in society and their remaining privileges, but embracing enthusiastically the opportunity to become once more a free church. In what might this freedom consist?

(1) Powerlessness

In a post-Christendom context, the church is liberated from the corrupting influence of political, economic and social power. As a powerless minority of resident aliens in a culture that no longer accords Christianity special treatment, the church is freed to live and witness in new ways. The church is released from any sense of responsibility for supporting the status quo, or ensuring that history turns out the way it should. It can concentrate on simply being the church, pointing toward a coming kingdom and, haltingly but with determination, embodying the values and ethos of that kingdom in its community life. Set free from the conceit that it should be involved in everything, running everything, influencing everything, it can concentrate on its primary calling—to participate in missio Dei, incarnating the good news of the kingdom of God.

Martin Robinson concludes: "The church in the West must now be thought of as a community without the power to determine key areas of public life and policy."[38] This should not be a cause for discouragement but welcomed as a relief. Powerless churches have an opportunity to abandon the Constantinian "moral majority" stance that understandably irritates a post-Christendom culture, and recover their biblical calling to be a "prophetic minority." This is a stance that befits their role in contemporary society and helps them recover their sense of perspective. It also calls them back to the model of the incarnation, which is the pattern for Christian mission in any culture. John Drane reminds us that "at the center of the gospel is the fact that God became a child. Weakness, vulnerability and powerlessness are central to Christian belief—and to the extent that Christians fail to model that in both lifestyle and evangelistic communication, they are betraying the very gospel that they claim to represent."[39]

Rather than pontificating on what people *ought* to do, or moralizing about how they *ought* to behave, post-Christendom churches will concentrate on living distinctively and provocatively, inviting others to consider new possibilities. Powerless churches are not interested in imposing morality. They offer alternatives, rooted in their own communal experience, and they speak winsomely, not arrogantly. A key element in their testimony will be *surprise*. One of the problems facing evangelism in a post-Christian society is that many people assume they already know what Christianity is. The Gospel is not perceived as news of any kind. They also know how churches will react to various issues. Each time churches indulge in these predictable attitudes, comments, and activities, they reinforce these assumptions and perceptions.

But this is so different from the model of Jesus, whose unpredictable words and behavior surprised, shocked, disturbed, outraged, puzzled, and intrigued his contemporaries. It is different also from the impact of pre-Christendom churches on their culture, whose deviant lifestyle and distinctive ethos were primary reasons for their growth.[40] Christendom inculturated Christianity and robbed the churches of this distinctive nonconformity. Post-Christendom churches will search for ways to recover this, not through gimmicks, but through radical Jesus-centeredness, sensitivity to the Spirit, and authentic contextualization.

They will understand the spirit of the age, but often choose to live in an opposite spirit. They will sometimes seem conservative, sometimes liberal, sometimes radical. They will not be easy to pigeon-hole as right-wing or left-wing, for their agenda will be broad and they will make unusual connections between different issues. They will provoke a similar mixture of reactions to those in the crowds who met Jesus,[41] because they will say and do surprising things which suggest they owe allegiance to another kingdom. Their ethos will be attractive and yet disturbing, familiar and yet strange, conformed and yet deviant, as befits communities of resident aliens.

(2) Good News to the Poor

Post-Christendom churches, freed from pretensions to kingship, recognize that the kingdom of God is an "upside-down kingdom,"[42] that grass roots action is more significant than trying to influence the "movers and shakers" of society. They choose to be identified with the poor, the weak, the marginalized, those without voices or status. They adopt as their agenda for mission the Nazareth Manifesto:[43]

"The Spirit of the Lord is on me, because he has anointed me to preach good news to the poor. He has sent me to proclaim freedom for the prisoners and recovery of sight for the blind, to release the oppressed, to proclaim the year of the Lord's favor."

What might this mean? Wholistic mission which refuses to separate social justice from evangelism? Decades of Justice as well as Decades of Evangelism?[44] Church planters prioritizing poor communities as they decide where to plant churches? Evangelists discovering how to bring good news to the "sinned against" as well as to sinners? Pastors empowering the weaker and less articulate members of their churches? Apostles urging each other not to neglect the poor?[45] Prophets summoning churches to demonstrate justice within their communities and to work for justice in society?[46] Churches becoming communities of liberation and hope? Morris Stuart writes: "When our strategies for justice emerge, matching in every way the plethora of already existing strategies for evangelism, church growth, healing, times of refreshing, and so on, then we shall know for certain that we have been captured by this passion of God."[47]

The "year of the Lord's favor" is thought by many scholars to be a reference to the neglected "year of Jubilee," the foundation of Old Testament economic legislation.[48] Every fifty years, there was to be a radical adjustment of wealth throughout society, as debts were cancelled, slaves were released, property was returned, and resources were redistributed. Regular observance of the Jubilee legislation would preclude both endemic poverty and excessive wealth. Between Jubilee years, minor adjustments were made through various other systems, such as Sabbath years, tithing, gleaning, and first-fruits. Although the adjustment mechanisms were used, and occasional attempts were made to achieve more radical results, it is unlikely that the Jubilee legislation was ever fully implemented. It is not difficult to understand why. Jubilee was wonderful "good news to the poor," but it was not good news to the powerful, rich, and successful.

Was Jesus announcing that it was time to practice Jubilee? Certainly, in his teaching and his ministry, he indicated that radical changes were needed in the way in which wealth was handled. His disciples were initially appalled at the implications, but it is arguable that the economic life of the Jerusalem church, described in Acts 4-5, was a determined attempt to contextualize the Jubilee provisions. A national Jubilee was not feasible, but within this growing church radical steps could be taken to remove the extremes of wealth and poverty and to share resources. The result—"there were no needy persons among them"[49]—certainly represents the aim of the Jubilee legislation.

Post-Christendom churches, responding to the challenge to be good news to the poor, may explore creative ways of practicing Jubilee. They may set aside the system of tithing, recognizing that it has no New Testament warrant, was not practiced by pre-Christendom churches in the first three centuries,[50] was introduced reluctantly as the churches adapted to the increasing nominality of church life under Christendom,[51] and, divorced from its Old Testament setting, often constitutes "good news to the rich" and further oppresses the poor. Liberated from the system of tithing, and inspired by the Nazareth manifesto, churches in a post-Christendom society may no longer be alienated from the poor, but communities of good news to the poor.

(3) Humility

Post-Christendom is a pluralist culture, with diverse ideologies competing for adherents, and with an aversion to any of these attaining the status once accorded to Christianity. As such, this culture is similar to the situation into which the earliest churches were planted and in which church planters in most areas throughout history have operated. Western churches are gradually coming to terms with a pluralist society, but often this appears to be a reluctant and grudging acceptance. This does not result in an ethos conducive to bold and sensitive mission in a pluralist society.

If Christendom attitudes are partly responsible for this, confusion between *plurality* and *pluralism* is also partly to blame. Christianity is implacably opposed to pluralism, a philosophical position that denies ultimate truth claims. In the name of tolerance, pluralism absolutizes relativism and emasculates religious convictions in an attempt to homogenize and harmonize a multifaith society. But this is an insipid and painless tolerance that lacks the courage to grapple honestly with divergent views. It tends to result in new forms of intolerance, masquerading in liberal dress. But plurality is to be welcomed as an excellent environment for evangelism and the exercise of choice in matters of faith. Historically, the church has often thrived in pluralist cultures, but it has generally struggled to impact monolithic societies.

Post-Christendom churches will revel in the freedom this pluralist society offers to commend the gospel humbly, boldly and sensitively to any who will listen, including those who are currently adherents of other religions or secular ideologies. The self-confident, imperialistic, crusading mentality of the past can give way to gracious faith-sharing. These churches believe that the gospel is good news to everyone but claim no privileged position for the gospel. They respect and learn from the convictions of others, and defend their freedom to reject the gospel as passionately as they attempt to communicate this gospel to them.

Vinoth Ramachandra, whose analysis of mission in a pluralist environment should be standard reading in post-Christendom churches, explains why evangelism can be confident but must also be humble: "Since the gospel announces the sheer grace of God toward unworthy sinners, it can be commended to others only in a spirit of *humility*. . . . It is all of grace. This forbids me from thinking of the gospel as my possession and of evangelism as a matter of demonstrating the superiority of my 'religion' over all others."[52] Humble evangelism may include "asking forgiveness *from* others" for perversions of the gospel and atrocities committed in the name of Christ, as well as offering divine forgiveness to others. It will certainly involve more listening than talking, starting where people are rather than where the church is, not limited to the agenda of contemporary society but certainly engaging with this.

There are encouraging signs that a new evangelistic paradigm is currently emerging,[53] several aspects of which we have noted at least in passing in earlier chapters. It is crucial to note that this paradigm shift involves a change of ethos as well as of methodology, and that attitudes toward other faith communities in a pluralist society are included within this revised thinking. Post-Christendom churches will give much greater attention than ever before to the question of relationships with members of other faith communities. If they are wise, they will draw gratefully on the insights of those with cross-cultural experience as they struggle to escape unhelpful attitudes and perceptions.

Post-Evangelical/Post-Charismatic?

How will churches with an evangelical charismatic ethos fare in a postmodern and post-Christendom culture? Will they continue to thrive, but predominantly in the areas of society where they are currently strongly represented? Will they find in their theological and spiritual roots resources and precedents to guide them? Will they fail to adapt to this changing context and become less able to win new adherents? Will they seize the opportunity to grapple with the challenge of being communities of resident aliens, thoroughly engaged, but prophetically distinctive? Will we witness the emergence of post-evangelical and post-charismatic churches?

In line with the comments in chapter 6 on the meaning of "post" in our discussion on postmodernity, post-evangelical and post-charismatic can be interpreted as implying either a period of transition and deconstruction, or the emergence of a new shape and ethos, or the reemergence of charismatic evangelical churches in chastened mode.

It is likely that some radical and uncomfortable changes will be needed. Humility and powerlessness are not concepts readily associated with churches in this tradition. The issues of power and authority will need to be confronted and new ways of thinking will need to be nurtured. Most evangelical and charismatic churches are identified not with the poor but with the more affluent areas of the country. Relocation through strategic church planting and changes in ethos will be required to redress this imbalance. Evangelical attitudes toward other faiths will need to be re-examined[54] and evangelistic practices will need to come under demanding scrutiny.

Any attempt to move away from propositional truth, evangelism as proclamation, or authoritative preaching will meet stern resistance. The art of dialogue will need to be taught and modeled. New attitudes to doubt will be required. Living with questions and uncertainties, rather than neatly packaged theology, will seem very threatening. Church leaders will be especially vulnerable and may be less willing than members of their churches to make such changes. The use of story and an emphasis on spirituality will require courage in the face of accusations that the gospel is being watered down, and wisdom if such watering down is to be avoided.[55] The balance between the objective and the subjective must somehow be retained. But propositions are not the only way in which truth can be communicated. Incarnational mission allows for truth to be encountered relationally and experientially, as well as propositionally: "the law was given through Moses" (propositionally); "grace and truth came through Jesus Christ" (relationally).[56]

Charismatic evangelical churches, which have tried to hold together "Word" and "Spirit," the objective and the subjective, may feel that their form of spirituality is attractive in contemporary culture. Their growth in recent years may appear to confirm this. But this confidence may be misplaced. This is partly because this spirituality is often set within an ethos that is profoundly unattractive in contemporary culture (as well as lacking theological warrant). Hierarchical leadership structures, sexist attitudes, activism, and triumphalism do not encourage many with spiritual interest to pursue their quest in charismatic evangelical churches. But it is partly also because this spirituality may be deficient or lopsided in in a variety of ways.

First, charismatic evangelical spirituality often fails to integrate the elements of *transcendence* and *immanence*. Evangelical theology and spirituality have reflected a wider Western Protestant tendency to concentrate on the transcendent: worshipping an awesome God, an exalted Christ, and a mysterious Holy Ghost. Important though these aspects of spirituality are, unless they are infused with the dimension of immanence, they tend to produce a view of God as remote and passionless, a docetic view of Christ which devalues his humanity, and a fearfulness that marginalizes the work of the Holy Spirit. Charismatic renewal has given renewed attention to the immanent: worshipping a loving Father, a friendly Jesus, and a dynamic Holy Spirit.

Valuable though this recovery of intimacy with God has been, however, unless it is set in the context of transcendence, it tends to result in sentimentality, overfamiliarity, and myopia. Charismatic evangelical churches sometimes manage to combine the least attractive features of both emphases! Postmodern churches will face the challenge of integrating these elements in more creative ways.

Second, spirituality sometimes degenerates into *superstition* in charismatic evangelical churches, especially where certain understandings of demonology and spiritual warfare are taught. Rejection of the reductionist worldview of materialism is vital if churches are not to find themselves less aware of the supernatural dimension than the culture around them. So is our recognition of the cosmic conflict which forms the backdrop to human life. However, dualism, gnosticism, paranoia, and speculation are not helpful components. Postmodernity opens the door to all kinds of weird beliefs, irrationality, and superstitious practices, which need not be imported into the churches. The greatly underrated gift of "distinguishing between spirits"[57] will be needed if this is to be avoided.

Third, the *noise* and *energy* of charismatic evangelical expressions of spirituality do not commend these churches to those who are looking for spiritual resources to sustain them in a culture which is rapidly changing, noisy, and busy. Although for some subcultures, energetic and high-decibel expressions of spirituality may be appropriate, for others these will be unhelpful. Stillness, peace and the space simply to be are vital components in a spirituality for contemporary living (as the popularity of various forms of meditation demonstrates). Robert Warren is surely right to include stillness in his list of "marks of a missionary congregation": "A missionary church will be an oasis of peace and quiet, in a frantic world, able not to be driven by doing but reflecting on experience before moving on." [58]

Fourth, a spirituality disconnected from daily life does not offer much to a culture which, despite a tendency toward fragmentation, is replacing compartmentalism with wholism. Charismatic evangelical escapism must give way to what David Bosch calls[59] a "spirituality of the road," a spirituality to sustain those whose journey involves all aspects of life rather than church meetings. Among other things, this may mean that worship becomes more world-conscious; that prophecy embraces issues of social justice as well as internal church concerns; that the imbalance between singing and intercession is redressed; and that church meetings are seen as refueling stops rather than the final destination.

Fifth, a spirituality dominated by the motifs of *fall* and *redemption*, rather than rooted in *creation*, is inappropriate in a postmodern culture. It also fails to reflect a biblical balance. Morris Stuart calls for "a theology that is inspired by the original creation" and complains that in charismatic evangelical churches "its starting point . . . has been the 'fall' of the human creature and consequently the redemption work of Christ. This has bequeathed to it a negative and pessimistic view of human nature and of the world."[60] This theology and spirituality may have flourished under modernity, where the natural world was regarded as a resource for human exploitation, but in a postmodern culture the fourfold movement of creation, fall, redemption, and the new age of the kingdom of God needs to undergird the spirituality of evangelical charismatic churches.

The Contribution of Church Planting

Some charismatic evangelical churches will fail to see why such changes are needed and will resist them. Those which are large and self-confident, and those which are convinced they are following *the* New Testament pattern, will find this challenge especially difficult to cope with. Others will draw gratefully on the resources within their heritage and engage courageously in the process of authentic contextualization. They will become missionary congregations, with an ethos that is appropriate for their missionary calling.

Charismatic evangelical churches may also draw on the resources of two past church planting movements, to which we have referred on several occasions: the Celtic and Anabaptist traditions. Both represent non-Christendom expressions of European Christianity. The Celtic tradition offers perspectives on (among other things) wholistic mission, cultural adaptation, powerlessness, humility, world-affirming spirituality, the use of story, nonhierarchical structures, and concern for the poor. The Anabaptist tradition offers a thorough critique of the Christendom mentality, and perspectives on cultural distinctiveness, community, the use of story and dialogue, social justice, nonviolence, and the humanity of Jesus.

Contemporary church planting could contribute in various ways to the renewal of charismatic evangelical churches. It may enable churches which realize that change is needed but are uncertain about the implications to learn from the experience of pioneering ventures. It may offer those disillusioned with their own churches an alternative to dropping out of church life altogether. It may enable those who are concerned about the ethos of their church, but who are unable to implement the necessary changes, opportunities to move forward without causing offense or dividing churches.

Cloning will not achieve the changes needed, nor will establishing churches which are different in shape but similar in style and ethos. Church planting *per se* is not the answer. But creative church planting that results from a genuine missionary engagement with a postmodern and post-Christendom culture may well be part of the answer.

8. CHURCH PLANTING AND THE STRUCTURES OF THE CHURCH

Church Planting and Church Buildings

Church planting offers fresh opportunities to think radically about church buildings. What kinds of buildings might enable churches to engage effectively in mission? More fundamentally, what are the advantages and disadvantages of having church buildings?

Several church planting movements have concentrated on establishing congregations rather than erecting buildings. The churches planted by the early Christians met in homes or used public buildings like the Jerusalem temple[1] or the Hall of Tyrannus.[2] Churches planted by the sixteenth century Anabaptists met in homes or in the open air. The home-based "class meetings" of early Methodism remained fundamental to this movement after Methodists began to build church buildings. Churches planted in Britain in the 1960s and 1970s used homes so extensively that a movement became known as the *house churches*.

Various factors may have discouraged these movements from erecting their own buildings, including persecution, lack of finance, and legal restrictions. But it is arguable that ecclesiological and missiological reasons were also involved. Some contemporary church planting initiatives adopt a similar policy of using homes or secular venues. Cell churches operate primarily in groups small enough to use homes for meetings. Their ecclesiological convictions are often not conducive to ownership or extensive use of church buildings. Youth churches frequently use secular venues for contextual and missiological reasons.

Other church planting movements have erected church buildings but have consciously built different kinds of buildings from those used by existing churches. Often this has involved a rejection of pomp and splendor, and an emphasis on simplicity. The Donatist

181

churches of North Africa in the fourth and fifth centuries white-washed the walls of their meeting places as a protest against the or-namentation of the Catholic churches.[2] Celtic missionaries in fifth and sixth century England established churches and monastic train-ing centers that were much simpler than the buildings used by the Roman churches that predated and succeeded them. Plymouth Brethren churches planted in the nineteenth century[3] often erected buildings that expressed their desire to return to a simpler pattern of worship.

There are also examples of church planting initiatives that have constructed buildings which are consciously different from existing church buildings, but which have moved, for missiological reasons rather than self-indulgence, in the opposite direction, toward very high standards of architecture, decoration, and facilities. The Willow Creek Community Church building is an excellent example of this, with a multipurpose building that is designed for a particular con-text, target community and mission strategy.

Some church planting initiatives, however, have demonstrated less missiological and ecclesiological awareness in relation to church buildings. These have involved the erection of buildings as a prereq-uisite for establishing new congregations, excessive multiplication of church buildings, and raising huge sums of money to provide lavish and extensive, but disappointingly unimaginative premises. Baptist church planting in Britain in the nineteenth century was accompa-nied by the construction of large and imposing church buildings, which were mostly underused and inappropriate. Indeed, the prolif-eration of denominational churches in the nineteenth century, each with its own building, led to a ridiculous situation in some areas. If every man, woman, and child had been in these buildings on a Sun-day, there would still have been plenty of spare seats.

Professor Robin Gill has argued,[5] on the basis of extensive re-search into this era, that this situation had a negative impact on the spiritual life of the church and the nation, as it conveyed the impres-sion that churches were weak and declining, since so many church buildings were underused. Some church planting ventures devote more creativity and resources to premises than to mission and con-gregation-building. Local ecumenical projects and denominational ventures are especially prone to this, which may be one reason (though not the only reason[6]) for the struggles experienced by such initiatives.

Critics of contemporary church planting sometimes assume that planting churches implies the construction of more church buildings and argue that there are already enough church buildings. This criticism is sometimes dismissed by church planters, on the grounds that church planting is concerned with multiplying congregations rather than buildings.

Evidence from history and from the contemporary scene suggests, however, that neither the assumption behind the criticism nor the dismissal of this concern are wholly justified. Church planting *need* not involve the erection of church buildings, but it frequently does. Even where there is initially no intention to build or buy a church building, pressure grows for the new congregation to move into its own premises, until only groups with a strong aversion to such a development are able to resist. Gradually, the early churches moved out of homes and the catacombs and into church buildings, which became larger and more elaborate as the status of the church grew in the Roman Empire. This shift took place over a period of three or four centuries: subsequent church planting movements were rarely able to resist this shift for more than a few years.

We need to analyze carefully the relation of church buildings to the task, shape, and ethos of the church. Such analysis can be undertaken without reference to church planting, as existing churches review their role and requirements. But church planting stimulates thinking on the issues involved and provides models of alternatives to traditional patterns. Many church plants are currently meeting in rented halls. They know from experience the advantages and disadvantages of not having their own premises. Few are likely to resist the pressure to invest in their own building sooner or later, unless they reflect seriously and creatively on the implications of obtaining a building. Conversations with churches that do own buildings, and who can explain the disadvantages as well as the advantages of owning buildings, might be illuminating.

Disadvantages with Church Buildings

In a context where, among church planters and newly planted churches, there is an underlying bias toward eventually obtaining a church building, it is important to explore the significant problems associated with church buildings. Some appear to be practical problems, which might be overcome by practical solutions. Most, however, have underlying missiological and ecclesiological significance,

significance which needs to be identified if the issues are to be properly addressed.

An immediate problem, of which churches with older buildings are fully aware, and which gradually becomes more apparent to churches looking for buildings, is the sheer expense of maintaining these premises. This necessitates pouring into bricks and mortar resources that could be used in other ways.

The underlying issue is not whether a congregation can raise sufficient funds, but whether spending its money in this way is consistent with its priorities and principles. Having a building imposes severe restrictions on a church's financial freedom.

A second problem is the possibility of an idolatrous attitude to the building, whether it is old and full of memories, or new and precious because it represents the result of sacrificial giving. This is signaled by the use of inappropriate terminology like "the sanctuary" or "the house of God" to refer to the building; by placing unnecessary restrictions on activities that can take place in the building; and by the assumption that certain activities should take place nowhere else. Sacred buildings are almost universal within human religions, but this does not mean that Christianity requires them. Many people in newly planted churches look forward to having their own church building, so that they will be once again be part of a "proper" church. This mindset is deeply rooted and will not be changed merely by reminders that "the people are the church, not the building."

A third and insidious problem is the temptation for congregations that own buildings to be busy with activities to justify the use and upkeep of these buildings. Churches with buildings tend to have many more meetings than churches without buildings, but unnecessary activities can seriously damage the health of a church and hinder its mission. Congregations that have renovated their buildings are especially prone to this temptation, as are church plants when they move into their own premises. The underlying issue is that the buildings have ceased to be a resource for mission and ministry. They have begun to drive and direct the energies of the church. An extreme, but quite common, expression of this is the suggestion that the existence in a certain locality of a church building (with or without a remnant congregation) requires the planting or replanting of a church there. Missiologically, the existence of this building may be an advantage, a disadvantage, or irrelevant, but it is only a minor component in assessing the feasibility of planting a new church.

A fourth problem is that buildings impose limitations on congregations and affect their shape and style. This is true for congregations that meet in homes and rented halls as well as in church buildings, but it is easier to recognize this and to work through the implications. Church buildings intrude as much and often more, but there is a tendency to regard these as sacrosanct and to be less aware of their influence. Again, some of the problems are practical. Older buildings with fixed furniture often cannot be used for innovative forms of worship, teaching, or witness. Large buildings make it difficult to develop an atmosphere of intimacy. Some newer buildings are difficult to relax in.

But there are also deeper issues. The design of the church building may contradict or undermine the ecclesiology to which the church that uses it is theoretically committed. Church buildings which are designed to enable an audience to listen to an orator, or to watch a church leader perform ceremonies, are appropriate for churches that subscribe to a clerical understanding of ministry, but they are quite inappropriate for churches committed to the priesthood of all believers and every member ministry. Hundreds of church buildings not only contradict the ecclesiology of the denomination which built them, but have much greater influence on the ecclesiology of the congregation than the sermons which are preached in them.

A fifth problem is that church buildings can seriously hamper the witness of the church in its community. The proliferation of special buildings coincided with the acceptance of Christianity as the state religion and the progressive identification of the church with a powerful and wealthy establishment. The fact that the church is a major landowner, and that this represents a huge amount of wealth that could be released to meet the needs of a hungry world, is an offense to some sectors of society—especially those which the churches find hard to reach with the gospel. Frequent appeals to the general public to provide money to repair or renovate church buildings confirm the suspicion of many people that churches are after their money; whereas buildings in disrepair communicate powerfully the message that the church is a decaying institution.

And sixth, having their own buildings may encourage churches to operate with a centripetal ("come") rather than a centrifugal ("go") mentality in mission, inviting nonmembers onto church territory at times convenient to church members, rather than going into society to meet people on neutral territory, reversing the apparent thrust of mission in the New Testament.[7] Peter Nodding's warning is apt: "It's surprising how many of us can begin with the word 'go' and still base our outreach around the word 'come'. We are challenged by stirring sermons which clearly expound the imperative to go into all the world, and yet most of the events are centred on our church buildings. Clearly we are expecting people to come."[8]

Church Buildings and Mission

In a Christendom context, the centripetal model of mission, whereby the church could expect people to come to its buildings and events, worked tolerably well (indeed church attendance was often legally required and absence penalized). Attempts to export this model into pre-Christian mission contexts through building "mission stations," where the missionaries lived, and into which they gradually drew converts, have been widely criticized. Donald Mc-Gavran exposed the folly of such a strategy and urged the adoption of practices which would build bridges into the community rather than isolating converts from it.[9] Lesslie Newbigin has observed that "since 'mission' means going and 'station' means standing still, one might think that 'mission station' was the perfect contradiction in terms."[10] In a post-Christian context, it is illegitimate, as well as ineffective, to rely on expectations that people will come to church buildings if they are interested in the gospel. Mission will require the recovery of strategies based on a centrifugal model.

Churches may, in fact, need to develop mission strategies that combine elements of both models: the Old Testament vision of the nations coming to meet God at Jerusalem,[11] and the New Testament vision of a missionary community that encircles the earth in its quest to make disciples of all nations.[12] Research into how people have become Christians in recent years underscores this. Most people identify relationships with Christian friends or relatives as the major factor in their coming to faith, relationships that do not primarily involve church attendance. However, for many people, these relationships encouraged them to attend church events before they came to faith: belonging preceded believing.[13]

Nevertheless, it is arguable that the centrifugal model should be primary. Church buildings may still have a significant role in this mission, but their impact on the congregation needs to be carefully assessed. Some have argued that church buildings can be "heretical" if they "encourage within the congregation a feeling of religious security inside the walls of an isolated holy place. They are to be rejected if they stimulate introversion and escapism."[14]

Undue attachment to church buildings may also hinder the development of church planting initiatives. This may be financial or psychological. A congregation that has spent significant sums of money renovating its buildings is likely to look askance at proposals to use these buildings less in order to plant a new church elsewhere. The reduction of income that may result from committed financial supporters joining a church planting team and, sooner or later, redirecting their giving may increase the burden of upkeep on the remaining members of the congregation. And where church members identify a building as the place where they meet God, it is not easy to adjust to meetings in the local school hall or community center, as those who form the core of a new church may be asked to do.

Despite all these concerns, there are undoubtedly advantages in churches owning buildings, sufficient in the minds of most church members to outweigh these and other disadvantages. Here we will do no more than list some of the more obvious benefits: stability, the demonstration of commitment to a locality, facilities to develop social ministries, facilities to make available for community use, a sense of belonging for the congregation, freedom to meet at convenient times, no rental costs, storage room for equipment, and the intangible but often deeply felt sense of peace that seems to imbue buildings used over long periods for prayer and worship.

Given these benefits, it is not surprising that most church plants anticipate having their own building. But this near-identification of church and church building is not essential to church planting. Church planting is about multiplying communities of the kingdom, not about extending the real estate owned by these communities. The practice of church planting, if it is defined as the establishing of new congregations rather than the erection of church buildings, does not prejudge this issue.

There may be pressing practical and missiological reasons for building or buying church premises. Churches whose understanding of mission includes social action often regard their buildings as vital assets for such ministry (although this may be a centripetal approach to social action that is no more appropriate than a centripetal approach to evangelism). But the experience of church planting without a church building, and the insistence that good reasons are needed before church plants obtain their own buildings, can remind churches that buildings are optional, not compulsory. Vision and mission should be determinative, rather than congregational comfort or traditional concepts.

If church planting challenges the necessity of church buildings, it may also encourage fresh thinking about what kinds of buildings might be appropriate if churches do choose to own buildings. Churches that build their own buildings may have greater freedom than those which take over existing church buildings or other premises, although creative planning can transform initially unpromising sites. Opportunities for change may be limited, as may financial resources, but a number of issues might be considered. It is important to explore these ecclesiologically and missiologically, rather than simply aesthetically or pragmatically—although aesthetic considerations may themselves have missiological significance.

Our concern here is neither to be prescriptive nor to intrude upon areas that require the expertise of architects, interior designers, builders, decorators, and furnishing consultants (among others). Church buildings will need to be as creatively diverse and contextually appropriate as the congregations which use them, if they are to contribute toward mission in a multicultural society. All we can do is raise certain questions. The fact is that a church building, old or new, conveys a message, and this may not be the message intended by the congregation which uses it. Architecture, size, design, furnishings, color, light, temperature, ease of access, audibility, "feel," and a host of other factors powerfully affect those who use a building. Churches cannot escape such realities, but they can choose to consider them in terms of the mission and ministry of the church.

Decisions about church buildings often fall within the dimension of maintenance rather than mission, so it is encouraging to note the production of an Anglican report, *Mission and Mortar*, by the Council for the Care of Churches as a contribution to the Decade of Evangelism. A mission-oriented approach, albeit one that is predominantly centripetal, might be to consider environments in which those whom the church is concerned to reach feel at home or relaxed. Designing a church building with this in mind might result in very different styles of buildings in different communities. Some might be like cinemas or theatres, some like the lounge bar of a public house or a working men's club, some like a large living room, some like a community center. If mission activities rather than church meetings are prioritized, the building might function as a multipurpose community building that can also be used for church meetings, rather than a church meeting place that can be used for other purposes. A more centrifugal approach to mission might result in the development of a training and resource center, from which church members can disperse to engage in mission.

Questions a church might ask about its buildings include these: Which sections of the local community are most or least likely to feel at home here? Are there any in the community who would be unable to use the premises? For what kinds of community events or church activities is the building best or worst suited? How will those who are unfamiliar with the building find their way around it? If a home says something about the family or individuals who live in it, what does the church building say about the church which uses it? Are there aspects of the building which help or hinder the ecclesiological priorities of the congregation? How flexible are the premises to cope with changes of use? To what extent are the buildings characterized by simplicity, beauty, utility, and homeliness? Are the buildings compatible with the ethos of the congregation?

However the mission of the church is understood, if the church perceives its primary task to be mission rather than maintenance, questions about church buildings will be answered in relation to its primary task, rather than secondary considerations. Church planting both can recall churches to this primary task and give fresh opportunities for reflection on the use of church buildings.

Church Planting and Church Size

We return now, as promised in chapter 1, to church size (an issue not unrelated to the kinds of buildings churches need). The issue of size is multifaceted and affects church planting at theological, strategic, and methodological levels. Is there an optimum church size? What are strengths and weaknesses of larger or smaller churches? How does the multiplication of churches anticipated by church planting policies relate church growth goals? Should church planters aim to plant churches of specific sizes or anticipate unlimited growth? How large does a church need to be to plant another? Should questions about church size be answered biblically, theologically, missiologically, contextually, psychologically, or pragmatically?

Large and small are relative terms, and the dividing lines between small, medium, and large may appear somewhat arbitrary.

Within a British church context, congregations with over 250 members are generally regarded as quite large, and very few churches have more than 1000 members. Many churches operate over long periods with 75 to 175 members. "Small" churches begin to chafe at this designation once they have reached a membership of 50 (especially if they are aware of statistics such as those in a report by the Baptist Union of Great Britain entitled "Half the Denomination," which noted that half of all British Baptist churches have fewer than fifty members).

In some other Western nations, churches with many thousands of members are relatively common, although not as numerous as popularly supposed. As significant as the numbers themselves are the transition zones between different kinds of churches. This is a subject on which the church growth movement has provided helpful insights to many growing congregations, drawing on the insights of sociologists concerning group dynamics.

The "200 barrier" is the most familiar of these zones. Many growing churches have experienced difficulty in maintaining numerical growth beyond a membership of about 200. Church growth consultants indicate various reasons for this, including the style of leadership, pastoral structures, buildings that are nearing capacity, an inadequate administrative base, and resistance to team ministry. Further transition zones are identified as the congregation grows larger still, although not many British churches have faced the challenge of these.

Three-Level Churches

More significant for many churches has been the discovery of what sociologists have identified as *primary, secondary,* and *tertiary* level groups, and the recognition that at each of these levels different activities, resources, and purposes are appropriate. The primary level group—the *cell* group, with up to about twelve participants—works well if it does not attempt to mimic the style of a secondary level group—a *congregation* of up to about 175 people. Similarly, the congregation will function effectively if it does not try to recreate the atmosphere of a larger *celebration* event. Each level provides opportunities for group activity that is less effective at other levels, and wise church leaders will learn to respect these limitations rather than fighting against them. But there are still many churches where basic principles of group dynamics are ignored. Telltale signs are sizeable congregations which sing "Happy Birthday" to members every other Sunday, and small, often recently planted, churches with an array of unnecessary microphones, and guitarists who play more loudly than they or other worshippers need.

There is wide agreement that tertiary level churches need primary level groups if they are to be effective pastorally and evangelistically. Whether such churches transition themselves into "cell churches" and devolve responsibility to the primary level groups, or retain the traditional structure whereby the smaller groups service the larger, subdivision is crucial for the health and further growth of these churches. There has been less certainty about the benefits of developing three-level churches, with congregations as secondary level groups.

Several difficulties have been encountered. Pastorally, there have been uncertainties about the connection between the three levels. Churches have found that members, who valued belonging to groups at two levels, are unsure how to belong to groups at a third level, and are wary of making commitments to another kind of group. Restructuring as a three-level church need not result in additional church meetings, but frequently this is the outcome. This is compounded by confusion among the leaders of these various groups as to what each group is trying to achieve, and how the groups differ from each other. Church members are sometimes unable to understand the thinking behind the new structure, and tend to opt out of at least one of these groups.

In relation to mission, a three-level church might seem well-equipped, offering opportunities for diverse forms of social action and evangelism, from the intimate to the anonymous. But this model has two particular weaknesses: the amount of energy required to run such churches, diverting members from building relationships with nonmembers and so hindering evangelism; and the danger that newcomers will not be effectively integrated into this complex organism, or nurtured within it. In his discussion on three-level churches, Eddie Gibbs asks, "To what extent do our structures act as a maze to confuse and divert people, rather than a channel which leads them into the heart of the fellowship?"[15]

Some church planting ventures have attempted to operate with a three-level structure, either by planting congregations in new locations which do not become independent, but remain connected to the mother church (the "satellite congregation" model); or by the development of different congregations in the same location, often reaching different communities or subcultures (the "multicongregational" model).

Although some of the difficulties remain, in church planting ventures there tends to be greater clarity about the purpose of each level than in cases where these levels result from internal restructuring. In addition, the primary focus is neither on the celebration (as in the megachurch model) nor on the cell (as in the cell church model), but on the congregation. It may be that this focus is crucial for effective three-level churches. A semiautonomous model, whereby the secondary level congregations develop their own style, mission priorities, leadership and mode of working, but remain networked together for various purposes, offers perhaps the best way forward.

Even so, the development of multiple groups at the secondary level can be difficult to retain within a three-level church. Whether the congregations meet within the same premises at different times, or in different locations, the relationship of these congregations to the church as a whole can become strained, especially at leadership level. Some denominations find this less problematic than others, so it is likely that ecclesiological factors rather than interpersonal dynamics are dominant. In traditions where the responsibility for the work and ministry of this congregation rests with congregational leaders, who are primarily answerable to the congregation rather than to external groups, secondary level groups tend to pull away from the three-level church and become independent churches.

Many Baptist churches that have planted daughter congregations with no intention that these should become independent churches, at least in the near future, have been dismayed by the discovery that the congregation wants much greater autonomy, and sooner than had been envisaged. This appears to have been less of a problem for church plants from house church or Anglican churches. David Wasdell commented in 1975 that Anglican church planting is sometimes "strangled by its insistence on one secondary group at the heart of each parish."[16] But where this stranglehold is broken, Anglican ecclesiology operates much more happily than many other traditions with a network of interrelated congregations.

Although this discussion has important implications for church planting, the issue here is essentially one of structure rather than size. Perhaps churches can grow to any size, provided they can develop structures to help this growth. Large churches that do not develop smaller units, whether through church planting or a cell group structure, may continue to grow numerically for some time (although not indefinitely), but they will be very limited in their internal life and external ministry. They may operate as preaching centers, or celebrations, but there are vital dimensions missing. Cell church advocates argue that churches can grow to any size if appropriate structures are in place. But there may be reasons for limiting such growth.

Megachurch or Multichurch?

(1) Contextual Factors

Are there any contextual factors that need to be considered in assessing whether large churches or many smaller churches are appropriate in a particular context? Some have suggested that British culture is less open to megachurches than other cultures, and various reasons have been put forward to explain this observation. Others have interpreted this as evidence of restricted faith and limited vision, and have contrasted this with the North American scene. They have challenged the fear of large churches and endorsed their importance, especially in large urban areas. Graham Dow, Bishop of Willesden in North London, writes: "Impact for Christ in big cities is likely to involve big churches. Among the teeming, anonymous culture of networks, it is important for the people of Christ to be visible if an impact is to be made."[17] Martin Robinson notes four contributions a megachurch makes to mission: it is a repository of creativity; its size and visibility demands attention; it has resources to reach unchurched people; and it provides anonymity to seekers.[18]

However, thoughtful critics of North American megachurches have discerned in the drive to establish large churches worrying evidence of unwitting cultural conformity, rather than contextual planning. Os Guinness, in the provocatively titled *Dining with the Devil*, raises concerns about ways in which large churches appear to be held captive by the methodology, values, and goals of the culture of modernity. He questions the reasons for their growth, their sustainability, and their relevance to an emerging postmodern culture. Comparing these churches with the development of huge shopping centers, he warns that "the grand and gleaming megamalls will soon become an anachronism themselves and so will the megachurches that have copied them."[19]

It is arguable that in a post-Christian and postmodern mission context, large churches are inappropriate. In a culture where grassroots activism and networks are replacing hierarchical structures, large churches may appear increasingly out of date, however contemporary their decor, style of music, and language.[20] In a context where churches need to grapple with the challenge of a pluralistic environment and develop models of mission that are humble and courageous rather than overbearing, large churches may convey the wrong message and hinder the development of appropriate attitudes. In a context where spirituality is back in vogue and evangelism is easier, but where commitment to institutions is out of favor and discipleship is harder, large churches may be ill-equipped for mission strategies that will make disciples rather than converts. The cell church is one alternative model. Planting many smaller churches is another.

The contemporary church planting movement owes much to the church growth movement, and church planting is endorsed by church growth teachers and strategists as an effective form of evangelism. But those unfamiliar with these strong links might be excused for thinking that, on the question of size, the two movements are moving in opposite, even incompatible, directions. In fact, although some have advocated the enlargement of existing churches, while others have argued that multiplication of churches is the more effective means of sustained growth, the validity of both approaches has been recognized, and this issue has not been contentious. It may seem naive, especially in contexts where overall church growth is small or nonexistent, to assume that there is no need to choose between these two strategies, but this assumption has been subjected to surprisingly little scrutiny in either movement.[21]

In a growth context, it is arguable that church planting and the growth of existing churches are complementary and mutually enriching. Evidence can be assembled which suggests that recently established churches, with relatively low numbers but high levels of commitment to evangelism, tend to grow rapidly; that the planting of a new church may stimulate growth in the planting church, as hitherto dormant gifts are awakened and the church as a whole responds to the challenge of replacing members who have left to plant the new church; and that denominations or networks which adopt church planting policies tend to experience overall growth, which will in some situations result in the enlargement of existing churches.

Not all of this evidence is as persuasive as advocates sometimes claim, with some interpretations of statistics lacking rigor and others apparently confusing causal and incidental factors. Attempts to explain church growth on the basis of limited information and without proper consideration of contextual factors are simplistic and misleading. Nevertheless, the conviction that church planting stimulates church growth is widely held.

The reverse also appears to be true. Churches that engage in church planting are generally churches which have experienced growth. The experience of growth not only provides the personnel and resources for church planting, but morale is generally high in such churches, and there is energy, enthusiasm, and faith for new ventures. If the church has been successful in one location, expectation of a similar experience elsewhere seems legitimate. The planting of a new church may result in temporarily reduced numbers in the planting church, but the vision is for overall increase, through the anticipated growth of the new church, and the recovery of numbers in the planting church.

Where church growth and church planting reinforce each other as harmoniously as this, there is no reason to consider these strategies as even potentially contradictory. But there are other situations where the question of *megachurch* or *multichurch* requires more careful consideration. Not all church planting ventures result in the expected growth. Some merely redistribute church members, others actually lead to decline in overall membership. The attempt to run two churches rather than one may prove to be beyond the resources of the available personnel. The effort involved for little obvious benefit may lead to some members experiencing burnout and leaving the church. Nor do all growing churches choose to plant new churches: some opt to redevelop their overcrowded premises or move to a larger site. And some churches grow by siphoning off members from other churches, leading to the closure of these churches. This may leave areas unchurched, and so militate against a church planting vision of saturating the nation with churches.

Church growth and church planting may, therefore, be working at cross-purposes in some contexts. And in those nations (such as the United States and Britain) where overall church membership remains stubbornly static or in decline, despite the implementation of church growth principles and church planting programs, the continuing endorsement of both policies seems increasingly problematic.

In such contexts, church growth may be balanced by church decline, and church planting by church closures. Both strategies are crucial in averting further overall decline. But success in both strategies at the same time in contexts of overall nongrowth or decline can only be at the expense of the decline and closure of other churches. Although this may still be advocated as the most effective policy, the wastage rate implied by the number of churches declining or closing begins to raise serious missiological and pastoral issues.

Do efforts to enlarge substantially a small number of churches justify the neglect and marginalization of many smaller churches? Are programs to multiply churches in regions where there are already many churches strategically preferable to efforts to resource struggling churches in underchurched regions? Does the coexistence of church growth and church planting strategies result in an unacceptable imbalance, which will have serious and detrimental long-term consequences? Perhaps a more comprehensive approach is needed, which considers regions strategically and looks creatively at ways of combining strategies for planting new churches, resourcing older churches, enlarging some churches and relocating members from others.[22]

(2) Missiological Factors

Underlying this discussion is a question about the most effective size for churches to fulfill their God-given mission. If this mission is interpreted primarily in evangelistic terms, there are a number of related issues to consider. How large can a church grow before its maintenance needs significantly detract from the ability of its members to build with nonmembers the quality relationships which are essential for sharing faith effectively? At what point does the size of the church provide church members with sufficient diversity of social interaction, so that they begin to insulate themselves from meaningful relationships with others? Are some churches too small to attract new members? Are some churches too large to continue attracting new members? Are nonmembers more likely to respond positively to and be incorporated into larger or smaller churches?

Does this vary from one culture to another, or according to individual preferences? Should an evangelistic strategy draw on churches of varying sizes, to offer different options to nonmembers? Are some forms of evangelism more effective through primary, secondary, or tertiary level churches?

Different answers are given to these questions. Some suggest that the anonymity offered by large churches to those who are exploring the Christian faith is helpful and allows them time to consider the gospel without pressure. But it is arguable that this implies that the gospel is propositional and that it undervalues the role of the Christian community in evangelism. Some contend that relational evangelism is primary and that involvement in a small group is a more appropriate setting within which to encourage people who are exploring the Christian faith. The presence or absence of pressure, they argue, relates more to the ethos of the church rather than its size. Others think that exposure to a larger group of Christians can be beneficial, whether through the witness that this makes to the attractiveness of Christianity, or through the increased likelihood of finding others with similar interests, or through the impact of worship in a celebratory atmosphere. However these issues are assessed, the question of size has tactical, and probably also strategic, significance for evangelism.

But mission need not be interpreted only with reference to evangelism. The tendency within church growth writings to equate mission with evangelism lacks biblical and theological warrant. As a reaction against contrary trends in some circles to redefine mission without reference to evangelism, this tendency is understandable, but, as with many reactive positions, it has become an overreaction. Churches that operate with this reductionist interpretation of mission and only measure growth numerically will either tend to regard indefinite enlargement of membership as legitimate, or they will plant new churches which replicate the same limited missiological vision as their own.

However, if church planting (and church growth) initiatives are placed within the theological framework of missio Dei, incarnation, and the kingdom of God,[23] a broader and more complex mission emerges. If churches, whether established churches or newly planted churches, are to be involved in other aspects of mission than evangelism, the question of appropriate size must be revisited. Some forms of social action and community involvement can be undertaken effectively by small churches; others appear to require larger groups. Small churches may need to focus on single issues. Larger churches may be able to develop programs which address a range of social issues. Alternatively, issues requiring greater resources might be addressed by partnerships between smaller churches in a locality.

These are not just questions that require pragmatic answers in terms of resources. An underlying issue is whether size drives vision, or vision drives size. If an initiative to plant a new congregation includes a vision for some form of social involvement, this may require sufficient numbers in the planting team to make this project feasible. Or if a church is planted with a certain number of founder members, this may restrict the social ministry of this church, at least in the early stages of its development.

Another underlying issue is whether the size of the church will be significant in enabling it to gain a hearing for its concerns. This relates especially to situations where mission is understood to include political engagement. Some argue that only large churches will have enough "clout," or a loud enough voice, to be taken seriously in the political arena. Church planting, by dividing available resources, hinders such a witness. But it is arguable that this "top-down" approach to political involvement is theologically inappropriate in a post-Christian society and contextually inappropriate in a postmodern culture, and that grass-roots activism by small, prophetic communities is preferable.

(3) Ecclesiological Factors

In chapter 5, we contrasted planting and "cloning" and advocated creativity and flexibility in the development of new churches. The question of size is relevant also to this issue. In a typical mother/daughter church planting venture, the likelihood of cloning increases as the number of people in the planting team increases. This is partly because the new church can adopt more of the practices of the planting church than it could if the size of the new church were significantly smaller than the mother church. Also there are many members of the mother church involved with shared experiences of church life, who reinforce each other's assumptions. Small teams cannot simply recreate the planting church (although some try to do this and fall foul of the principles noted above about primary, secondary, and tertiary groups); there is less expectancy from the planting church that they will reproduce the same ecclesiastical structure; and the amount of baggage carried by the team is less.

Some church planting advocates urge churches to begin with a sizeable core group. The suggestion that at least 50 people are involved is widely quoted[24] but appears to have numerous disadvantages: it excludes many churches from attempting to plant a new church and thus contributes to the marginalization of church planting; it significantly reduces the membership of medium-sized planting churches, with possibly enriching but potentially damaging consequences; it limits the speed with which church planting can be attempted, since churches cannot frequently spare fifty members; and, as we have commented, it tends to limit the ecclesiological flexibility of the venture. Planting a new church with fifty or more people diminishes the risk of failure, but it may also diminish the possibility of creative rather than replicative church planting.

Church planting, if it is not merely cloning, offers opportunities for ecclesiological reflection and renewal. Are there vital aspects of church life which have been lost as churches have aged and grown numerically? In the context of smaller and younger church plants, some of these may be recovered. Of course, if the emphasis is on numerical growth and the venture is a "success," there may be only limited time (and little incentive) to examine such things. But if growth is slower coming, or if there is scope for fresh thinking about church life, some neglected areas might be explored.

What might these areas be? We will consider two examples, not because these are the only areas, or necessarily the most crucial, but to avoid any inference that we are constructing an exhaustive and prescriptive list. What is needed among church planters is not the adoption of someone else's ecclesiological agenda, but creativity under God to develop churches that are both faithful to biblical revelation and able to incarnate the gospel into diverse cultural contexts. Our two examples are multivoiced worship and the exercise of church discipline.

Multivoiced worship. The New Testament gives surprisingly little information about what the earliest congregations did when they met together, and few instructions for the conduct of corporate worship. However, one emphasis that appears frequently in the New Testament,[25] and has been lost frequently in subsequent centuries, is that worship should be participatory rather than passive. Participation in worship is not to be restricted to a clerical caste, a choir, or a "worship group." Paul's response to the charismatic chaos at Corinth was not to restrict participation, but to suggest guidelines that would enable maximum participation and maximum edification. His understanding of worship was multivoiced: "When you come together, everyone has a hymn, or a word of instruction, a revelation, a tongue or an interpretation."[26] The expectation that several prophets will speak and that others will weigh their contributions[27] indicates multiplicity in exhortation and encouragement; and the much-debated restriction on women asking questions in church meetings[28] seems to suggest that dialogue, rather than monologue, was the familiar mode of teaching.

This multivoiced worship has been a feature of several church planting movements. It characterized British house church meetings in the 1960s and 1970s. For the Plymouth Brethren, a century earlier, it was a crucial outworking of their insistence on the "priesthood of all believers" (or at least the "priesthood of all *male* believers"). Earlier still, Anabaptists quoted Paul's instructions to the Corinthians and questioned the legitimacy of churches where such participation was discouraged. An early tract from the Swiss branch of the movement asked: "when someone comes to church and constantly hears only one person speaking, and all the listeners are silent, neither speaking nor prophesying, who can or will regard or confess the same to be a spiritual congregation."[29] But few movements retain this beyond the second generation. This may be regarded as another aspect of the institutionalization that impacts all movements, but the impact of growing numbers on this should not be ignored.

Multivoiced worship becomes increasingly difficult as numbers grow. There are ways to retain elements of participation, but the celebration style of worship that seems to be appropriate within tertiary level groups does not help this. Congregational participation is often reduced to (sometimes interminable) singing or individual contributions by a very small percentage of the church. Teaching is the prerogative of a minority. Various responses can be made to this: defining participation in terms of personal involvement, rather than audible contribution; extolling the virtues of celebration worship, the quality of music, or level of articulation in the preaching; or pointing to small groups as the forum for participatory worship.

Increasing musical complexity, the reintroduction of actual if not theoretical clericalism, and a transition from participation to performance, from congregation to audience, signal movement away from multivoiced worship. Some revel in the change. Some see it as a necessary accompaniment of growth. Some mourn a lost opportunity to recover an important dimension of new covenant post-Pentecost worship, where the Spirit is poured out on all.

Again, the challenge of the cell church model seems relevant, relegating celebration to a secondary, though still important, place.

Cells give opportunity for participation; celebrations provide inspiration. The primacy of the small group ensures that multivoiced worship does not become marginalized. However, it is doubtful whether the typical cell group is adequate in scope to provide the richness and diversity that is the essence of multivoiced worship. A cell-and-celebration structure runs the risk of neither element providing such worship. Cell churches which operate through three levels may find their congregational level to be the most appropriate place to explore this dimension of corporate worship.

It may be that multivoiced worship is best helped by the multichurch approach, whereby churches do not expand indefinitely, but establish new churches which are large enough for diverse contributions and small enough for full participation. There are still important roles for cells and celebrations, but multivoiced worship functions best at the congregational (secondary group) level.

Church discipline. We suggested in chapter 3 that attempts to plant "New Testament churches" often draw heavily on Acts and the Epistles, but make sparing use of the Gospels. We noted also that one of the very few recorded references to the church in the Gospels describes a community that is committed to accountability and mutual admonition. We know very little about the kind of church anticipated by Jesus, but we do know that he envisaged a community practicing what has generally been defined as church discipline. The subject of church discipline is not popular today, for various reasons,[30] but it has particular relevance to church planting and to the question of the size of the church.

Accountability is an important issue for church planters. Its absence can create major problems in a context of dangerous liberty, inexperienced leadership, enthusiasm, and creativity.[31] Where a new church is planted from an existing church, accountability can be provided through relationships between the churches and their respective leadership teams. This sometimes works well and enriches both churches, but on other occasions it proves inadequate or unworkable. This may be due to friction between the churches, to disagreement over the degree of autonomy given to the new church and the time frame for increasing this, to difficulties encountered as the new church develops its own rather different identity from the planting church, or to the absence of anyone with the capacity to oversee and guide this new venture. In such situations, church planters may need to develop another structure for accountability, drawing on denominational resources or those with appropriate skills and experience. This may involve inviting the participation of a consultant, or the integration of the new church into a wider network.

Partly as a response to the perceived need for accountability in a new and liberating context, and partly through reflection on biblical teaching about the church, several church planting movements have recovered the often neglected practice of church discipline. For early Anabaptists, the absence within the state churches (Catholic and Protestant) of biblical church discipline was a substantial cause for disaffection. To the Protestant insistence that the preaching of the Word and the proper administration of the sacraments were the defining marks of a true church, Anabaptists added the proper exercise of church discipline. The early Methodists and early Baptists similarly took church discipline very seriously, and the practice has been a familiar aspect of the churches planted by the house church movement.

These movements have all been criticized by their contemporaries for their application of the principles of church discipline, but each has served to recall these contemporaries to a practice that has support from all the main strands of New Testament teaching, and yet has been persistently misinterpreted or marginalized. This is another example of the potential of church planting to stimulate ecclesiological renewal, as well as to multiply churches.

But in what kind of church can church discipline be exercised effectively? To attempt to introduce this practice without asking fundamental questions about how members of the church understand their membership is to court disaster. Time is needed to teach the principles on which it is based, to explore the implications of this teaching, and to develop the relationships that are crucial for it to function positively. Churches that have operated without a church discipline policy for many years will not be able to introduce such a policy quickly.

As with many other such issues, church planting offers an opportunity for progress. In a context where relationships are being forged, commitments are being clarified, and new structures are being invented, it is feasible to introduce church discipline as a foundational component within the new church. If the vulnerability of church planting prompts the adoption of accountability structures, the liberty accorded to church planters helps the recovery of the practice of church discipline.

The smaller size, as well as the newness, of the church plant may be an important factor in this recovery. The kind of community envisaged by Jesus in his teaching on mutual admonition is a church whose members are sufficiently involved in each other's lives to notice spiritual and moral problems, and where relationships are strong enough to risk misunderstanding or offense. Furthermore, the process Jesus describes includes a command to move beyond private admonition to public confrontation. If there is no response to such admonition, the matter cannot be ignored: "Tell it to the church."[32] This instruction requires careful handling and a level of maturity within the community if it is to achieve its intended purpose, but arguably it also requires a community small enough to provide a relational rather than an institutional context.

A form of church discipline may still operate within larger churches, but the tendency there will be for this to become a leadership function rather than the community activity that appears to be envisaged in Matthew 18 (where no mention is made of church leaders). Such church discipline may be exercised graciously or harshly, but will be much more prone to abuse than where discipline is exercised by and within the church community. An alternative possibility is for cell groups to function as "the church" for the purpose of church discipline. This has the advantage of setting the process within a context of committed relationships and retains the communal rather than clerical dimension. But if the cell is a component part of a larger church, whether as a home group within a traditional church or a cell within a cell church, it may not be clear if and how action taken in this group should be communicated to the rest of the church.

Our intention here has not been to suggest that there is an optimum size for churches, whether as targets for newly planted churches or ceilings for growing churches. The creativity and diversity required for churches to engage effectively in a pluralistic culture may require churches of varying sizes and structures. For church planters, the freedom to ask radical questions about size and structure is vital, and it is important that missiological and ecclesiological considerations are not outweighed by practical factors. But when these considerations are weighed carefully, it is surprising how well the traditional congregational model fares.

The congregational model of church, which operates at the secondary group level identified by sociologists, has significant benefits for the implementation of various important aspects of church life.

204 • *Church Planting*

This model is very familiar in church history;[33] its strengths and weaknesses are well-documented; its durability may be testimony to its adequacy rather than evidence of enslavement to tradition; and it is for this kind of church that most church leaders are trained. It is under attack both from those who advocate the development of larger churches and from those who advocate cell churches, where the primary commitment is to a smaller group. Church planting that is not merely cloning will want to subject the congregational model to a searching critique. But it is possible that in time church planting experience and reflection on this will lead to a recovery of the dynamism of congregational structures. Asking radical structural questions does not always result in the rejection of tried and tested answers.

9. CHURCH PLANTING AND THE LEADERSHIP OF THE CHURCH

*A*nother aspect of ecclesiology that is influenced by the size of a church is leadership. Churches that want to "break the 200 barrier" are recommended to increase their paid staff and develop a leadership structure that will help ongoing growth. Team leadership becomes a necessity, although church growth writers generally insist that one person should continue to function as overall church leader, with primary responsibility for direction. If the leader of a small church can adapt to the requirements of being the leader of a larger church, there is no need for a change of personnel, although new staff will be needed alongside this leader. Otherwise a new leader will be needed.

But the role of the leader in a larger church is significantly different from the role of the leader in a smaller church. Lyle Schaller has suggested[1] the term *rancher* rather than *pastor* might be used to signal this change. Peter Wagner is grateful for this imagery and uses it extensively in his teaching. He explains: "in a church led by a rancher the sheep are still shepherded, but the rancher does not do it. The rancher sees that it is done by others."[2]

Eddie Gibbs draws on parallels with industrial skill levels to describe the kinds of leadership needed as a church enlarges. In a small church (up to 65 members), the leader functions as a foreman, who leads the work team and is involved in all aspects of the work. In a medium sized church (66-150 members), the leader is a supervisor, operating through delegation of tasks and general oversight of the work team. In a large church (151-450 members), the leader operates as a middle manager; in a larger church (451-1000 members), the leader operates at top management level. As numbers grow, the leader becomes less involved in day-to-day decisions and more concerned with strategic issues. In a very large church (1000+ members), the leader is the equivalent of the chairman of the board, responsible for overall vision, policy decisions, and key appointments.[3]

The importance of leaders adapting to the different responsibilities and tasks involved in leading larger churches is widely acknowledged. The alternatives appear to be premature burnout and deceleration or reversal of church growth. But the legitimacy of applying to church leadership principles derived from industry or business has been challenged as a further example of the unhealthy and uncritical dependence of the church growth movement on secular management techniques. There are certainly a number of ecclesiological issues here, that need to be identified and weighed carefully.

One concern about the emphasis on the role of the leader within the church growth movement is that it appears to reinforce clericalism and the dominance of professional church leaders. Despite the apparent counterbalance of emphases on the mobilization of all church members and the importance of team ministry, the "church growth leader" seems to exercise a directive role that marginalizes the discernment of the congregation and usurps the authority of the gathered church. Churches may regard these losses as the price paid for a growing membership, but it is important that this price is recognized and its implications explored. A related concern is the effect of such power on the character of leaders in large churches.

Despite protestations of church growth writers to the contrary, it is not easy to combine this role with the quality of "servant leadership" presented by Jesus to his disciples[4] as a radical alternative, which would distinguish their community from other institutions and organizations. The recent use of "servant leadership" terminology in some secular organizations is intriguing, and may be an example of influence in an opposite direction,[5] but similarity of terminology does not necessarily imply equivalence of meaning. Can large churches escape power politics and hierarchical leadership?

A practical difficulty with the "rancher" model of church leadership is that very few church leaders have any appropriate training for such a role. Ministerial training tends to assume that churches will be small enough to require "pastors" and concentrates on the skills and practices needed in such contexts. Secular management principles may be very helpful for those who find themselves in larger churches, but the absence of theological and pastoral undergirding may be perceived as a serious weakness. If larger churches led by "ranchers" are to be encouraged, more thought needs to be given to the training of these leaders, or the retraining of leaders whose experience has previously been in smaller churches.

But a more fundamental ecclesiological issue is whether such leadership is appropriate in most contexts. If the kind of leadership modeled and taught by Jesus precludes the kind of leadership required for large churches, perhaps large churches are not a helpful development. Perhaps the "200 barrier" is there for a purpose and should be respected rather than breached. Advocates of large churches may reject this conclusion, often on the grounds that right attitudes are crucial and that these can be maintained however large a church grows.

Examples can be given of humble and gracious leaders of very large churches. It is also undoubtedly true that some people have the strategic skills and capacity to lead large organizations, and that they will not flourish as leaders of small churches. Is it not better to recognize diversity of gifts among church leaders, and try to ensure that appropriate leaders are appointed to lead churches of different sizes?

This may be our conclusion, but it is important that we examine the implications and recognize that there are alternatives. One of these alternatives is church planting. Rather than allowing churches to expand indefinitely, new congregations can be planted that will be of the size that will require the kind of leadership for which most church leaders have been trained. If these congregations relate to each other in a network, there is still a role for strategic leaders, but without some of the inherent problems associated with leadership of large single churches. Church planting may also help to avert the leadership bottlenecks that can occur in larger churches, where those with leadership gifts are frustrated in their attempts to find ways to exercise these gifts.

Another alternative is to transition the church into a cell church, where leadership is devolved to the small group, and where a very large number of people are involved in leadership (1 in 5 members in some models). The apprenticeship model for developing new leaders in such churches is impressive: every leader has an assistant, who is being trained to take over. However, this model requires a large numbers of leaders, and some cell churches struggle with chronic shortages of leaders.

Advocates express the hope that as cell churches become more common, they will help to develop different perceptions of leadership, so that more people will be prepared to become leaders. A key feature of cell churches is that, by comparison with traditional churches with house groups, leaders of cell groups do not carry other major responsibilities in the church, and so are less liable to burn out. In cell churches there is still a role for strategic leaders, but it is less clerical and more compatible with the "servant leader" model.

Thus, church planting and the development of alternative models of church may make contributions to discussions about leadership styles within growing churches. But the establishing of new congregations raises several other significant questions about the nature of church leadership. Among many issues that churches must address when they are planting new congregations are those relating to the leadership of these groups. Although in some cases ready-made leaders are available (an Anglican curate or Baptist assistant minister, for example), more often the leadership base has to be broadened and new patterns developed. Structures and styles taken for granted elsewhere often seem inappropriate and unhelpful in church planting situations, especially where the motivation for planting is missionary.

Sometimes the new church faithfully adheres to the accepted pattern of leadership, despite the limitations that result. More often a compromise solution is reached, whereby a traditional structure is maintained, but the way in which leadership is actually exercised is quite different. Where there is sufficient freedom, more radical changes may be adopted.

An example may be helpful. The leadership structure of Baptist churches traditionally involves a minister and a group of deacons. Proposals for action are normally discussed within this leadership group before being brought to the church at regular business meetings. Decisions are made by the gathered congregation, usually through a voting procedure. There are variations from church to church, with some churches operating with a two-tier leadership structure involving elders and deacons, some larger churches having more than one paid minister, and with different levels of support required for decisions to be made. There are differences also, of course, in style, and in the balance of power between the congregation and the leadership. In some churches, the church meeting is little more than a rubber stamp on leadership decisions; in others the minister lives in fear of the deacons and the church meeting.

As a newcomer into Baptist circles, I have been impressed by both the strengths and weaknesses of this system. Conversations with Baptist ministers, deacons, and church members have revealed considerable disquiet about this structure, but an almost equal loyalty to it. This dual reaction brings to mind Winston Churchill's comment about democracy being the worst form of government—except for all the other forms that have been tried![6]

But when Baptist churches plant new congregations, the style of leadership often changes. Although there may still be formal commitment to a democratic form of church government, the recognized leader (often untrained and nonordained) may exercise a rather more directive role than his or her (usually trained and ordained) counterpart in the planting church. The democratic decision-making process, which worked tolerably well in a more settled church context, is now perceived as time-consuming, cumbersome, and unable to respond quickly enough to the challenges and opportunities of a mission context. The style of leadership in recently planted churches may resemble that in a mission agency.

There are obvious dangers in this situation, especially where leaders are inexperienced and there is inadequate accountability, and some church plants have failed to thrive as a result. But where relationships are strong within the planting group, where the leader consults widely if informally, and where the church has a clear vision owned by all the founding members, directive leadership is often appreciated and effective.

The planting church may express concern about this more directive style of leadership and more informal process of consultation. But to the discerning, and to those who are struggling with the shortcomings of more established procedures, the benefits may also become increasingly apparent. If relationships between the planting church and the new church remain strong, both may learn from the experience of the other. The planting church may learn to honor those with gifts of leadership, and give them greater freedom to use these gifts. Many church leaders are really involved in management rather than leadership—either because they do not have leadership gifts, or because they are disempowered by the structures within which they have to operate. The church may also loosen up its decision-making procedures.

The church plant may tend, over time and as numbers grow, to return to a more democratic style of leadership. This is part of the transition from a core group to a congregation. Informal consultation works well in a small committed group, but more organization is needed if those who join the church are not to be excluded. Both churches may move some way toward each other in the way they reach decisions.

A second important aspect of leadership in Baptist church planting ventures is the discovery of the benefits of team ministry. This partly counterbalances the more directive style of leadership. Although team ministry is not restricted to church plants, frequently the quality of relationships, clarity of task allocation, level of accountability, and strength of commitment to a shared vision in church planting teams challenge those whose experience and understanding of team ministry has been less developed. A minister with deacons may describe this structure as team leadership, but the reality may be qualitatively different from that enjoyed in many church plants.

Where church planting is not cloning, and where there is mutual respect between the planting church and the new church, ecclesiological renewal can take place in relation to models and styles of leadership. Within Baptist circles, this particularly relates to issues of team ministry and models of decision making. Similar and quite different issues will be encountered by Presbyterian, Methodist, Pentecostal, and other churches as they engage in church planting.

Leadership in Church Planting Movements

Ecclesiological renewal in relation to patterns of church leadership has characterized various church planting movements. Although there are significant differences between these movements, it is interesting to observe some common features in movements that were operating in quite different contexts. Recurrent tendencies include a movement from pastoral leadership to mission leadership; the recovery of neglected ministries; freedom for women to be leaders; and rejection of clericalism.

(1) Mission leadership

The mission focus of many church planting initiatives challenges the assumption, resulting from centuries under Christendom, that pastoral ministry is normative for church leaders. The equation of *minister* and *pastor* has been made for so long now that these terms are often used interchangeably. It is assumed that the senior leader in larger churches will be a pastor, and that this is the first appointment a smaller church should make. If a church can afford one full-time staff member, their choice will be someone with pastoral gifts, who can hopefully teach as well. In churches oriented toward maintenance, pastors and teachers play a dominant role. If there is finance for a second staff member, an assistant pastor, a youth pastor, or an administrator may be appointed. Evangelism and other aspects of mission are the responsibilities of church members rather than priority activities for church leaders.

But in church planting, the obvious need in selecting leaders may be for those with evangelistic gifts or abilities to initiate new projects. Those with pastoral and teaching gifts will be needed if the new church is to thrive, but these gifts may be found within members of the core group rather than within the church leader.

Most theological and denominational training is based on the same assumption, that pastoral ministry is normative. Lesslie Newbigin writes: "We have lived for so many centuries in the 'Christendom' situation that ministerial training is almost entirely conceived in terms of the pastoral care of existing congregations."[7] In similar vein, and drawing on the imagery of "resident aliens," Hauerwas and Willimon ask, "What does it mean for the pastor to have as his or her job description, not the sustenance of a service club within a generally Christian culture, but the survival of a *colony* within an *alien society*?"[8] This assumption is evident at every stage of the process of recognition and training. Those within local churches who aspire to leadership, and show promise, are encouraged to exercise pastoral ministry by leading home groups or some equivalent task. Those who display evangelistic enthusiasm are more often encouraged to work with a "parachurch" agency.

Those responsible for interviewing applicants for accredited denominational ministry place greater emphasis on pastoral ability than on commitment to mission. Many ministerial training courses still treat mission studies as a bolt-on component, rather than setting theological and pastoral studies within the context of mission. Where training is provided for evangelists, these are generally regarded as having a secondary ministry compared to those perceived as having a broader pastoral calling.

Martin Robinson describes the "self-perpetuating cycle" that operates here. "The model that is used for the selection of potential candidates is one which is looking for pastor/teacher qualities. Once in college, training is geared toward producing pastor/teacher ministers. The result is that pastor/teachers, both by gifting and training, are what tend to emerge from our colleges. Because so many pastor/teachers emerge from our colleges and then take up positions of leadership in our churches, the model is reinforced when the issue of selection is again raised."[9] Ellis and Mitchell agree that the use of the term "pastor" for local church leader marginalizes those with other kinds of gifts and conclude: "this has resulted in a lopsided, safe church leadership which often lacks a cutting edge and the ability to evangelize effectively."[10] This marginalization of those with the gifts that are needed for mission, at local church and denominational levels, is inappropriate in a post-Christian culture where *all* church leadership must be missionary. It must be challenged if missionary congregations are to flourish.

Church planting provides an opportunity to challenge this monochrome and maintenance-oriented view of leadership. Here, the main leader or full-time staff member might be an evangelist, or a community worker. As the church grows, the appointment of a person with pastoral gifts may well be considered, but there is no necessity for this person to be the senior leader. A mission-oriented church will be concerned to appoint staff who will help them to move forward in mission, rather than maintaining the status quo. If the missionary task of the church is recovered, the leadership required to help churches to fulfill this mission must also be recovered.

Some pastors clearly have such a mission mentality, and some evangelists are also effective pastors. What is needed is not arbitrary division, or unhelpful stereotyping, but an understanding of leadership that is defined in relation to mission, and which recognizes the need for different gifts in different leadership roles. This might involve in different contexts a refusal any longer to equate the terms *pastor* and *minister*, the recognition of evangelists as ministers, or a redefinition of the role of pastor. Such redefinition is needed to bring this role into line both with the contemporary mission context within which all leadership gifts must be set, and with New Testament images of shepherds as those who seek lost sheep as well as caring for those already in the fold.[11]

The Anabaptists recognized evangelists in the early sixteenth century, despite the insistence of the Reformers that this office was obsolete. The Waldensians recovered the evangelistic ministry in the fourteenth century, but found similar resistance from the established churches, who were locked into static pastoral models of leadership. Perhaps the contemporary church planting movement can emulate previous church planting movements, which restored to the churches the ministry of the evangelist.

(2) The Recovery of Neglected Ministries

But these movements did not only recognize evangelists. They discovered, as they read the New Testament, references also to other leadership roles, especially apostles. And they discovered within their churches those with gifts that seemed to justify their recognition as apostles.

Other church planting movements have recognized such leadership roles. Early General Baptist churches in England were served, not only by elders and deacons as local church leaders, but by those who moved among the churches, acted as consultants, evangelized, and planted new churches.[12] These were generally referred to as *messengers*, a term with missiological connotations, and they were engaged in activities that could be regarded as apostolic, by comparison with the roles of those recognized as apostles in the New Testament.[13] The British house church movement is a contemporary example of a church planting movement which has recovered the apostolic ministry. Those recognized as apostles within this movement have been extensively involved in church planting initiatives, and many continue to exercise a strategic leadership role that is mission-oriented.

The opposition from some Baptists to the recognition of apostles within the house church movement is surprising in light of this very similar phenomenon in their own early years. It is interesting also that historians who chart the activities of leaders of church planting movements where the term *apostle* was not used, quite often use this term themselves to describe the role of these leaders. Examples include early Celtic missionaries, Ninian, Columba and Aidan; John Wesley in eighteenth century England; "praying Hyde" in India; and Watchman Nee in China. This may be an imprecise use of the term, but no other word appears adequate to describe the breadth of ministry exercised by such leaders.

For church planting movements, the identification and deployment of apostles (and prophets[14]) is arguably highly significant. Various interpretations have been given of the role of New Testament apostles in the planting of early churches. Many churches were planted by unknown men and women, rather than by recognized apostles. There is certainly inadequate support for any attempt to equate the terms *apostle* and *church planter*. But there are passages that seem to link apostles closely with church planting. Some have suggested that apostles and prophets are *foundational* ministries in a way that neither pastors nor evangelists are. Although Jesus himself is the "cornerstone," churches are built on the "foundation of the apostles and prophets" (Eph. 2:20-21).

A mark of Paul's apostolic ministry was that he laid foundations (1 Cor. 3:10), and that he did not build on foundations laid by others (Rom. 15:20). Teachers and pastors like Apollos, Aquila, and Priscilla, and many unnamed local leaders, built on these foundations. Noting that more individuals are designated in the New Testament as apostles than as evangelists, Mitchell and Ellis argue that "the neglect of the apostolic would appear to be a major contemporary ecclesiological oversight."[15] Perhaps the contemporary church planting movement can play a part in the restoration of this dimension.

One of the questions facing the church planting movement is whether there are apostles operating within it who need to be identified as such, and released into strategic pioneering roles. Another question is whether churches being planted by those with evangelistic or pastoral gifts can draw on those with apostolic skills, to ensure that they are built on solid foundations. Some church plants seem to struggle because they are limited by the pastoral or evangelistic perspectives of those who lead them. The contribution of apostles (and prophets) to such church plants could provide breadth and depth to the vision of the new church, and ensure that they are well founded.

Church planting movements appear to provide scope for the emergence of those with apostolic roles, and are significantly strengthened by such people. The use of the term *apostle* is less important[16] than the effective deployment of apostles, by whatever term they are known. Apostles are translocal rather than local leaders, and their focus is on mission rather than maintenance. It is this focus that differentiates them from bishops, cardinals, moderators, superintendents and others with roles that are not restricted to local churches.

All denominations have leaders with translocal responsibility. But in most contexts, these leaders tend mainly to exercise administrative and pastoral roles, rather than being mission leaders. In this way the bias toward maintenance, which is reflected in the predominance of pastors in local churches, is repeated in other kinds of church leadership. Within church planting movements, translocal leaders are mission-oriented, even though they may also carry pastoral responsibilities.

The perennial need for the recovery of apostles within church planting movements is testimony to the persistent tendency for mission to be swallowed up in maintenance. Sometimes this takes three or four generations; sometimes it happens much more quickly. Anabaptist apostles were replaced by Mennonite bishops. Roger Hayden traces the disappearance of English Baptist messengers to the unwillingness of local churches to release their most gifted leaders to this translocal role.[17] There are indications that some (though by no means all) house church apostles are increasingly involved in maintenance roles, and may have become bishops in all but name. Perhaps the contemporary church planting movement can help to recover this ministry once more, not only within the house churches, but throughout the church.[18] The challenges such movements offer to the wider church are to release those with appropriate gifts into pioneering and translocal roles, and to redress the imbalance between mission and maintenance roles in their denominational appointments.

(3) Women in Leadership

A recurrent feature in the history of the church has been the significant role played by women in first generation church planting movements, and their marginalization in subsequent generations. Institutionalization and reversion to a maintenance mentality seems to be accompanied by displacement of women from leadership responsibility. It is possible to interpret this in various ways: as a result of greater theological reflection that recovers biblical restrictions on women; as a sign that the movement has let slip a significant aspect of ecclesiological renewal; as an ecclesiastical example of the sociological observation that men prefer hierarchies and women prefer networks; or as evidence of the pervasive nature of male oppression that has prevented church planting movements from accomplishing more for the emancipation of women.

Women certainly appear to have played a significant role in first century church planting. Interpretations of Pauline teaching on the role of women in church life, that fail to consider his inclusion of women in his mission teams and warm commendations of them, risk substantially distorting the biblical evidence. The emergence of the Montanist movement a hundred years later is explicable in part as a protest against the subsequent marginalization of women in the mainline churches.[19]

Both the Celtic and Anabaptist church planting movements gave much greater scope for women to exercise leadership roles than the contemporary Roman or Reformation movements. The Celtic movement not only encouraged women and men to work together in mission teams but benefited from wise leadership of several women in their monastic training centers. The names of Hilda at Whitby, Brigid at Kildare, Ita at Kileedy, and Ebba at Coldingham are familiar to historians, but there were many more. Anabaptist churches were sometimes planted and led by women, and there are many accounts of how Anabaptist women under interrogation astonished their captors, both by their biblical knowledge and by their courage.[20]

The annals of cross-cultural church planting are filled with stories of heroic women in pioneering situations, often exercising far greater responsibility and more effective ministries than those in their sending churches who resisted recognition of women as church leaders in any other than cross-cultural mission contexts.[21] In more recent times, Pentecostal church planting has relied heavily on women leaders, despite doctrinal statements within many Pentecostal denominations that would appear to restrict the ministry of women.[22] The emergence of cell churches in many parts of the world would have been impossible without women leaders. Most cell leaders in the largest cell church in the world, Yoido Full Gospel Church in Seoul, are women; and it has been estimated that 99% of China's house churches are led by women.

But the contemporary church planting movement appears to be an exception to this trend. Widespread anecdotal evidence suggests that women are crucially involved in church planting initiatives, that many are highly effective in evangelism, and that in church planting situations many women find greater freedom to exercise leadership roles than in the planting churches of which they were previously members. Accounts of women church planters have begun to appear in print and these comprise some of the more innovative examples of church planting. Some churches that are deeply committed to church planting also encourage women in leadership (Ichthus Christian Fellowship and Kensington temple are well-known examples in London). But most of those leading church planting teams are men.

Most books on church planting are written by men[23] and appear to assume that church planting is done by men. Some contain particularly unenlightened examples of noninclusive language.[24] Denominational and network leaders who advocate church planting and speak at conferences are men.[25] Most of those involved in training and consultancy for church planters are men.

It seems that contemporary church planting depends as heavily as earlier movements on the contributions of women, but that, unlike many of these movements, this has not generally been translated into the recognition of women as leaders. There may be several reasons for this. First, the contemporaneous debate about the ordination of women in the Anglican church may provide an alternative context for exploration of this issue. Second, the social context is such that recognizing women as church leaders may be regarded by some churches as a radical step, but it can hardly be perceived elsewhere as anything more than a belated move by a male-dominated institution. The deployment of women as church planters today has less missiological significance than previously, although it has considerable ecclesiological importance. Third, the unusually ecumenical nature of contemporary church planting, though this has many advantages, has tended to hinder ecclesiological reflection and to ensure that the movement operates within established (male-dominated) parameters.

Is there any reason to anticipate that the contemporary movement might develop in an unusual way for church planting movements with regard to the recognition of women in leadership roles? Whereas previous movements have progressively marginalized women leaders, might the present movement increasingly value women as church planters? Realization of the vital role of women in church planting (albeit not often in leadership) might have this effect, although there are inherent dangers here.

In her research paper on "Women in Church Planting," Rosie Nixson notes a standard feminist observation that "when an idea/concept/task is new, interesting and challenging, men tend to keep it to themselves, but when it becomes mundane, routine, and has lost its original charisma, anyone can do it. When the typewriter was invented, it was a new and complex machine which could only be operated by men. When typing was perceived to be dull and repetitive, it became a woman's job." She comments: "My perception is that church planting has so far been 'owned' by men. If and when it ceases to be the latest thing, will it be fully opened up, or even left, to women?"[26] This issue invites ecclesiological reflection among church planters, who may be grateful for the availability of resources for such reflection in past church planting movements.

Debate will doubtless continue concerning the biblical and theological legitimacy of recognizing women as church leaders. The practice of church planting does not offer fresh insights on this dimension of the discussion, beyond the provision of evidence that in pioneering contexts, where leadership is perceived as mission-oriented rather than pastoral, women have often emerged as effective leaders. It is arguable that the marginalizing of women leaders is a further instance of the distortion that results from a maintenance mentality within church life. But church planting does give opportunity for churches uncertain about this issue to experiment in contexts that are less bound by traditional expectations. As with other such experimental developments, the appointment of women leaders in church plants may in due course result in changing attitudes and roles in the planting churches.

Furthermore, those who reflect on the context within which churches are called to engage in mission (as effective church planters are required to do) may recognize at least two further reasons why gender restrictions on church leadership need to be removed. First, it is widely acknowledged that the popular perception of the church as a sexist institution hinders its witness to a significant segment of society. Some have suggested that women taking part publicly in the church at Corinth risked offending those who might otherwise have become members of the church, and thus hindered the church's mission. But it may be the male-dominated structure and ethos of churches in Britain that offends our contemporaries, and hinders the mission of churches today.

At the least, new churches are needed which will operate differently with regard to this issue, and so be able to incarnate the good news that God has poured out his Spirit on all people, has given his gifts to women and men, and is building a new inclusive community where gender stereotypes and male domination are no longer welcomed. The continuing prevalence of churches which fail to embody this dimension of the gospel will hinder the witness of these new churches, but may not completely destroy their credibility.

Second, mission in a postmodern environment requires careful consideration of media and methodology. Among the diverse fea-

tures of this environment are a number which may encourage
churches to value contributions of women leaders. Networks are replacing hierarchies, and it is recognized that women are often more
comfortable within networks and flexible structures.[27] Spirituality,
rather than doctrine, is the contact point between church and society, and women are seen as having much to offer in this area. Evangelism is increasingly operating through dialogue rather than monologue, in small groups rather than in large auditoria, and this is a
context where women are often more skilled and effective than men.

There are, therefore, some reasons to hope that those who engage in the reflection necessary for effective church planting may
recognize the importance of women exercising leadership. There are
certainly dangers to be avoided: not only the danger identified above
of women being left with church planting once it has ceased to be
fashionable, but the ever-present dangers of gender stereotyping
and evangelistic pragmatism. Identifying features of postmodern culture or the church's mission to this culture as reasons for encouraging women to be church leaders carries such risks. There are more
fundamental theological, biblical, and ethical reasons for action.
There may be other ways of interpreting the features of postmodern
culture that we have highlighted, and other ways the church might
respond to these. But reflection on the context within which church
planting is taking place may at least provide an initial stimulus for
challenging the status quo, and lead on to theological reflection that
is needed for any enduring changes.

(4) Rejection of Clericalism

Church planting frequently raises questions about the meaning
and legitimacy of ordination, and the division of church members
into *clergy* and *laity*. Rediscovery of the priesthood of all believers is
not limited to church planting movements but is a common feature
of such movements. Sometimes this begins pragmatically, as church
plants begin to question the necessity of relying on visiting clerics to
perform certain functions, or as churches find themselves operating
without ordained leaders. Church planters often find themselves exercising responsibility in ways that are not allowed by the denominational polity to which they owe allegiance, and which would not
be winked at in the same way in more established situations.

Not only does church planting provide new opportunities for
women to exercise leadership: nonordained men are also given new

freedoms. Once this new liberty is experienced and accepted by the church plant, there may be resistance to attempts to normalize the situation through the reimposition of clerical leadership for certain functions. Pragmatic solutions may open the door to theological reflection.

Sometimes churches are planted to escape from clericalism. Anabaptist congregations were consciously operating without clerical leadership, not only because they lacked sufficient ordained leaders, but because they discerned in the New Testament a model of church life that depended on all church members exercising ministry. They had heard Martin Luther and other Reformers talking about the priesthood of all believers and were determined to follow through the implications of this revolutionary concept, in ways that the Reformers seemed unwilling to countenance.

Just as institutional development and increasing concern for maintenance results in the marginalizing of women as leaders in second and third generation movements, so clericalism tends to return in due course. Few church planting movements have been able to resist this development, and the decline of a group like the Plymouth Brethren, which has done so, does not commend such resistance (even if the decline is arguably due to other factors). The influence of Brethren ecclesiology on many house church leaders may discourage this movement from quickly reverting to clericalism, but there are indications in some sections of the movement that this development may not be too long postponed.

Church planting, therefore, raises questions about clerical structures and encourages more relaxed attitudes and greater participation in leadership. If the focus of a church planting movement is on numerical growth rather than ecclesiological renewal, these tendencies may be short-lived. The reversion of such movements to familiar clerical patterns may occur too soon for the challenge of an alternative possibility to be felt within other churches. But the persistent rejection (or at least modification) by church planting movements of clericalism, ordination as implying the creation of a separate class of church members, and the hierarchical model of church leadership, may eventually lead to significant changes of perception. This will require the conjunction of various factors, including ecclesiological reflection on this issue among church planters; dissatisfaction with clericalism in existing churches; and a cultural context conducive to the development of a different model of leadership.

There is some evidence that each of these factors is present today, although it is unclear whether, separately or together, they are sufficiently powerful to bring about change to a long-established tradition, buttressed by powerful vested interests. Within a postmodern culture, authority of all kinds is unpopular, and hierarchies are regarded as disempowering and inflexible. Churches may respond to this cultural change in various ways. An inadequate response is uncritically to endorse this attitude toward authority and adapt their leadership structures accordingly. Another equally unhelpful response is to insist on maintaining traditional views of authority, assuming that these views are sacrosanct.

A better response might be to take the opportunity to look afresh at biblical and historical models of leadership through the lens of postmodernity, in an attempt to develop forms of leadership that are both contextually appropriate and theologically undergirded. We may do this, aware of the lens we are using, and not uncritical of this worldview, but open to the possibility that God might be active in this and calling for parallel changes in the churches. What form of leadership is appropriate for communities of resident aliens?

There is also evidence of some ecclesiological reflection among church planters on this issue, especially among Anglican church planters. Nigel Scotland complains that "almost from the moment a church plant is born, the bishop or diocese start looking toward getting leaders ordained."[28] He quotes with approval the comments of Roger Ellis and Roger Mitchell, church planters identified with two of the British house church networks: "Planting and church growth will not be achieved by a church adhering to a professional or elitist approach to ministry and serving God. The concept of clergy and laity (priest and congregation) will need to be discarded from our thinking if we are to move forward."[29]

Arguing both from New Testament research into the role of elders in the early churches, and from contemporary perceptions of the designation "priest" ("to the person in the street it smacks of ecclesiasticism, dogmatism, authoritarianism, irrelevance, humbug and hypocrisy"), Scotland urges the Church of England to allow church planters "freedom to establish new congregations which are informal in style, lay led, without robes, without liturgical requirements of canon law, and which meet on non-church premises."[30]

Other *Recovering the Ground* contributors raise similar concerns. Timothy Royle, in an essay on "Church Planting and Lay Presidency" asks: "Does ordination convey special and mysterious powers to an individual which then enables such a person to change the substance of the elements within the Eucharist and that, without this intervention, the Lord cannot convey his blessing to his people?"

Although Royle does not advocate abandoning the ordained ministry, he does identify problems with current practice that are exacerbated in church planting contexts: "It is always deeply unsatisfactory for a congregation when clergy unrelated to their corporate life appear, perform a ceremony and disappear. This is even more the case where a church plant is involved."[31] David Pytches writes: "On the one hand, the professional and ordained clergy claim a monopoly of many ministries in the life of the church. On the other hand, the laity are led to expect no one but the clergy to fulfill any of the proper ministries of the church. How can we mobilize the church and equip the saints (every believer) for the work of ministry if this traditional role of the clergy continues to be the exclusive model of ministry?"[32]

Included also in this volume is an abridged version of a lecture by Richard Holloway, Bishop of Edinburgh, entitled "Deconstructing the Church's Ministry." This lecture starts with theological principles, considers the "paradigm of structural power," and compares the impact of the present state of cultural transition on the monarchy with its potential impact on the ordained ministry. Holloway calls for ordination to be "demythologized" (rather than abandoned) and welcomes such initiatives as "NSMs [non-stipendiary ministers], locally ordained ministers, the apostolate of the laity." He refers with approval to the writings of Roland Allen, "who believed that each community of Christians should generate its own appropriate ministerial arrangements."[33]

These criticisms of ordained leadership are significant but limited. They are not yet representative of church planters within the Anglican church, many of whom are striving valiantly to assure church leaders that church planting can operate within present structures, and without fundamentally challenging Anglican policies. This is seen as vital if church planting is to receive the official support needed for this practice to become widespread. This is perhaps another example of concern for "how many?" taking precedence over questions about "what kind?" Furthermore, most of these contributors are not ready to abandon ordained ministry in the way suggested by Ellis and Mitchell, and they continue to use the language of "clergy" and "laity." But the appearance of this volume, and the level of dissatisfaction with clerical structures it records, are indicative of the potential impact on Anglican leadership patterns of church planting practice.

Church planting is not the only stimulus to discussion about ordination. The debate about the ordination of women has caused many to reconsider the ordination of men. Financial limitations and shortages of candidates for the ordained ministry in a number of denominations have prompted further thinking on this issue, and some relaxation of attitudes. Advocates of "missionary congregations" have identified "clericalism" as a feature of churches in maintenance mode. Robert Warren calls for a "change in the relationship between the respective roles of clergy and laity" and warns that without this, "decline in church life must inevitably continue."[34]

In *Anyone for Ordination?*[35], contributors from various traditions offer perspectives on this subject. Most endorse the concept of ordination but indicate areas of concern. A more radical critique is provided by Roger Forster, writing from a house church perspective, and Alan Kreider, representing the Anabaptist tradition. The title of Alan Kreider's chapter, "Abolishing the Laity," expresses the concern to recover once more the priesthood of all believers, which so many church planting movements have recovered and then let slip. It indicates also that the underlying issue is the empowerment of church members and the release of ministry from the grip of a special class. Church planting sometimes accomplishes this in practice, even where there is inadequate ecclesiological undergirding for such a shift.

The practice of church planting may be a catalyst for change in a context where, both within the churches and in society, traditional concepts of authority are under review. But the impact of church planting on patterns of church leadership will be greater if those involved in church planting invest energy in ecclesiological reflection. Without this, there is every prospect that the radicalism of first generation churches will wane and that a new clericalism will emerge. The new clergy may be called elders, apostles, or simply by their first names, but the many familiar features of clericalism—hierarchical structures, special roles and responsibilities, and the gradual disempowering of church members—are liable to reappear.

From past church planting movements, and from present experience of church planting, there are important lessons to be learned about church leadership. Appropriate and effective leadership is widely recognized as critical for successful church planting. What is less widely recognized, but of considerable significance, is the opportunity for ecclesiological renewal in the area of leadership, if the patterns of leadership evolving in new churches are allowed to challenge established practices and understandings. Despite the difficulty many have in differentiating between *leadership* and *clergy*,[36] such a distinction is possible and vital. Abolishing clerical concepts and structures does not require abdication of leadership. Indeed, it may release leadership within congregations. It is the conjunction of effective leadership *and* non-clerical leadership in many church planting situations that provokes consideration of the possibility both of abolishing clericalism and releasing leadership.

Finally, in this discussion of leadership, we will consider two further issues which are relevant to many churches but of particular importance in church planting: bi-vocational leadership and leadership training.

Bivocational Leadership

The significance of bivocational leadership for growing churches has been recognized for some time. The church growth movement identifies bi-vocational leaders as one of five main types of church leader, and suggests that they are particularly useful in new initiatives.[37] Church planting is an obvious example, where new churches can be freed from the onerous financial commitment of supporting a full-time leader, but can benefit from the part-time availability of a leader to concentrate on the development of the church and its mission. Church plants have suffered both from overreliance on a full-time leader and from the absence of anyone with time and energy to devote to the venture.

Bivocational leadership is not just a cheap option. There are advantages both for the churches who employ them and for the leaders themselves. Churches with bi-vocational leaders are less likely to become dependent on professional leaders; they are more likely to have a substantial proportion of their members mobilized; and the lure of clericalism is easier to resist. In church plants, the higher than average level of commitment and participation among church members may make a full-time leader seem redundant. A bivocational leader can give enough time to the church to prevent overcommitment from other members, but not so much that participants become passengers. If the role of the bivocational leader is to equip church members for mission and ministry, rather than doing most of this personally, this may be a valuable and liberating form of leadership in a new church.

The advantage for leaders is the possibility of being involved in society as well as in the church. For leaders whose gifts are primarily evangelistic, bivocational leadership offers an attractive alternative to a full-time appointment that reduces their contact with those who are not Christians. But whatever gifts leaders have, bivocational leadership offers opportunities to escape an immersion in church culture that arguably hinders effective teaching, pastoral care, and spiritual leadership, as much as it reduces evangelistic impact.

A perennial problem for full-time church leaders is their seclusion from the world beyond the church, which can lead to several consequences, including an orientation toward maintenance rather than mission; practical if not ideological clericalism; ecclesiocentric attitudes and interests; insensitivity to the context within which most church members live and work; a tendency to multiply church activities and to use centripetal methods of evangelism; and teaching that does not engage with contemporary issues, especially issues in the workplace.

Bivocational leadership does not guarantee that these features will be absent, but it offers some protection to leaders and to churches. It may enable church leaders to be more effective in recognizing that their main responsibility is to equip and sustain church members for ministry, not only or even primarily in church activities, but in daily life and work. It may help with the transition advocated by Margaret Kane as vital for mission in contemporary society, a transition from a perception of the church where church leaders have a crucial ministry, assisted by church members, to a perception of the church where church members have a crucial ministry, assisted by church leaders.[38]

Bivocational leadership has too often been regarded as second class, suitable only for churches unable to afford a "proper" minister, and for leaders lacking the skills to be full-time ministers. Perhaps it is time to reconsider the advantages of such leadership. Church plants which have discovered the value of such arrangements might then be able to resist the temptation to appoint a full-time leader. Growing churches in need of additional staff might opt to appoint further bivocational leaders. This, more than any other strategic decision, might enhance the ability of the church to engage in effective mission.

Leadership Training

Some church planting movements have given little attention to leadership training, and second generation churches have suffered from the consequences of this neglect. The Anabaptist movement took many years to recover from the effects of failing to provide adequate training for congregational leaders. By contrast, the training provided for Celtic church planters was a significant component in the vibrancy of this movement. There are various reasons for neglecting training: the energies of church planting movements are expended in planting churches rather than education; leaders are needed immediately, rather than after a period of training; training agencies may be perceived as belonging to the old ecclesiastical structures, which are now being replaced; and reliance on the Holy Spirit is often seen as preferable to reliance on training programs.

In addition, the rejection of clericalism can be interpreted as negating the validity of training those who exercise leadership in the churches. This interpretation is understandable, and the introduction of leadership training processes runs the risk of reinventing a clerical class, but it is vital that these issues are separated. Anti-clericalism need not result in inadequately trained leaders.

There is increasing awareness in the contemporary church planting movement of the importance of leadership training. Much church planting in the past twenty years has taken place without such training, and this kind of church planting will doubtless continue. But some of the weaknesses of this methodology are becoming apparent. Several training courses have emerged in recent years, mainly in-house programs for particular denominations, networks, or local areas, which have begun to address this area of concern. Among the positive aspects of such training have been its practical and experiential basis, its accessibility and rootedness in local situations, and its provision of training for other than recognized leaders. This broader concept of training is particularly helpful in avoiding a return to clericalism.

However, some of the training provided seems rather narrowly conceived, lacking theological depth and exposure to other ecclesiological and missiological perspectives. This training may be appropriate for basic instruction of those who will be involved in church planting, but unless at least some of those with leadership responsibility are equipped with the tools for theological reflection, the result may be effective cloning rather than creative church planting.

But the kind of training which might provide such tools often appears to be set within institutions oriented toward academic rather than applied theology, and maintenance rather than mission. The ethos of these institutions is often unattractive to those with the vision and gifts for church planting, but whose culture, gender, or educational background are different from others in training. And those who have received theological training in such contexts have frequently felt ill-equipped when confronted with the challenge of church planting. Lesslie Newbigin concludes that "ministerial training as currently conceived is still far too much training for the pastoral care of existing congregations, and far too little oriented toward the missionary calling to claim the whole of public life for Christ and his kingdom."[39]

Some attempts have been made recently to bridge the gap between these models of training.[40] If the strengths and weaknesses of each are recognized, perhaps partnerships between local churches, networks, and training institutions can provide leadership training which will equip church planters with theological insights, spiritual resources, and practical skills to plant churches with solid foundations and the potential for creative reproduction.

It is at this point that we need to recall the discussion in a previous section about the recovery of neglected ministries. Although theological institutions are still primarily concerned to train pastor/teachers, some colleges are now training evangelists and church planters. Creative interaction between such colleges and the church planting movement might enable church planters to draw on the resources of the colleges, and encourage the colleges to embrace a mission framework for leadership training. This may involve the development of further training pathways for those with apostolic and prophetic ministries, many of whom would benefit greatly from theological and contextual training. Resistance to the idea of training apostles and prophets may indicate unhealthy attitudes to such ministries, tending toward superspirituality or reemerging hierarchical thinking.

But, more fundamentally, such interaction might stimulate progress toward the recognition, urged by David Bosch[40] and others, that "mission is the mother of theology." For all church leaders, whatever their specialism, this means that mission is not an additional item on the curriculum but the basis for their entire training. Biblical studies, church history, systematic theology, ethics, philosophy, contextual studies, pastoralia, and all the other elements of theological education fit within this mission context. In a post-Christian society, no other basis for training Christian leaders can be justified. Pastors, teachers, evangelists, church planters are all involved in a missionary enterprise. They need to be trained for mission, not for maintenance.

10. CHURCH PLANTING: MODELS AND METHODS

Church planting literature identifies various models of church planting. If we are to plant the kinds of churches which are needed to incarnate the gospel in contemporary society, we will need to consider these models and ask whether some of them are more likely than others to establish such churches. There are common features in church planting that transcend the model used. Quite similar churches may be planted by very different methods, especially where the expectations of the planting agency dominate the ecclesiological development of the new church. But different models do employ different methods, and these may result in the planting of different kinds of churches.

Since we have argued in previous chapters that many kinds of churches are needed in a complex culture, we will not assume here that one church-planting model will be appropriate in all circumstances. Nor will we attempt to derive models or methods from the New Testament. There are significant lessons to be learned from the ways in which the early Christians planted churches, and various books on church planting have attempted to summarize these, but there are no blueprints.

Attempts to establish biblical precedents frequently do no more than justify preferred models, and sometimes hinder creative engagement with the contemporary context. Different social contexts will need different approaches. Different ecclesiastical structures will employ different methods.[1] Sociological analysis, theological reflection, and prayerful planning will be more effective than attempts to operate within "biblical" straitjackets.

There are many different ways of planting churches, although not quite as many as one might assume from the diverse terminology used. The imagery found in church planting literature is drawn predominantly from horticulture and obstetrics, but there are also nautical, astronomical, and military terms. However, different terms are often used to describe the same model, or the same stage in the process. There is no agreed morphology or standard terminology; those involved in teaching and training work with their own categories and preferred imagery.[2] But, as we examine the strengths and weaknesses of the more popular models, and consider the potential of some less familiar models, the limitations of much contemporary church planting will become increasingly clear.

Church planting models can be categorized in three ways: by reference to the *planting agency*, the *motivation*, or the *result*. The planting agency may be a local church, a pioneer, a mission team, a group of local churches, an evangelistic organization, a house group, or a combination of agencies. The motivation may be evangelistic, logistical, remedial, ecclesiological, expansionist, or a mixture of motives. The result may be a church with multiple congregations, a renewed church, an autonomous church, or a network of semi-independent churches. Categorization using all three referents can enable church planting ventures to be described with greater accuracy than is possible through the use of terms that are familiar in church planting literature.

Our primary concern here, however, is not with precise categorization, but with the identification of those forms of church planting which are liable to contribute most effectively to planting the kinds of churches needed to engage in mission in a post-Christian, postmodern, and pluralistic environment.

The Mother/Daughter Model

The most popular contemporary method of church planting is usually referred to as the mother/daughter model of church planting. The planting agency is a local church, the motivation may include various factors, and the anticipated result is a new church in the locality that will attain at least some degree of autonomy. This model normally involves the selection and commissioning of a sizeable group of church members to become the founding members of the new church. Church planting literature contains many examples of this model, and a wealth of practical advice. Other models are mentioned, and some examples given, but most books and training programs focus predominantly on this model.[3]

This model would not have attained its popularity if it did not have significant strengths and advantages. Our intention is not to dismiss these, nor to suggest that this may not be an appropriate model in many situations. It is a tried and tested model, that has been used by churches in various parts of the country, and with very different structures and resources. The fact that it is popular means that considerable experience has been developed, advice is available from those who have planted not one but several churches in this way, and there are mother churches and daughter churches which can be visited by those who are embarking on a similar venture. There is enough accumulated wisdom here for churches to avoid repeating the mistakes that have caused problems elsewhere— although a depressingly large number of mother/daughter church plants seem oblivious to this.

Critics of church planting sometimes express concern about the risks involved.[4] Mother/daughter church planting is a relatively safe form of church planting. The planting team is normally quite large, often comprising a ready-made congregation, rather than just a core group. The new church usually has ongoing support and supervision from more experienced church leaders in the mother church. Although in time it will be expected to become more self-sufficient, the new church may rely initially on significant financial and administrative backing from the sending church. There is also a fallback position if the venture is unsuccessful: the team can be gathered back into the mother church.

Although any kind of church planting is demanding and challenging for those involved, the mother/daughter model appears feasible to more church members than many other models. It does not generally involve major changes in terms of cultural adaptation, moving homes and jobs, or settling children in new schools, although any of these may be necessary. This model can mobilize a significant number of people. Not only those who are seconded to form the new church, but those who take up new responsibilities in the mother church, those who help to plan the new venture, and those who support it prayerfully and financially can all legitimately claim to have been involved in church planting.

And this form of church planting may have a very positive impact on the planting church. If the process is well managed and the result is encouraging, the morale of the mother church can be significantly affected: its members have become a mission agency, they have given away some of their finest people, and they have risen to the challenge of a demanding initiative. The empty seats that, whenever the church meets, are poignant reminders of those who have gone may also stimulate renewed evangelistic efforts. In addition, the speed with which the membership is replenished over the coming months may surprise and further encourage the church. Those who would not previously have felt able to contribute toward the ministry of the church now discover hidden gifts, once those perceived as more able or experienced have transferred to the new church. Furthermore, if the relationship between the mother and daughter churches remains strong, initiatives taken by the new church may challenge the planting church and lead to ecclesiological and missiological renewal.

There are, however, several significant disadvantages of using this method to plant new churches. It is very labor intensive. Most mother churches can only plant out once, or perhaps twice, without suffering serious strain. It is not only that many church members are given away each time, nor that for the plant to be successful the most able members are needed. But, each time a new church is planted, there is an upheaval in the mother church, various adjustments have to be made, and responsibilities have to be allocated to new people again. There is a limit to the number of times a church can cope with this emotional, psychological, and spiritual upheaval.

Stephen Ibbotson, an experienced English church planter, has warned about the "planting fatigue" that afflicts planting churches if they plant too many daughter churches. This fatigue is a factor even where the church planting is perceived as a positive venture, but the impact on a planting church may not be as positive as the situation described in rather glowing terms above. Some mother churches have been badly damaged by planting a new church. Loss of vision, inertia, feelings of bereavement, disappointment with the new church, strained relationships, and financial pressures can all take a heavy toll. Of all the models of church planting we will consider in this chapter, the mother/daughter model has the greatest capacity to damage planting churches.

One response to this is to ensure that there are substantial periods for recuperation before embarking on a further church plant. But this wise pastoral strategy exacerbates another problem with this model: mother/daughter church planting is a slow process. It tends to involve a great deal of planning and preparation, which cannot be rushed or diminished without risking damage to mother church, daughter church, or both. Most mother/daughter plants involve people who have not been involved in church planting before. Each church starts from scratch, learning from others if it is wise, but needing to take time sharing the vision, training participants and those who will replace them in the mother church, answering questions, reassuring those with fears and doubts, and working through decision-making processes. These processes provide useful safeguards, but they may also require considerable patience from those who are itching to move forward with new initiatives.

We have argued that it is more important to plant the right kinds of churches than to plant churches rapidly, but the predominance of the mother/daughter church planting model ensures relatively slow progress toward any goals that may be set. It will tend to result in reduced levels of church planting as mother churches recover from their initial ventures. There is some evidence already that the first wave of church planting associated with the Challenge 2000 movement has begun to subside, as many of the churches that were in a position to plant daughter churches have done so, and are not yet ready to repeat this.[5]

One way forward would be to encourage daughter churches to plant out again (grand-daughter churches?), so that a reproductive cycle is established, rather than expecting mother churches to continue planting daughter churches indefinitely. Churches that have themselves recently been planted would be familiar with what is required for effective church planting, and the process need not take so long. This was the hope of many as they set goals for church planting in the 1990s, which would require exponential growth in the number of churches planted year after year. But it seems that relatively few daughter churches have been able or willing to rise to this challenge.[6]

A further weakness of this model is its limited strategic awareness. The decision to plant tends to be made by individual local churches, usually but not always after some measure of consultation with other churches in the locality. The location of the church plant is likely to be determined as much by where church members live as by the needs of the wider community, or the mission priorities of a city or region. Such reliance on local church initiatives, rather than national or regional initiatives, may result in the proliferation of churches in certain areas and the neglect of other communities.

A report on church planting in the Church of England Newspaper in 1995[7] commented that many of the Anglican churches which had been planted in recent years had been "in the wrong places." Flourishing suburban churches have the resources and personnel to plant daughter churches, and so increase the number of churches in areas which already have many churches. Churches in rural or urban areas with fewer resources are unable to plant daughter churches in the areas where more churches are desperately needed. Different models of church planting will be needed, both to establish new churches in underchurched areas, and to help churches in well-churched locations with the resources to plant new churches to develop effective church planting strategies.

Many who advocate the use of the mother/daughter model also advise (as we noted in chapter 8) that the planting team should be relatively large. This results in an additional disadvantage: the effective restriction of church planting to larger churches. If church planting is equated with the mother/daughter model, and this model requires a church to commit thirty or more members to this venture, few churches with a membership of less than one hundred will feel able to consider this. Church planting is in danger of becoming a hobby for large churches, rather than a mission strategy for the re-evangelization of the nation. Furthermore, if church planting can only be achieved in this way, many members of smaller churches with a pioneering spirit and suitable gifts for church planting will not be able to participate.

The most serious problem is the danger that the mother/daughter model will result in cloning rather than planting. The factors identified in an earlier chapter that tend to produces clones rather than plants are particularly associated with this model. Where the planting agency is a local church, the resources for ecclesiological reflection are limited, the influence of tradition may be more pervasive than the planting team realizes, and the expectation of the planting church may be that the new church will be "made in its image."

The larger the planting team, and the stronger the links with the mother church (both regarded as positive aspects of mother/daughter planting), the less flexibility and creativity there is likely to be. Although there will be exceptions—where the daughter church is significantly and purposefully different from the mother church—if this model remains dominant within the church planting movement, the ecclesiological creativity required to develop churches with the ethos, focus, shape, and structure necessary to meet the challenges of mission in contemporary society is in danger of being stifled.

There are other models. Our intention in the remainder of this chapter is to examine some of the alternatives, to assess their strengths and weaknesses, and to indicate some of the contexts in which each might be particularly effective. But the fundamental point is the insistence that church planting is not restricted to large and wealthy churches, nor suburban areas, nor the mother/daughter model. Church planting is too important to be so restricted.

Models for Urban Church Planting

During the past thirty years, "urban mission" has received renewed recognition as a vital, but frequently neglected, dimension of the mission of the church. An extensive literature on urban mission now offers theological, biblical, historical, sociological, and biographical studies. Various studies and reports (including the familiar, but still challenging, *Faith in the City*[8]) have noted the long-term alienation of inner city communities from the churches, the failure of past attempts to engage in mission and to plant churches in urban communities, and the continuing marginalization of urban priority areas in the allocation of resources and deployment of personnel by most denominations. These reports led to consultations, reorganization, increased funding for urban ministry, and several new ventures.

But evidence from the English Church Census at the beginning of the Decade of Evangelism confirmed what some had suspected, that inadequate attention had been given to evangelism and ecclesiology,[9] and that many urban[10] churches were still losing ground. Adult churchgoing in England was declining fastest in city centers and inner city areas. The Census did not reveal the true extent of ethnic church planting which had been occurring (since many of these new churches were impossible for those responsible to locate), and which in some urban areas has transformed the face of the church. But it did indicate that many of the good intentions of the previous decade had not been translated into action, and that those which had, had failed to arrest the decline of urban church life. Although there had been explosive growth through the multiplication of Caribbean and African churches, most white, working class communities and many other ethnic communities remain predominantly unchurched.

As urban mission began to slide back down the ecclesiastical agenda, church planting was one of the items which was commanding greater attention. Very few advocates of church planting, however, were also advocates of urban mission. Furthermore, the popular models of church planting seemed to require resources that were unavailable to most urban churches. Church planting might be an interesting hobby for suburban church leaders with time, people, and energy to spare, but it did not seem relevant in contexts where survival rather than reproduction was the main concern.

But church planting is of key importance for mission in urban areas, and urban church planting critical to the church planting movement. The diverse projects and ventures initiated by Christians in urban areas represent arguably some of the finest models of incarnational and kingdom-oriented mission in the United Kingdom. Their wholistic approach, partnership with other agencies, perseverance, and creativity offer rich resources for the wider Christian community to draw on. Church leaders and church planters have much to learn from these unheralded initiatives. But the continuing decline of churches in urban areas and the paucity of church planting in these areas threatens the survival of such ventures.

New churches are needed. Suburban churches transposed into urban areas will not suffice, nor will further attempts to plant the kinds of churches which failed to take root in previous generations. The normal mother/daughter model is inappropriate, both for the available personnel in urban areas and for the creativity needed to establish authentically contextualized urban churches. Cell churches may be needed, although the perception and use of homes in some urban communities may not be compatible with these. Further network churches will almost certainly be crucial if the many subcultures of the urbanized West are to be evangelized.

Churches designed for "the unchurched" will discover whether models developed for cultures where churchgoing is still socially acceptable can be translated into cultures where people have been unchurched for generations (memorably described recently by Bob Mayo[11] as "pre-nonChristian," lacking even the understanding of Christianity not to believe it). New shapes of church life will be needed, but above all, churches with a different ethos, churches which may be perceived by suburban church members as chaotic, raw, unspiritual, immoral, or heretical. Urban mission literature contains numerous examples of creative attempts to plant such churches, which have received lukewarm support or outright condemnation from suburban Christians.

What church planting models and methods might help church planting in urban areas? The three models presented for consideration here are not without their difficulties. They will certainly not guarantee that the kinds of churches needed are in fact established. Nor are they relevant only in an urban context. But they do have features which may make them, individually or in combination, more appropriate than many other models for urban church planting.

(1) Colonization

This church planting model, which is sometimes referred to as the "helicopter" model, is similar structurally to the mother/daughter model. The planting agency is a local church, and the planting team comprises members of this church who are "hived off" (in church planting jargon) to form the core of the new church. The aim is to establish a new church which will not be dependent on the planting church. It differs from the mother/daughter model in that most daughter churches are planted within the vicinity of the planting church, but colonization operates over a greater distance. Colonization enables churches to establish new congregations in quite different communities, tens or even hundreds of miles away.

This model has several important implications. For churches with the capacity to plant another church, colonization presents the challenge and opportunity to target an area which is considerably more underchurched than its immediate locality. Rather than adding another suburban church to the tally, a new church might be planted in a community that is almost devoid of churches.

Suburban churches have for many years grown numerically through the addition of those who were converted in urban areas but have moved out to the suburbs. This drift to the suburbs is a demographic trend in which many Christians have participated, exacerbated by the phenomenon of what sociologists call "redemption and lift": in a society where the church is located predominantly in suburban areas, suburban culture is perceived by new converts from other areas as more "Christian," and many aspire to belong to this culture and the churches which are rooted within it.[12] Colonization is one way of reversing this trend, which has decimated urban churches, by relocating Christians into urban areas.

Colonization demands much of participants. They will need to find new homes, new schools for their children, and possibly also new jobs. They will move away from friends and familiar surroundings, and into a community which is quite different, and which will take time to understand. Their ongoing contact with and the support they receive from the planting (or, perhaps more accurately in this context, "sending") church will be quite limited, not only because of the distance involved, but because the different context will require fresh thinking rather than the adoption of structures and practices from the mother church. Consultation, prayer support, and friendship can continue, but if the leaders of the sending church are wise, they will be sensitive to the contextual differences and will encourage the planting team to develop their own style.

There are several significant risks involved in the use of this model. Will participants be able to adjust to the new context? Will they be sensitive to cultural issues, rather than imposing their cultural norms on the community? Will there be sufficient support for them? To whom will they be accountable? Since the size of the planting team is generally smaller than in mother/daughter church plants, will there be an adequate base on which to build a new church? If it takes longer to establish a new church, will the planting team be prepared to persevere? Do they have the necessary leadership gifts to operate autonomously much sooner than a daughter church would normally?

If the venture does not flourish, what will happen to the members of the planting team? With the mother/daughter model, they can quite easily be drawn back into the mother church, but with colonization this would involve a second major upheaval.

These are weighty concerns and indicate that colonization should not be attempted without careful and realistic consideration. Nor should it be undertaken without very sensitive exploration of the target community. Indeed, even the terminology of colonization is not without problems, with echoes of the colonialism which has often characterized cross-cultural church planting in Africa, Asia and Latin America.[13]

We have retained this terminology, partly because it is familiar in church planting literature, and partly because it expresses well the goal of planting churches in various cultures which are communities of resident aliens, representative of the kingdom of God. But the prospect of well-meaning, but unprepared, suburban church planters descending unannounced and uninvited on an urban community, imposing their own cultural norms and operating independently of other churches and community groups, is not one to relish. Urban communities have suffered long enough from such invasions.

But if new churches are to be planted in many urban communities, resources from other areas will be needed. Existing urban churches do not have the personnel to plant these. Provided certain procedures are established, colonization offers one response.[14] Time will be needed for research, consultation, and preparation: this is not a method for planting lots of churches quickly. Those who participate in such ventures will need the same kind of induction and training that cross-cultural missionaries receive. Rather than relying on the methods advocated by most North American and European church planting manuals, the insights and experiences of cross-cultural church planters will be needed.[15] Above all, the experience and views of urban church members will be regarded as essential.

Colonization, despite its drawbacks and risks, offers the possibility of church planting in areas currently almost untouched by the contemporary church planting movement. It does not guarantee that new kinds of churches will be planted, since participants will bring with them all kinds of assumptions, preferences, and expectations. But there are reasons for hope: the commitment required of participants, the freedom from planting church domination, the awareness that cultural issues will impact ecclesiology, the smaller core team, the enhanced training provided, and interaction and consultation with the local community. These factors may enable church planting colonists to think fresh thoughts about church life, differentiate between gospel and culture, between nonnegotiable and negotiable aspects of ecclesiology, and prayerfully discover new ways of being church in an urban context.

(2) Planting Teams

The dependence of contemporary church planting strategies on the mother/daughter model, and indeed on local churches as the main planting agency, not surprisingly has no parallel in New Testament church planting strategies or other pioneering contexts. For saturation church planting strategies, this model may be appropriate and effective, but in contexts where unchurched communities are involved, there are no local churches to plant further congregations.

In most urban areas there are still some churches, although there are now housing estates and communities of significant size which have no church that is in any way a part of the local community. The parish church is now combined with another parish church, and the resulting "super-parish" is completely unrealistic even for a combined parish staff team to cover. Other churches and mission halls have withdrawn or closed down. But even where there are still churches, few have the energy or resources to engage in church planting. In these contexts, where pioneer planting or replacement planting is required, a different model of church planting will be needed. Colonization is one possible response. The deployment of planting teams is another.

The planting team model has New Testament and other historical precedents, including the Celtic missionary movement explored in chapter 4. Within several denominations, networks, and evangelistic agencies, teams are used for evangelistic initiatives,[16] and there are contemporary examples of church planting teams, the most familiar of these being those used by the Belgian Evangelical Mission.[17] This model may operate in various ways, and our concern here is not to be unduly prescriptive, but to indicate the potential of such a model for the urban context.

We are interested here in teams deployed, not by local churches, but by other agencies. Although a large local church might employ a version of this model, sending out teams to establish new churches in different locations, this scenario is not easy to distinguish from the colonization model. The numbers involved in each team may be fewer than in a typical colonization planting group, but similar comments to those made in the previous section would apply here.

The planting team model has a number of features which differentiate it from this model. First, the planting agency is likely to be an evangelistic organization or mission society. Second, team members will be drawn from various local churches, may continue to receive support of various kinds from these churches, and may report back periodically to them, but they will not be operating under their auspices. They are primarily trained and supervised by, and accountable, to the planting agency. Third, the team is responsible for raising its own financial support, rather than being dependent on outside funding. This may involve some members of the team working to support others who are released to concentrate on evangelism or other aspects of mission. The team might live in community, or operate as a "common purse" group. Fourth, the expectation is that once a church is planted, some or all of the team will move on to plant churches elsewhere.

This model has a number of inherent advantages. It allows for the mobilization of gifted and committed members from a wide range of sending churches, including those who would not otherwise become involved in church planting. The formation of teams drawn from several churches does not weaken these churches as significantly as is true of planting churches using the mother/daughter model. And each team comprises members with diverse experiences of church life, giving the team the potential to draw selectively on different traditions and ecclesiologies. Financial self-sufficiency benefits both the sending churches (who may choose to contribute financially but are not obliged to do this) and the team itself, since financial dependence tends to hinder flexibility.

The anticipation that the team will not comprise indefinitely the core of the new church encourages the development of indigenous leadership. And, if the venture succeeds, the team can move on to plant again, drawing on the lessons learned and experience gained.

Inevitably, there are also risks and drawbacks. First, unless the planting agency provides ongoing training, pastoral support and accountability, team members may tend to become isolated, feel overwhelmed, or develop unhelpful independent attitudes. But if the planting agency is too heavily involved, the team may not feel free to experiment. They may be free from the ecclesiastical traditions of their own churches, but could feel under pressure to plant churches approved by the planting agency.

Second, the selection and integration of team members is critical. Unlike core groups drawn from one church, these teams come from different backgrounds, will need time to be welded into units, and will need to develop a united vision if their energies are not to be dissipated.

Third, the sharing of finances in this way is not without difficulties and may place significant strains on relationships. Drawing on the experience of other kinds of communities may be very helpful here as part of the preparation of such teams.

Fourth, the stronger the team relationships become, the greater the danger that any church planted will consist of the planting team as an inner core, and other people as peripheral members.

Fifth, pioneer teams, like colonization ventures, will need time to adapt to the local context and build relationships in the community.

Some of these risks are inherent in the model itself, but some can be addressed by effective training and careful supervision, or minimized by ensuring that team members are alerted to potential problem areas. Tom Steffen's book, *Passing the Baton: Church Planting that Empowers*, is a helpful resource for planting teams.[18] Once again, this is not a model for planting many churches quickly, at least in the early years, although successful teams may be able to plant further churches more quickly. Unlike the mother/daughter model, where most planting groups start from scratch, planting teams can build on their previous experience of church planting. Provided this does not make them dependent on one model, or insensitive to contextual factors, this is a valuable asset.

The relevance of this model for urban church planting should be obvious. Significant factors include the following: the financial independence of the team, the freedom to develop new forms of church life, the opportunity to select team members with the ability to operate in another culture, the possibility of drawing some team members from urban churches without weakening them unduly, and the concern to develop and empower indigenous leaders.[19]

(3) Planting via Social Action

Much church planting concentrates on the evangelistic dimension of church mission rather than embracing a broader understanding of mission that includes social and community involvement. This may not be a position that derives from a particular theological or missiological stance, although the influence of church growth thinking on church planters is likely to discourage the inclusion of social action, on the grounds that this may hinder evangelism and numerical growth. This proposition is frequently asserted, but does not appear to be as well supported by the evidence as proponents claim. Church growth and social action are often assumed to be incompatible, but this may be a misinterpretation of the evidence.

Kirk Hadaway has investigated this, among several aspects of church growth teaching which he suspects are ill-founded, and concludes: "social activism *per se* does not lead churches to decline. Instead it is the constellation of other characteristics typical of the white, social-activist church which leads to decline. If white congregations could disassociate social activism from its theologically liberal, non-evangelistic, upper-class, intellectual connotations, the negative relationship probably would not exist."[20]

It may simply be, however, that the energy required to establish a new congregation, the absence of suitable premises in which to develop social action projects, and reticence to develop such projects until a congregation is properly functioning, militate against this more wholistic approach. Evangelism and church planting are accorded chronological, rather than ideological, precedence. Indeed, urban churches generally may conclude that evangelism and congregational growth are prerequisites for broader mission strategies and social programs.[21]

Understandable though this tendency is, it may have unhelpful consequences for the growth and balance of the developing church. Once a church has established its priorities, allocated its finances and deployed its personnel, it is less easy to introduce major new initiatives. Social action projects are often seen as just that—projects—which can be bolted on to churches and detached again without affecting the heart of the community or its mission. Social action initiatives that are not integrated into the core vision of the church may have the effect of making extra demands on church members, who are already heavily committed in other ways, demands which do in fact detract from their evangelistic impact or involvement in other aspects of the mission and ministry of the church.

Furthermore, churches that are planted without engaging in social action may find it less easy to convince members of the local community that they are serious about social involvement, after operating for many months or years without expressing any such concern about their neighborhood. "In some Urban Priority Areas the concept of church qua church may simply be too much of a luxury," suggests the report of the Mission Theological Advisory Group.[22]

In urban areas, the dislocation of evangelism and social action, which is equally illegitimate but apparently less crucial in other contexts, significantly impairs the credibility of local churches. Whether in their relationships with individuals and families, or in their engagement with social structures and systems, attempts to proclaim good news without demonstrating good news in practical ways will not endear churches to urban communities. Social action cannot be postponed until the church is established without jeopardizing the ability of the church to gain a hearing in the community.

However, the kinds of social action that are taken, and the attitudes with which the church operates, are also of fundamental importance. Patronizing approaches, programs that are designed for the community rather than in partnership with the community, projects that create dependence rather than empowering people, and initiatives that have strings attached and use social concern as a cover for evangelizing, will damage the witness of the church and ensure that any growth in membership which does occur is offset by the diminution of the church's ability to operate indigenously.

Relatively few church planting ventures have included from the outset significant social action initiatives. Fewer still have regarded social action as fundamental to their success in establishing a local church. One reason for this may be that much church planting has occurred in suburban areas, where social needs and social injustice may be less obvious, rather than in areas of deprivation and powerlessness. But if social action is recognized as an important aspect of the mission of the church, church planters may be willing to explore the possibility of incorporating social action into the initial phases of strategy, rather than leaving this to a later stage. Rather than appointing an evangelist, the new church might employ a community worker. Instead of running seeker services, the church might develop a launderette, a community shop or a community center.

A recent and influential WCC publication that provides a theological rationale for such an approach, together with a simple strategy and several practical examples, is *The Isaiah Vision* by Raymond Fung,[23] then Secretary for Evangelism in the WCC's Commission on Mission and Evangelism. Subtitled *An Ecumenical Strategy for Congregational Evangelism*, this booklet argues for a three-pronged approach to evangelism that includes social action, an invitation to worship, and an invitation to discipleship. The social action will vary enormously from context to context, but will concentrate on achievable aims and working in solidarity with others "of good will" in the community. The worship of the church will be related to its community action, not disconnected from its social context.

Out of the partnership with members of the wider community, opportunities will arise for sharing faith with those who already know church members through shared involvement. Although this booklet is concerned primarily with the development of evangelistic strategies for existing congregations, it is set in the context of a WCC document that affirms that "the multiplication of local congregations in every human community" is "at the heart of Christian mission,"[24] and the approach outlined is equally applicable to church planting situations.

Of fundamental importance to "the Isaiah vision" (which refers to the vision in Isaiah 65:20-23 of a community where children are protected, the elderly are respected and working men and women receive a fair return for their work), and to social action in urban mission, are attitudes which enable churches to avoid the pitfalls of many past initiatives. Urban communities are littered with abandoned mission halls, representing the efforts of a previous generation to engage in church planting via social action. In their heyday, these mission halls were packed with people, drawn by the offer of food, warmth, clothing, and other practical benefits. But rarely did such initiatives aim at or result in the planting of indigenous congregations. This was social action for others rather than with others, social action alongside evangelism rather than integrated into a wholistic mission strategy, social action that created dependence rather than empowering individuals and communities.[25]

But social action that involves solidarity and partnership between the church and the community, that welcomes help with church projects from nonmembers, that participates in social projects without dominating or manipulating these, may lead to very different outcomes. Roy Williamson reflects that in his predominantly urban ministry, "I probably saw more people make the journey from the fringe to the centre of the church family by placing a paint brush rather than a prayer book in their hands. Enlisting their help in a practical project often resulted in their dormant faith becoming alive."[26]

The temptation is to write off church planting via social action as a failed approach and concentrate on establishing churches rather than engaging with social issues. But the failure of the mission hall methodology need not imply that this approach to church planting is invalid, any more than the ineffectiveness of traditional "guest services" should discourage the development of sensitively designed seeker services. The principle may be right, even if some attempts to practice this are rejected. Church planting via social action may be a vital component in urban mission.[27]

There are a limited number of contemporary examples of church planting via social action. None of those I am aware of have been in operation long enough for proper evaluation, but three reports of such ventures have recently been presented to me by students, who have monitored these church plants over an eighteen month period. One has developed from a social action program among homeless people in Colchester, Essex; another employed two community workers rather than evangelists in Tilbury, Essex; a third operated as a community shop in Birmingham and employed a youth and community worker. I know of another venture which aims to plant a congregation as one aspect of a program involving the renovation of a pub and development of a multipurpose community center. It is likely (though not inevitable) that numerical growth in such ventures will be slower than in church plants that concentrate on evangelism, but the long-term impact and rootedness of such initiatives may be greater.

Models for Rural Church Planting

Since my experience of church planting has been entirely within urban communities, it is with considerable caution that I include even a brief section on rural church planting. My intention is not to pretend to expertise that I do not have, but to raise questions about appropriate models for planting churches in rural areas. The rural environment is as diverse and complex as the urban scene, and no one model of church planting will fit every context, but the suburban methodology of mother/daughter church planting may be as inappropriate in many rural contexts as it is in many urban areas.

There appears to be more resistance to the idea of rural church planting than church planting in urban or suburban areas. Are more rural churches really needed? But this reaction may be based on an outdated understanding of the rural scene. There are several reasons why church planting needs to be considered:[28] village communities are expanding as a result of population shifts toward rural areas; those who live in the countryside but commute to work and to shops prefer not to drive to church as well; the church needs a relevant presence in the countryside if it is to connect with the boom in leisure and tourism in these areas; and there are many ready-made buildings waiting to be reclaimed by congregations. But rural church planting faces difficulties.

Graham Licence, in his booklet, *Rural Church Planting?*[29] gives examples of church planting initiatives in rural areas and highlights some of the particular problems faced by rural church planters. Among these are the rural suspicion of strangers; the relatively slow growth often experienced; the difficulty in obtaining premises; the demoralizing effect of Christians travelling to the larger towns to belong to churches there rather than participating in village church plants; and the fact that in many situations there is little prospect of the new church becoming independent from the planting church.

However, the employment of church planting models other than the mother/daughter model, evident in some of the examples given, has the potential to redefine or remove some of these difficulties. If the goal is to plant churches which operate independently and self-sufficiently (the typical suburban mother/daughter scenario), rural church planting is fraught with difficulties and unlikely to succeed in the short term, if ever. But if the goal is to establish communities in rural areas that incarnate the gospel and are rooted in small towns, villages, and hamlets, different criteria will apply and other models will be useful. Very few of the examples given in this booklet can be classified as mother/daughter plants; and it is arguable that this is why they have flourished.

Colonization and planting teams are not likely to be appropriate models in most rural situations, particularly in the "deep country-side."[30] Strategies which depend heavily on newcomers arriving from outside the local context are problematic, in a way that is less true of urban areas. For rural church planting two other models appear to have more to offer.

(1) Satellite Planting

This model of church planting involves a local church planting out groups of church members who operate in a semiautonomous way. It differs from the mother/daughter model in a number of important ways: there is no expectation that the groups will become fully autonomous; the number of people involved in each group can be quite small; and the groups can limit the scope of their activities, rather than attempting to function as omnicompetent congregations.

Structurally, this may initially resemble a church with house groups, but it differs from this in several ways: there is no limit to the numbers who can join each group; the group may choose to meet in a public hall or other venue rather than in a home; there is a greater degree of autonomy than in most church house groups; and the focus of the groups is on mission. The commitment of church members is both to the local group and to the central church, each of which provides what is lacking in the other (a version of the metachurch model).

The advantage of this model for rural church planting is that it can enable churches to establish worshipping and witnessing groups in small communities without having to constitute these as separate churches with full-orbed programs. A church in a town can act as a resource church for several satellite groups in surrounding villages, each of which can adapt to its own local context and develop in ways and at rates which are appropriate. Aspects of church life which require greater resources can be provided centrally, whilst each group can concentrate on dimensions of witness and nurture that are relevant to the local community. Even in quite small villages, there may be enough church members to form a satellite, without the pressure of self-sufficiency. Those who might otherwise choose to travel to a church in a nearby town can benefit from their involvement in a larger congregation, but they can also continue to participate in a local group.

Crucial to the success of such ventures is an ecclesiology that does not insist upon the autonomy of the local church, but is happy to operate indefinitely with a network of interrelated semiautonomous congregations. Satellite planting does occur in some suburban contexts, but often this represents a transitional phase before the new church attains full autonomy. In a rural context, such a transition may be neither feasible nor desirable. Crucial also is the willingness of the central congregation to be a resource rather than a drain on the satellites, recognizing that placing undue demands on the members of satellite churches in terms of their involvement in central activities will hinder the mission of the satellite groups.

This decentralized and empowering model has great potential, but requires a centrifugal rather than centripetal attitude among the leaders of the central congregation.[31] Care must also be taken not to cause damage to existing rural churches, especially those struggling to survive and wary of new ventures that appear to ignore them. Consultation is important in all kinds of church planting, but in rural areas the damage done by failing to consult is likely to be significant and long-lasting.

(2) Planting by Adoption

Church planting by adoption refers to the situation where one local church adopts another struggling church, resources it, and enables it to rebuild and grow. This may require varying degrees of involvement and lead to different outcomes. The adopted church may retain its autonomy but work as partner of the adopting church; it may surrender its autonomy temporarily but then regain this; or it may surrender its autonomy permanently and remain in some way within the adopting church, perhaps functioning as a satellite congregation.

It is arguable that this process is not really church planting, in that the number of churches remains constant or even declines. But in reality, if the process is successful, there is growth rather than decline, and the adopted church may become a new church in all but name. In a rural context, this might mean a larger town church adopting one or more struggling village churches.[32]

Adoption planting may be initiated by a struggling church, which comes to realize that it is no longer able to operate independently. This may be quite evident to others long before the church or its leaders will acknowledge the situation, but churches with an ecclesiology that emphasizes autonomy will be especially hesitant to reach such a conclusion. The initial approach to a neighbor church may be for help with a specific aspect of ministry (for example, preaching, youth work, or music), rather than for adoption. Alternatively, the initiative may come from a larger church that is aware of and concerned for a struggling neighbor. Their approach may be prompted by a mission concern for the local area, or by a pastoral concern for the members of the struggling church. A third possibility is of a strategic denominational initiative being taken. Rationalization or streamlining of parish structures has been occurring among Anglicans for many years, combining congregations in what sometimes amount to adoptions.

Many of these situations are retrenchments rather than initiatives designed for growth. But there is potential for such initiatives to be taken with a view to mission and growth. Church planting by adoption through combining the available resources may be a viable alternative to spreading these resources more thinly and developing a new church plant. This may involve some form of planting team methodology, drawing members from several local churches, not to plant a new church as may often be appropriate in an urban context, but to resource a struggling church.

This model is fraught with potential difficulties. There may be various reasons why the church has declined which will impede progress even if it is adopted. These include unsuitable premises, which are poorly located, poorly maintained, inappropriate in size and style for their context; internal problems such as introversion, traditionalism, inflexibility, disunity, and cultural distance from the community; the reputation of the church in the community and the fact that an adoptive plant does not benefit from the "newness" factor that often attracts people to church plants; the difficulty of ensuring compatibility of vision and values between the churches; and the time that may be required to build trust, develop relationships, and clarify plans.

Planting by adoption risks investing people and time in a venture that may come to nothing. If a larger church attempts to take the initiative to adopt another church, there are likely to be serious reservations on the part of the smaller church, unless there is substantial trust between the churches. Fears of imperialism and being "taken over" may stymie the venture, whatever terminology is used. Even offers of help may be perceived as threatening.

However, there are some potential advantages: the availability of local knowledge and networking; the availability of premises which many church plants lack; the availability of financial resources (often limited, but sometimes substantial); and the availability of church members, who may be well respected in the local community, who have a commitment to the church and a desire to see it flourish. In suburban areas these advantages may not seem adequate, but in a rural context, they may be sufficient to outweigh the problems.

Great care will be needed in assessing the situation[33] if attempts to plant by adoption are to avoid the many possible pitfalls, and church planters will be needed with rather different temperaments and gifts than in pioneering situations.[34] But in communities which are suspicious of outsiders and innovations, church planting by adoption (where outsiders are at least working with local people) may be preferable to models which involve breaking with tradition or introducing new structures.

Strategic Church Planting

Whatever the merits and limitations of the above models for church planting in areas where mother/daughter planting seems less effective, approaches to church planting are needed which will enable mission to advance strategically rather than haphazardly. The development of strategic church planting may involve several stages.

Consultative church planting. A distinctive feature of contemporary church planting is the attention given to research and consultation. Congregational audits, community surveys, and discussions with local church leaders often precede decisions to establish new congregations. Although some local churches act precipitately and independently and disregard concerns expressed by others, much church planting today is based on careful planning and is consultative rather than competitive.

Where the mother/daughter model is used, this may mean that the location of the new church is chosen with reference both to where members of the planting group live and to where other local churches are not actively involved in evangelism. This model, as we have seen, may not be effective for planting churches in urban or rural communities which are significantly underchurched, but it may enable churches to be established in underchurched pockets of otherwise well-churched areas.

Cooperative church planting. Research and consultation enables local churches to act responsibly and to deploy their resources effectively. On occasions, consultation leads to cooperation, as other local churches commit personnel or resources to this venture. If the motivation is not sectarian but missionary, local churches can work together to plant churches in their town or borough. The level of consultation and cooperation in contemporary church planting is unusual by comparison with past church planting movements, and is very welcome.

However, church planting that depends on initiatives taken by local churches, with or without consultation, will be limited in its strategic awareness. Some of the gaps may be filled in otherwise well-churched areas of the country, but success in such ventures may increase the imbalance between these areas and those which are substantially less churched.

Beyond consultative or cooperative church planting lies *collaborative church planting*. Although the role of local churches will continue to be crucial, church planting need not rely solely on local church initiatives. If personnel and resources are to be deployed effectively, and if the church planting movement is to break out of its suburban heartland, a more strategic approach is needed. The church planting needed in rural and urban areas will not be achieved by individual churches operating independently. The disparity between different parts of the same city in terms of mission resources will be redressed only by collaboration and citywide initiatives. Opportunities to plant new churches in major new housing developments will be missed, unless joint initiatives are planned and implemented, involving local churches and mission agencies.

Consultative and cooperative church planting is strongly advocated by the DAWN strategy. Its "10 Principles for Responsible

Church Planting"[35] (referred to in chapter 4) encourage mutual respect, sensitivity to the impact of church planting on existing churches, the sharing of resources, the prioritizing of unreached communities, the development of teamwork, and the importance of reconciliation if conflicts arise. There are also indications in these principles that collaborative church planting may be possible. The final principles commend partnerships between local churches and parachurch organizations, and common planning.

What is envisaged by the concept of collaborative church planting is that local church leaders, denominational or regional church leaders, and representatives of mission agencies will meet together to consider the needs and opportunities of their region or city. Their task is the identification of underchurched communities (geographical and cultural); the selection of appropriate models and methods to respond to the challenge of planting churches in these communities; the discovery and calling of the personnel and resources available; and the development of a strategic initiative which is owned by participating agencies. Such a strategic initiative can also identify struggling churches. Working to renew and revive these churches may diminish the need for church planting in the future.

This kind of collaboration is demanding, but many church leaders have experiences of working together regionally in connection with large-scale evangelistic initiatives. The levels of trust and friendships developed during these initiatives have transcended denominational differences and parochial attitudes, and there has sometimes been a sense of loss once the initiative has ended. Working together in mission has broken through ecclesiastical barriers and focused attention on fundamental areas of agreement. Might it not be possible to draw on these experiences and memories, to recapture this level of partnership in mission, and to develop collaborative church planting strategies?

It is important to differentiate collaborative church planting from *ecumenical church planting*. Various attempts have been made in different parts of the country to plant ecumenical churches, with support from a number of denominations. Although there are occasional exceptions,[36] these have generally struggled and have sometimes failed quite spectacularly. Certainly concern to work together and not to proliferate denominational division in underchurched or unchurched communities is laudable. But experience suggests that planting ecumenical churches or establishing Local Ecumenical Projects is fraught with difficulties and may not be worth pursuing except in unusual circumstances.

George Lings notes the suggestion in the Anglican report, *Breaking New Ground*, that ecumenical planting should be "encouraged from the start wherever possible." He recognizes, however, that the priorities of ecumenists and church planters are rather different and that "local planting activists have seen ecumenical involvement as another layer of bureaucratic administration without sufficient gains to justify it."[37]

In his seminar at the Challenge 2000 congress at Nottingham in March 1995, Rob Frost presented a devastating critique of ecumenical church planting, drawing on extensive research into LEP's, and with particular reference to attempts to plant ecumenically in Milton Keynes, a new town in central England. His research underlined issues familiar to those who have been involved in or observers of such initiatives: a focus on ecumenism at the expense of mission; unwieldy consultation processes; the faltering of ecumenical attitudes when general statements have to be translated into practical decisions; the lack of enthusiasm within the target community for an ecumenical church. Ecumenical church planting appears to be fatally weakened in most situations by cumbersome bureaucracy, the absence of an agreed ecclesiology, wearisome internal negotiations, and consequent loss of vision for mission.

But collaborative church planting allows participating agencies to develop initiatives in partnership with one another, sharing resources and ideas, contributing toward a common vision, without having to endorse every detail of each other's theology and ecclesiology. Collaborative church planting concentrates on strategic rather than tactical issues, leaving participating agencies to work out the details within an overall mission framework. As new churches are planted, lessons can be learned and shared, questions asked, methods refined. If strong relationships are forged, and if planting rather than cloning is encouraged, such partnerships are likely to result in animated ecclesiological and missiological discussions, but church planting initiatives need not wait until these are concluded.

Effective collaboration in church planting may result in more substantial progress toward unity among participating churches than decades of ecumenical dialogue, or desperate attempts to create ecumenical churches, which frequently fudge issues rather than resolve them and place severe strains on relationships. This pragmatic, grass-roots "ecumenism" may not appeal to ecumenists hoping for official partnerships and structural integration, but it relocates ecumenism in the mission context out of which it emerged.[38] There is growing evidence that we are moving into a postdenominational era.[39] Collaborative and strategic church planting initiatives may accelerate this process and provide helpful models of united witness and sharing resources in this new context.

Collaborative church planting is vital if new churches are to be planted in the urban and rural areas where these are most needed. Strategic planning for a city or region enables "mission priority areas" to be identified and appropriate resources to be allocated. If church planting is left to local churches, these priority areas will continue largely to be neglected.

There are already some examples of attempts to collaborate in church planting, some within denominations and some across denominations. Church planting has been undertaken by Anglicans through diocesan initiatives and by Baptists through association initiatives. The DAWN acronym can be translated as "Disciple a Whole Neighborhood" as well as "Disciple a Whole Nation." Under this banner, church leaders from different denominations have gathered to share research on their region or city, to reflect on recent initiatives and to plan for future church planting.[40] Some of these initiatives have faltered, but others have begun to see encouraging results. If they are to proliferate and achieve their potential, important sociological, missiological, and ecclesiological questions will need to be considered.

One concern is that multidimensional strategies should be developed, rather than strategies that operate only in relation to parishes or territorial divisions. Collaborative church planting in a region or city may not simply be a way of helping neighborhood churches to plant more neighborhood churches, through sharing research and resources. Research will be needed into networks as well as neighborhoods, with a view to developing initiatives that will connect with people in their various networks of relationships, rather than assuming that they will be evangelized and nurtured exclusively through churches near their homes.

The WCC report, *The Church for Others*, advocates the recognition of "zones" and regards the development of "zonal structures" as crucial if the church is to fulfill its mission in contemporary society. The report gives two reasons for this:

"First, social life takes place in a much larger territorial area than the normal 'parish' and this increase in scale requires churches to see their work in a larger context. Places of work, leisure and education may be some distance away from places of residence. The various spheres of social living may be geographically dispersed throughout a wide zone, regardless of civil or ecclesiastical boundaries. Second, people belong to many different social groups and so play many different roles. This social differentiation requires the churches to work within a variety of strategic social groupings by means of appropriate functional structures. Church organization based on zones, much wider than the parish, can be the means of establishing such structures."[41]

The important point to note is that these "zones" are multidimensional. The issue is not simply whether evangelism and church planting strategies should be developed at parish or diocesan level (for Anglicans), at congregational or association level (for Baptists), or at local church or circuit levels (for Methodists). Nor is it just a question of achieving interdenominational cooperation in planting new neighborhood churches in a region. Important though these developments may be, mission strategies are also required that will develop various structures—including neighborhood churches, but including also work-based groups, network fellowships, and issue-based groups—to reach and disciple people throughout the zone in which they live.

Many examples of the kinds of structures and groups required already exist: student Christian unions, Christian business fellowships, youth projects, social action ventures, and many more. What is required for a zonal or multidimensional approach is the recognition that such structures are ecclesiologically valid and missiologically potent, and the development of integrated mission strategies that result in the growth and multiplication of these groups, as well as neighborhood churches.

Such groups have too often been perceived as competing with neighborhood churches for the loyalty of church members, regarded as ancillary to the neighborhood church, or dismissed as illegitimate because of a restrictive and onedimensional ecclesiology. To achieve such a zonal strategy, zonal research will be needed that does not concentrate only on territorial divisions, but interprets the community in terms of networks of relationships.

A concern of those advocating the development of missionary

256 • Church Planting

congregations is that Christians are not restricted to internal church issues but embrace "whole life Christianity."[42] Although reorientation of neighborhood churches may help with this, such a transition is unlikely unless structures are developed to enable Christians to grapple with "whole life" issues elsewhere than in neighborhood churches. If network and neighborhood structures can be understood within a zonal strategy, rather than being perceived as competing for the limited time and resources of their members, a symbiotic relationship might develop which could significantly benefit both and enable more effective missionary engagement with a complex society. Among many possible implications of such a strategy might be the streamlining of church programs, dramatically reducing the number of activities and programs operating in the neighborhood church, to release church members to engage in mission through various network groups. The role of local church leaders would then no longer be to enlist the support of church members for items on their church agenda. Instead, church leaders may recover their commission to "prepare God's people for works of service."[43]

Some of the ecclesiological issues raised in earlier chapters are relevant here. First, the often neglected or domesticated ministries of apostles and prophets will need to be recovered and set firmly within a mission framework. Men and women will be needed with insight, strategic ability, and broad vision to help collaborative church planting. Skilled translocal leadership will be needed.

Second, the unhelpful division between "church" and "parachurch" will need to be abandoned in favor of a more dynamic ecclesiology that recognizes that "where two or three come together in my name, there am I with them."[44] Neighborhood churches, mission agencies, evangelistic organizations, network groups, and other expressions of the church-in-mission will all be needed, if strategic approaches are to be developed that will enable a postmodern and post-Christian society to be penetrated by diverse communities incarnating the gospel creatively and contextually. No one planting agency or church planting model will accomplish this, but collaboration might make it feasible.

Third, this strategic and multidimensional approach provides a healthy environment for homogeneous churches. Diverse homogeneous groups can be planted to engage in mission throughout the region, developing structures and strategies appropriate to their target communities. But these do not function independently or in isolation. Through strategic collaboration, heterogeneous celebration, sharing resources, and above all through the development of respect and friendship, these groups can be incorporated into a multi-faceted, multilingual, multicultural, intergenerational community.

There is no one right way to plant churches. Different contexts will require different approaches. But the development of church planting strategies that can employ a range of models to impact entire communities in diverse ways may be crucial.

11. CHURCH PLANTING: BEYOND 2000

*T*here are many reasons not to plant churches today. There are many kinds of churches not to plant. There are many ways not to plant these churches.

This does not mean that church planting is unnecessary or ill-advised, but that we need to give careful thought to various issues if church planting is to fulfill its potential. It may be that the final years of a millennium and the first years of the new one are not always conducive to the reflection necessary for church planting to develop in the ways suggested in this book. The recent emphasis on planting many new churches was in line with the rather frantic mood that characterizes the closing years of most centuries and understandably was exacerbated by the approaching new millennium. This mood was designated as "premillennial tension." Perhaps the missiological and ecclesiological reflection we have been advocating will need to wait until the twenty-first century is further advanced.

It will become evident that the Decade of Evangelism has not accomplished the reevangelization of Western society, or resulted in massive church growth. It will also be clear that we have not planted anywhere near the number of new churches envisaged by the goals endorsed by some church planting advocates. We will face some important choices at that point. Do we pretend we have achieved more than we really have? Do we lose heart and turn inward once again? Do we declare another Decade of Evangelism? Or a Century of Evangelism? Do we extend the time frame for reaching our church planting targets? Do we discard church planting as a failed strategy? Or do we learn from our experiences in the 1990s? Perhaps we will discover that the significance of the Decade cannot be measured by the number of new Christians or new churches, but by the new perspectives gained on evangelism and church planting.

This could so easily become a face-saving exercise. Churches which run mission weeks that fail to live up to expectations are prone to conclude that, although nobody was converted, the church learned a lot. But this learning was not what they were working and praying for. Nor is it what many have been hoping, working, and praying for during the Decade of Evangelism. Integrity requires us to own up when goals are not reached. Perhaps we set unrealistic targets. Perhaps they were realistic, but we made mistakes or fell short of the commitment required. Honest assessment of the 1990s will be crucial if we are to have a firm foundation for future strategy and action.

The Decade of Evangelism will have achieved some significant results. A paradigm shift will have taken place in our understanding and practice of evangelism. We have noted in earlier chapters some features of this "new evangelism": it is relational, contextual, humble, patient, and wholistic. John Finney summarizes the main features of this new understanding of evangelism: "[it] goes where people are and listens, binds together prayer and truth, celebrates the goodness and complexity of life as well as judging the sinfulness of evil, and sees truth as something to be done and experienced as well as to be intellectually believed. It walks in humility."[1] Not everyone will be happy with this shift, and it is not without its dangers, but we are unlikely to see a widespread return to evangelistic practices that rely heavily on dogmatic proclamation, mass events, and cold contact with strangers.

A shift will also have taken place in relation to church planting. No longer will this be regarded as an esoteric practice, indulged in by separatist groups and on the periphery of church life. Church planting will have been widely accepted as a normal feature of church life and mission. New models of Christian community will have emerged. Much experience will have been gained in planting new churches. Some of the foundations will have been laid for mission in the twenty-first century.

Nevertheless, this will be a critical period for church planting. Disillusionment, disorientation, and weariness—"postmillennial depression"—may rob us of the gains made and hinder us from building on these foundations. Church planting may begin to slip down the agenda and be consigned to history once again as other strategies and priorities are adopted. Alternatively, post-2000, released from the pressure of time constraints and able to draw on the experiences of the previous decade, church planting could develop into a significant component in the renewal of church life and the continuing mission of the churches. Long term strategies could emerge. Church planting could enter into a new and very creative phase.

Post-2000? We have encountered many varieties of "post-" words in previous chapters: postmodernity, post-Christendom, post-evangelical, post-charismatic, postdenominational. Such terminology is evident in many areas of contemporary culture: post-Marxist, poststructuralist, postfeminist, postindustrial, etc. As we noted in our brief discussion of the most far-reaching of these terms—postmodernity—the prefix "post" denotes change rather than indicating much about content. We live in an era of flux, where past certainties are being questioned, past structures overturned and past answers re-examined. There is no way to know how much will survive, what new features will gain acceptance, or how stable this new worldview will be.

Church planting is not the only response we can make in this exciting but unsettling environment. The renewal of existing churches and their transformation into missionary congregations is also vital. But in a time of rapid change, will churches be able to adapt quickly enough without the stimulus of church planting? John Drane warns that in the past, "it was possible for the Church to catch up gradually with the culture in which it had to minister. Today, that is no longer possible. Any institution that is not on the cutting edge of change is soon going to find itself cast on one side as irrelevant."[2]

Church planting offers the church opportunities to be on this cutting edge, to engage creatively with a changing culture, discovering what can be affirmed and what must be challenged, neither locked into past patterns nor deferring uncritically to new and possibly short-lived trends. For mission beyond 2000, the number of churches planted in the 1990s may not be as important as the kinds of churches which have been planted, and the foundations which were laid for a church planting movement which will continue to challenge and renew churches in the new millennium.

APPENDIX:
10 *DAWN* PRINCIPLES FOR RESPONSIBLE CHURCH PLANTING

1. **Responsible Pluralism**: A given area may have more than one group ministering in it.

2. **Mutual Respect**: A participating body considering the possibility of entering a locality where there are existing churches will consult with representatives of those churches with an attitude of respect.

3. **Proximity and Density**: When a group considers entering a locality, it will evaluate and minimize any possible adverse effects due to proximity to an existing group. A dense population may reasonably allow different groups to be closer together than in sparsely populated areas.

4. **Unity with Diversity**: There is an intrinsic unity of the Holy Spirit in the Body of Christ. There is legitimacy for diverse structural and doctrinal distinctives within the churches/ denominations/groups that cooperate together.

5. **Team Spirit and Fellowship**: Workers from different participating bodies working in a given locality are encouraged to arrange for communication and fellowship, to create a team spirit.

6. **Sharing Resources**: Each participating body in an area is encouraged to make their resources available to support evangelistic and church planting efforts.

7. **Reaching the Unreached**: Participating bodies are encouraged to give priority to areas or groups where there is no resident gospel witness or church.

8. **Reconciliation**: Every effort should be made to resolve conflicts between participating bodies consistent with Matthew 18:15-17 and 1 Corinthians 6:1-8.

9. **Church/Parachurch Relationship**: The centrality of local church life is emphasized, and the supportive ministry of parachurch

organizations recognized. Consultation between the two groups is encouraged.

10. **Common Planning**: Common planning amongst participating bodies should be done periodically, and each group's plans shared.

Notes

Introduction

1. 2 Corinthians 3:6, 9-11.
2. Although some of what follows may be applicable to non-Western contexts, this book is concerned primarily with church planting in Western societies. It draws inevitably on my own awareness of the British scene but attempts also to engage with issues in other European and North American contexts.

Chapter 1

1. These are listed in the Select Bibliography.
2. The findings of the Census are reported and analyzed in Peter Brierley, "Christian" England (London: MARC Europe, 1991).
3. The Census revealed that 28,000 adults and 19,000 children stopped attending churches *every year* between 1975 and 1989, and that membership of English churches had declined by 3% between 1979 and 1989. Throughout the UK, 3100 churches closed (six each week during the 1980s), while 3000 were opened.
4. A brief account of the emergence of "Christendom," a summary of its most significant features and consideration of the implications for mission of operating in a post-Christian society will be included in chapter 5.
5. Evidence for this is presented by Robin Gill in *The Myth of the Empty Church* (London: SPCK, 1993). We will return to this issue in chapter 8.
6. Evidence from research that updates the figures to 1994 suggests that, although the rate of decline has slowed, decline is continuing. A mid-decade report on the Decade of Evangelism in Britain acknowledges this situation and indicates some positive signs but concludes that the churches continue to face a major challenge if the trend of decline is to be reversed. See Robert Warren, *Signs of Life* (London: Church House, 1996), pp. 44-47.
7. This phenomenon has been helpfully explored in Grace Davie, *Religion in Britain since 1945* (Oxford, UK: Blackwell, 1994).
8. John Finney, *Recovering the Past* (London: Darton, Longman & Todd, 1996), p. 38.
9. Peter Wagner, *Church Planting for a Greater Harvest* (Ventura, Calif.: Regal, 1990), p. 25.
10. A more detailed examination of this form of church planting appears in chapter 10.
11. Alex Welby has written a booklet entitled *Replanting* (Self-published, 1992) that explores the challenges involved and the skills required of "replanters."
12. This issue is explored in greater detail in chapter 10.
13. *Breaking New Ground* (London: Church House, 1994).

14. An interesting survey of British Baptist church plants identifies these factors in their growth; see Derek Allen, *Planted to Grow* (Didcot, UK: Baptist Union, 1994).

15. See chapter 6.

16. See chapter 9.

17. Church plants seem to attract a disproportionate number of people with complex pastoral and social needs, who can be very time-consuming and emotionally draining. Sensitive strategies are needed to respond with integrity to these people but also to prevent them becoming the focus of the venture.

18. Peter Nodding, *Local Church Planting* (London: Marshall Pickering, 1994) p. ix.

19. David Bosch, *Transforming Mission* (Maryknoll, N.Y.: Orbis, 1991), p. 332.

20. See, for example, Charles Chaney, *Church Planting at the End of the Twentieth Century* (Wheaton: Tyndale House, 1986), p. 64.

21. This issue is revisited in chapter 10.

Chapter 2

1. David Bosch chronicles the emergence of this concept during the past sixty years, its implications for missiology and the different ways in which it has been used (Bosch, *Transforming*, pp. 389-393). Some have questioned whether this phrase adds anything substantial to missiology. Latin phrases may be pretentious rather than illuminating. Certainly the phrase *plantatio ecclesiae* does not seem to convey anything beyond its English translation as "church planting." But in the case of *missio Dei*, this phrase does seem to have been a catalyst for renewed reflection among missiologists and the emergence of some important emphases.

2. Acts 3:21.

3. Hans Hoekendijk, *The Church Inside Out* (London: SCM, 1967), pp. 38-39.

4. Robert Warren, *Building Missionary Congregations* (London: Church House, 1995), p. 26.

5. Although the terms *mission* and *evangelism* are often used interchangeably within churches, missiologists prefer to differentiate them. However, there is ongoing debate as to the relationship between these concepts, whether evangelism is the primary dimension of mission, how other aspects of mission relate to evangelism, and how the further term *evangelization* relates to both. A recent helpful definition of these three terms appears in a paper written by Donald Elliott and comprising the appendix to Warren, *Signs*, pp. 90-91.

6. Systematic coverage of a community by individuals listening and praying as they walk the streets, as advocated in Graham Kendrick and Steve Hawthorn, *Awakening Our Cities for God: A Guide to Prayer-Walking* (Milton Keynes: Word, 1993).

7. 1 Corinthians 3:5-9 uses this terminology in the context of church planting.

8. Practical reasons and biblical examples are helpfully summarized in

David Shenk and Ervin Stutzman, *Creating Communities of the Kingdom* (Scottdale: Herald Press, 1988).
    9. Hebrews 1:1-3.
    10. Luke 4:18-19.
    11. John 20:21.
    12. Warren, *Building*, pp. 28-29.
    13. A very helpful document which is both theologically responsible and designed for use in churches is the "Kingdom Manifesto," written in New Zealand. This comprises Appendix 1 in Brian Hathaway, *Beyond Renewal* (Milton Keynes, UK: Word, 1990).
    14. For example, Martin Robinson, "Church Planting and the Kingdom of God" in Martin Robinson and Stuart Christine, *Planting Tomorrow's Churches Today* (Tunbridge Wells, UK: Monarch, 1992), pp. 15-33; and the chapter entitled "The Gospel of the Kingdom" in Roger Ellis and Roger Mitchell, *Radical Church Planting* (Cambridge, UK: Crossway, 1992), pp. 13-27.
    15. Indeed, the use of "kingdom" terminology often obscures more than it clarifies. The term *kingdom* often seems to mean no more than "Christian," or the way a particular author or speaker thinks Christians should act. The fact that there are within the churches many different understandings of the term kingdom makes this a particularly inane and unhelpful use of language. Furthermore the imperial connotations of such language, and its past abuse, have caused some to question whether it is appropriate or helpful in contemporary culture. Perhaps it is possible to find alternative ways of talking about this crucial biblical theme, following the example of those New Testament writers who used other language ("the age to come," "eternal life," etc.) to interpret this Jewish concept into a Gentile culture. I have retained the familiar terminology here but I am not unaware of the problems.
    16. Robinson and Christine, *Planting*, pp. 25-26.
    17. Finney, *Recovering*, pp. 66-71.
    18. See, for example, Matthew 21:43; Luke 12:32.
    19. Matthew 16:19.
    20. Matthew 23:23-24.
    21. Wilbert Shenk, ed., *The Transfiguration of Mission* (Scottdale, Pa.: Herald Press, 1993), p. 100.
    22. Mortimer Arias, *Announcing the Reign of God* (Philadelphia: Fortress Press, 1984), p. 93.
    23. David Bosch, *Witness to the World* (London: Marshalls, 1980), p. 133.
    24. Bosch, *Transforming*, p. 332.
    25. Ibid, p. 499.
    26. Timothy Yates, *Christian Mission in the Twentieth Century* (Cambridge, UK: CUP, 1994), p. 127.
    27. Edward Dayton and David Fraser, *Planning Strategies for World Evangelization* (Grand Rapids: Eerdmans, 1980), p. 59.
    28. Carl Braaten, *The Flaming Centre* (Philadelphia: Fortress, 1977), p. 55.
    29. Gerrit Berkouwer, *The Church* (Grand Rapids: Eerdmans, 1976), p. 391.
    30. Orlando Costas, *The Church and Its Mission* (Wheaton: Tyndale, 1974), p. 8.
    31. J. D. Douglas, *Let the Earth hear His Voice* (Minneapolis: World Wide Publications, 1975), p. 3.

32. J. D. Douglas, *Proclaim Christ Until He Comes* (Minneapolis: World Wide Publications, 1990), p. 34.

33. Ibid.

34. Douglas, *Proclaim,* p. 33.

35. This theme reappears in one of the closing addresses by Thomas Wang, the Congress Director, who calls for strategies to "plant vibrant, multiplying churches" in the twelve thousand unreached people groups in the world, "so indigenous churches within each people group can evangelize their own people" (Douglas, *Proclaim,* p. 358).

36. Lesslie Newbigin, *The Open Secret* (London: SPCK, 1978), p. 1.

37. Quoted in Warren, *Building,* p. 3.

38. *Mission and Evangelism: An Ecumenical Affirmation* (Geneva: WCC, 1983) par. 25.

39. A helpful perspective from a working group report of the World Council of Churches, *The Church for Others* (Geneva: WCC, 1967), p. 26, referred to in greater detail in a later chapter.

40. We return to this issue in chapter 7.

41. Ramachandra, Vinoth, *The Recovery of Mission* (Carlisle, UK: Paternoster, 1996).

42. Robinson and Christine, *Planting,* p. 126.

43. Douglas, *Let the Earth,* pp. 331-333. See also Howard Snyder, *The Community of the King* (Downers Grove: IVP, 1977), p. 123.

44. Ellis and Mitchell, *Radical,* p. 73.

45. This may not involve the planting of an entirely new church. The renewal of an existing church, through the replanting or adoption models referred to in chapter 1, can sometimes be so radical as to constitute, in effect, the planting of a new church.

46. Robert Warren, *Being Human, Being Church* (London: Marshall Pickering, 1995), p. 20.

47. This movement is considered in more detail in chapter 5.

Chapter 3

1. This is not because the Old Testament is irrelevant to the development of a biblical framework for church planting, but because the Old Testament primarily offers perspectives on the mission of God, which is the overarching framework within which church planting should be set. There are already many helpful accounts of these perspectives, to which we can add nothing significant within the scope of the present discussion. See, for example, Robert Martin-Achard, *A Light to the Nations* (London: Oliver & Boyd, 1962); George Peters, *A Biblical Theology of Mission* (Chicago: Moody Press, 1972), pp. 83-130; Donald Senior and Carroll Stuhlmueller, *The Biblical Foundations for Mission* (London: SCM, 1983), pp. 9-138. The Old Testament does not provide models or perspectives that are specifically applicable to church planting, despite some attempts to discover these. See, for example, David Dunn Wilson, "Colonies of the Kingdom: A Biblical Image of Church Planting" in *Epworth Review* 23, no 1 (January 1995): 42-48.

2. It is easy to slip from legitimate conclusions drawn from biblical teaching to illegitimate applications. Martin Robinson, in a helpful discussion setting church planting in the context of the mission of God (Robinson and Christine, *Planting*, p. 22), emphasizes the importance of the planting of Gentile churches in the progress of this mission. He rightly concludes, "The establishing of churches among the Gentiles is, therefore, an inseparable part of the plan and purpose of God for his world." But his application in the following sentence— "church planting is not an optional extra for Christians, it is an intrinsic expression of the redemptive action of God in his world"—is at least open to being interpreted as meaning that all Christians at all times should be involved in church planting. This does not take into account the very different contexts in which Christians live and witness. Some may legitimately regard active involvement in church planting as essential; others may endorse the conclusion that church planting is essential in a global sense but conclude that it is inappropriate locally. For them it *is* an optional extra.

3. Matthew 28:19-20.

4. See, for example, C. Peter Wagner, *Church Growth and the Whole Gospel* (Bromley, UK: MARC/ BCGA, 1981), pp. 53-54.

5. Matthew 9:16-17.

6. Revelation 2:5.

7. For example: Jack Redford, *Planting New Churches* (Nashville: Broadman, 1978), pp. 8-15; Graham Horsley, *Planting New Congregations* (London: Methodist Church, 1994), pp. 6-7; Robinson and Christine, *Planting*, pp. 315-335; Harry Weatherley, *Gaining the Ground* (Didcot, UK: Baptist Union, 1994), pp. 115-122.

8. One of the most thoughtful and comprehensive is David Shenk and Ervin Stutzman's *Creating Communities of the Kingdom.*

9. The activities of Stephen (Acts 6:8-7:60) and Philip (Acts 8:4-40) seem highly inappropriate for those chosen to exercise responsibility for food distribution within the Jerusalem church.

10. For a recent exception, see Steve Mosher, *God's Power, Jesus' Faith, and World Mission: A Study in Romans* (Scottdale, Pa.: Herald Press, 1996).

11. Robinson and Christine, *Planting*, p. 22.

12. An exception is Ellis and Mitchell, *Radical*, especially pp. 170-173.

13. Other New Testament books are written within and are relevant to a second generation context (see for example Luke 1:1-4; Hebrews 2:3), but the early chapters of Revelation directly address second generation churches and appear to compare their characteristics with those associated with first generation churches.

14. Bosch, *Transforming*, pp. 15-16.

15. For a summary and evaluation of this quest, see Howard Marshall, *I Believe in the Historical Jesus* (London: Hodder and Stoughton, 1977).

16. On the Waldensians, see Malcolm Lambert, *Medieval Heresy* (Oxford, UK: Blackwell, 1992). On the Anabaptists, see chapter 4.

17. Matthew 16:18-20 and Matthew 18:15-20.

18. For a more detailed analysis of these passages and the teaching in Matthew 18, see Stuart Murray, *Explaining Church Discipline* (Tonbridge, UK: Sovereign World, 1995).

19. Matthew 16:18-19.

Chapter 4

1. Troeltsch distinguished sect-type groups from church-type and mystical groups in his 1911 essay, "Stoic-Christian Natural Law and Modern Secular Natural Law." This essay is included in a collection of translated essays in Ernst Troeltsch, *Religion in History* (Edinburgh: T & T Clark, 1991).

2. J. F. Bethune-Baker, *Introduction to the Early History of Christian Doctrine* (London: Methuen, 1903), p. 279. On the Nestorians, see further David Christie-Murray, *History of Heresy* (Oxford, UK: OUP, 1989), pp. 62-68.

3. Quoted in Bosch, *Transforming*, p. 360.

4. See Yates, *Christian*, pp. 35ff.

5. Roland Allen, *Missionary Methods: St Paul's or Ours?* (Grand Rapids: Eerdmans, 1962, 1912) p. v. This was originally published in 1912.

6. On the Celtic churches generally, see James Mackey, *An Introduction to Celtic Christianity* (Edinburgh, Scotland: T & T Clark, 1989) and John McNeill, *The Celtic Churches* (Chicago: University of Chicago Press, 1974).

7. That later historians and biographers undoubtedly exaggerated these phenomena and added stories of their own need not preclude the recognition of at least a core of truth in many of the accounts.

8. Martin Robinson includes the Celtic missionaries in his chapter on historical precedents for church planting in Robinson and Christine, *Planting*, pp. 59-63. Robert Warren has indicated that the Celtic *modus operandi* offers helpful perspectives on the development of missionary congregations in Warren, *Building*, p. 11. A more detailed study has recently emerged in John Finney's *Recovering the Past*.

9. On the Anabaptists generally, see William Estep, *The Anabaptist Story* (Grand Rapids: Eerdmans, 1975) and Arnold Snyder, *Anabaptist History and Theology: An Introduction* (Kitchener, Ont.: Pandora Press, 1995).

10. A global evangelical movement, working closely with the Lausanne movement, consisting of various Resource Networks, which uses the target date to mobilize and energize evangelism. Its priorities and commitments were spelled out in the great commission Manifesto that emerged from the Global Consultation for World Evangelization by AD 2000, in Singapore in 1989. Details can be found in Luis Bush (ed), *AD 2000 and Beyond Handbook* (Colorado Springs: AD 2000 and Beyond Movement, 1993).

11. Bush, *AD 2000*, p. 21.

12. Quoted in Ellis and Mitchell, p. 208.

13. For the story of the DAWN strategy in the Philippines, see Jim Montgomery and Donald Anderson, *Discipling a Nation* (Colorado Springs: Global Church Growth Bulletin, 1980). The principles of the DAWN strategy are explained in Jim Montgomery, *DAWN 2000: 7 Million Churches to Go* (Crowborough, UK: Highland, 1990).

14. Montgomery, *DAWN*, p. 12.

15. These appear in Appendix A.

16. Montgomery, *Discipling*, p. 171.

17. Jim Montgomery coordinates the "Saturation Church Planting Resource Network" of the AD 2000 And Beyond movement, as well as being the Director of DAWN Ministries.

18. Montgomery, *Discipling*, p. 168.

19. Robinson and Christine, *Planting*, p. 67.

Chapter 5

1. Warren, *Building*, p. 32.
2. George Peters, *A Biblical Theology*, p. 214.
3. Ralph Winter, "The Two Structures of God's Redemptive Mission" in *Missiology: An International Review vol. 2, no. 1* (January 1974), p. 121.
4. See Watchman Nee, *The Normal Christian Church Life* (Washington, D.C.: International Students Press, 1962), published originally in Chinese in 1938.
5. C. Peter Wagner, *Leading Your Church to Growth* (London: MARC/BCGA, 1984), p. 154.
6. At a consultation in 1996, Tom Houston commented that "parachurch" organizations now receive more financial support from Christians than local churches receive. Though denominational leaders and local church treasurers may bewail this situation, it can be interpreted as evidence of grass roots concern for mission and a recognition that other agencies than local churches are required for this.
7. Howard Snyder has argued for a retention of "parachurch" terminology so that such structures are not "sacralized" but recognized as temporary and flexible "wineskins," whereas the local church is part of the "new wine of the gospel" (Snyder in Douglas, *Let the Earth*, pp. 337-339). His concern for flexibility is important, but it may be more helpful to consider *all* human structures as transitional, local churches as well as mission agencies. Snyder's attempt to identify the differences between churches and parachurch structures is unconvincing. Both are "wineskins" that will need periodically to be renewed to contain the "new wine" of the gospel.
8. David Bosch concludes of one of the main Reformation streams: "Lutheran orthodoxy believed that the 'Great Commission' had been fulfilled by the apostles and was no longer binding on the church": Bosch, *Transforming*, p. 249.
9. Bosch, *Witness*, p. 102.
10. Bosch, *Witness*, p. 169.
11. For a more recent example of a positive assessment of Christendom, see the comment of Abraham Kuyper, quoted in Leonard Verduin, *Anatomy of a Hybrid* (Grand Rapids: Eerdmans, 1976), pp. 101-102.
12. For example, Alastair Kee, *Constantine versus Christ: The Triumph of Ideology* (London: SCM, 1982).
13. This seems to be the stance of Stanley Hauerwas and William Willimon, *Resident Aliens* (Nashville: Abingdon, 1991), p. 17, although they welcome the demise of Christendom as an opportunity for renewed Christian faithfulness.
14. *Secularism* is a philosophy, a system that rejects all forms of faith or religion and accepts only what can be derived from the senses. Secularism as such has a limited following, mainly among intellectuals. It is openly hostile to Christianity and other religious explanations of reality. *Secularization* is an ongoing process of cultural change that removes religious beliefs, practices and institutions from a predominant position in society. It may not be hostile to Christianity but indifferent to belief systems.
15. Stanley Hauerwas, *After Christendom?* (Nashville: Abingdon, 1991), p. 18.

16. Bosch, *Witness*, p. 4.

17. John H. Yoder, *The Priestly Kingdom* (Notre Dame, Ind.: University of Notre Dame Press, 1985), pp. 142-143.

18. Warren, *Building*, pp. 6-7.

19. Bosch, *Witness*, p. 14.

20. Lesslie Newbigin, *The Gospel in a Pluralist Society* (London: SPCK, 1989), p. 224.

21. Nigel Scotland insists that "the Church of England is not now, nor has it been for some considerable time, a parochial church. No matter what it is in name, in practice it is a gathered or congregational church. For this reason it makes no sense for the Church of England to try to force church plants into a parochial strait-jacket"; Nigel Scotland, ed., *Recovering the Ground* (Chorleywood, UK: Kingdom Power Trust, 1995), p. 44.

22. *Breaking*, p. 3. See also Scotland, *Recovering*, pp. 44, 124.

23. Sandy Millar, "Perspectives on Church Planting," the appendix to Ellis and Mitchell, *Radical*, p. 205.

24. WCC, *Church*, p. 29.

25. The parish structure has been memorably described as the "condom of the Church of England" by David Pytches and Brian Skinner, *New Wineskins* (Guildford, UK: Eagle, 1991), p. 20.

26. *Breaking New Ground* gives considerable attention to this issue. Although it recognizes the need for flexibility and speaks of "supplementing the parish principle," it is clear that church planting ventures are expected generally to operate within the parish system.

27. See the various contributions to Scotland, *Recovering*.

28. This is further explored in chapter 10.

29. "More Churches or New Churches?" *Planting Papers* No. 7, pp. 1-4.

30. Robinson and Christine, *Planting*, pp. 25, 31.

31. The same terminology appears in Rob Warner, *Twenty-First Century Church* (London: Hodder & Stoughton, 1993), pp. 115-116. A recent conversation with a North American church planter revealed that this terminology is common also in North America.

32. Newbigin, *Gospel*, p. 227 (italics mine). A few pages later (p. 234) he refers to the congregation as "the only effective hermeneutic of the gospel."

33. The final report of the Western European Working Group of the Department on Studies in Evangelism.

34. This report is contained in an appendix in Graham Horsley, *Planting New Congregations: A Practical Guide for Methodists* (London: Methodist Church Home Mission Division, 1994).

35. Although the terminology is associated particularly with Warren's writings, others have also explored the implications of this concept. Lesslie Newbigin's *The Gospel in a Pluralist Society* includes a chapter on the subject of "Ministerial Leadership for a Missionary Congregation" (pp. 234-241). A recent example is Martin Robinson's chapter on "The Elements of a Missionary Congregation" in Martin Robinson, *To Win the West* (Crowborough, UK: Monarch, 1996), pp. 199-221.

36. Warren, *Building*, p. 4.

37. Warren's report on the Decade of Evangelism, *Signs of Life*, similarly contains only brief references to church planting. The development of mission-

ary congregations seems, at least in the writings of one of its main advocates, to be anticipated predominantly through the transformation of existing churches.

38. Warren, *Building*, p. 16.

39. This perception of imbalance during a period of adjusting toward a more balanced stance has been helpfully explored by David Spriggs in an article entitled "Focusing on Balance" *Church Growth Digest* (Winter 1995/96), p. 8.

Chapter 6

1. Wagner, *Church*, p. 11.

2. An early British church planting conference was organized by the British Church Growth Association, who also published one of the first British books on the subject—Monica Hill, ed., *How to Plant Churches* (London: MARC/BCGA, 1984). The DAWN strategy emerged from a church growth background. Keynote speakers at recent church planting conferences have included Church Growth teachers Peter Wagner and Eddie Gibbs. Church growth perspectives permeate church planting literature and have been helpful to many practitioners. The influence of church growth on the church planting movement is summarized in Robinson and Christine, *Planting*, pp. 83-98.

3. Warner, *Twenty-First Century*, pp. 56, 78.

4. Robinson and Christine, *Planting*, p. 9.

5. Ibid., p. 54.

6. Scotland, *Recovering*, pp. 12-13.

7. Terminology varies in connection with this model. "Seeker-targeted," "seeker-oriented" or "seeker-driven" churches are more radical versions. "Seeker-sensitive" churches, or churches with "seeker services," attempt to incorporate insights from the basic model or develop similar events.

8. On this model, see Lynne and Bill Hybels, *Rediscovering Church* (Grand Rapids: Zondervan, 1995); Martin Robinson, *A World Apart* (Tunbridge Wells, UK: Monarch, 1992); Ed Dobson, *Starting a Seeker Sensitive Service* (Amersham, UK: Scripture Press, 1992). For a detailed critique of Willow Creek, see Gregory Pritchard, *Willow Creek Seeker Services* (Grand Rapids: Baker, 1995).

9. The seven steps are (1) building authentic relationships; (2) sharing a verbal witness; (3) providing a service for seekers; (4) attendance at the new community service (for believers); (5) participation in a small group; (6) involvement in ministry through the use of spiritual gifts; (7) the exercise of stewardship. Despite the insistence that the whole strategy is needed by churches attempting to use seeker services, there is actually little here that is unfamiliar in many growing churches. The point is that seeker services may be an effective component in churches that are already outward-looking and able to mobilize their members. They are not sufficient in isolation. But they are the feature of the Willow Creek church that is distinctive.

10. This terminology has become familiar to readers of John Finney's research in *Finding Faith Today* (Swindon, UK: Bible Society, 1992). Robert Warren has endorsed this shift but has warned against allowing the pendulum to swing too far, since a process is "a sustained series of events" (Warren, *Signs*, p. 66). Seeker services can be perceived as such a series of events in a process that leads people toward faith.

11. There has been an explosion of such churches in many British cities, especially in London, in the past ten years, although some ethnic congregations (e.g. Scottish Presbyterians or German Lutherans in London) are much older. There is no comprehensive guide to such churches, although resources like the *Newham Directory of Religious Groups*, produced by Aston Community Involvement Unit, indicate the amazing profusion of such groups in a single London borough. A booklet by James Ashdown, *A Guide to Ethnic Christianity in London* (London: Zebra Project, 1993) gives a brief but already dated overview of the situation in London.

12. Youth churches have developed in many places during the latter half of the 1990s. Better known examples include the Nine o'clock Service in Sheffield, the Late Late Service in Glasgow, Holy Disorder in Gloucester, Soul Survivor in Watford, Bliss in Bournemouth and Joy in Oxford.

13. Helpful background information and perceptive comments on alternative network-style churches can be found in an unpublished paper by James Ashdown entitled "Alternative Churches."

14. In the 1970s the Christian Union at Bart's Hospital in London provoked considerable criticism by forming itself into a church. Two student groups in Australia have also become churches.

15. Encountered and discussed at greater length in chapter 3.

16. Donald McGavran, *Understanding Church Growth* (Grand Rapids: Eerdmans, 1980), p. 223.

17. A particularly helpful discussion of concerns about the principle can be found in Rene Padilla's contribution to Wilbert Shenk, ed., *Exploring Church Growth* (Grand Rapids: Eerdmans, 1983), pp. 285-303. See also Newbigin, *Open*, pp. 135-180.

18. Although the seer's vision of the redeemed community (Rev. 7:9) can be interpreted as implying the transcending rather than the abolition of cultural distinctives.

19. See the evidence presented in Peter Brierley, *Reaching and Keeping Teenagers* (Tunbridge Wells, UK: MARC, 1993). Many youth churches are targeted both at unchurched youngsters and youngsters who might otherwise slip away from church life.

20. This is Rob Warner's conclusion in Warner, *Twenty-First Century*, p. 60.

21. Eddie Gibbs, *Winning Them Back* (Tunbridge Wells, UK: MARC, 1993). Peter Brierley's survey, *Nominal Christians in the 1990s*, is presented as an Appendix.

22. See Robert Banks, *Paul's Idea of Community* (Peabody, Mass: Hendrickson, 1994); Robert and Julia Banks, *The Home Church* (Tring, UK: Lion, 1986).

23. Ralph Neighbor, *Where Do We Go From Here?* (Houston: Touch Outreach Ministries, 1990).

24. For an account of these and reflection on their relevance for the West, see Margaret Hebblethwaite, *Basic is Beautiful: Base Ecclesial Communities from Third World to First World* (London: Fount, 1993).

25. For a particularly outrageous example, see Gene Edwards, *How to Meet* (Beaumont: Message Ministry, 1993).

26. Many house church leaders would dispute this, pointing to ecclesiological differences, such as the leadership of apostolic teams and the absence of de-

nominational headquarters, but it is becoming increasingly difficult to substantiate claims to distinctiveness.

27. Terminology associated with the writings of Carl George. See, for example, *Prepare Your Church for the Future* (Chicago: Revell, 1991).

28. INFORM estimated in June 1995 that there are about 1600 such groups in the UK, and that between 40,000 and 80,000 people participate in these. John Finney concludes that "there are a large number of groups with comparatively few people in each" and comments that "despite these limited numbers, the effect of New Age thinking has been pervasive." See Finney, *Recovering*, p. 76.

29. The story is told by, among others, Sisay Beshe, a Mennonite cell leader, in *Anabaptism Today* Issue 7 (October 1994), pp. 5-8. Editor's note: Nathan Hege, author of *Beyond Our Prayers* (Scottdale, Pa.: Herald Press, 1998) is more inclined to report 5,000 members in 1982 when the churches were closed and 50,000 in 1991. He indicates that exact figures are difficult to obtain and that at any given time there are about 20,000 receiving instruction for baptism. In the year 2,000 they spoke of a worshiping community of over 150,000.

30. We will explore other aspects relevant to the ethos of the church in chapter 7. For those interested in exploring further, there is a huge literature on postmodernity. The books mentioned in the next three footnotes may provide a useful starting point. An enjoyable and entertaining guide is provided by Richard Appignanesi and Chris Garratt, *Postmodernism for Beginners* (Cambridge, UK: Icon, 1995). Two recent treatments by Christian writers are David Lyon, *Postmodernity* (Milton Keynes, UK: Open University Press, 1994) and Gene Veith, *Guide to Contemporary Culture* (Leicester, UK: Crossway, 1994).

31. Barry Smart, *Postmodernity* (London: Routledge, 1993), p. 116.

32. Graham: Cray, *From Here to Where?* (London: Board of Mission, undated), pp. 2, 12.

33. Mike Featherstone, *Consumer Culture and Postmodernism* (London: Sage, 1990), p. 3.

34. Warren, *Building*, p. 37. Warren suggests that we will need to be "bi-lingual; able to relate to those who belong to the old order, as well as to those who live in the new" (*Building*, 7).

35. Bosch, *Transforming*, p. 366.

36. John 17:14-18.

37. Richard Niebuhr, *Christ and Culture* (New York: Harper & Row, 1951).

38. See, for example, Hauerwas and Willimon, *Resident Aliens*, pp. 39-40.

39. Ashdown, "Alternative," pp. 8-9.

40. Roy Williamson, *For Such A Time As This* (London: Darton, Longman & Todd, 1996), pp. 179-180.

41. WCC, *Church*, p. 19.

42. An initiative associated with David Tomlinson, author of *The Post-Evangelical* (see chapter 7).

43. Barry Lowden (June 1996), quoted in a report by Stuart Taylor for the Spurgeon's/Oasis Church Planting and Evangelism course.

44. Robinson, *Win*, p. 241.

45. Unchurched not only in the sense that a small proportion belong to churches, but in the sense that the church is perceived as an alien and irrelevant institution. Various studies have confirmed that in many inner city areas of

Britain, families and communities have been effectively unchurched for generations. Mission in such a context will require different models from those appropriate for semi-churched or de-churched communities. This issue will be explored further below in chapter 10.

46. The term "Asian" is used here for the sake of brevity. There are many
Asian churches already, but different Asian cultures will require different expressions of church life. Converts from Hindu cultures and converts from Islamic
cultures will not necessarily feel at home in each other's churches.

47. On these principles and concerns see, for example, John Drane, *What
Is the New Age Movement Saying to the Church?* (London: Marshall Pickering,
1991).

48. This appears to be the approach of the report, *Breaking New Ground*,
mentioned above. Some Anglican church planters regard talk of "supplementing the parish principle" as an encouraging sign: see, for example, George Lings,
New Ground in Church Planting (Nottingham, UK: Grove, 1994), p. 24. Others
are dismayed by the lack of radical thinking in this report and a missed opportunity for ecclesiological renewal. See, for example, the comments of various
contributors to Scotland, *Recovering*.

49. Warren, *Building*, p. 38.

50. WCC, *Church*, p. 38.

51. Dale Stoffer: "Church Planting: An Anabaptist Model" (unpublished
paper given at the Anabaptist Vision conference at Elizabethtown (Pa.) College,
1994).

52. Os Guinness, *Dining with the Devil* (Grand Rapids: Baker, 1993), p. 28.

53. A useful summary of the key issues is contained in Newbigin, *Gospel*,
pp. 141-154.

54. On this, see Newbigin, *Gospel*, p. 119.

55. See Finney, *Finding*, p. 33-34.

56. Newbigin, *Gospel*, p. 154.

57. Nigel Wright, *The Radical Evangelical* (London: SPCK, 1996), pp. 22-
24.

58. Warren, *Signs*, p. 53.

59. Philippians 3:20; Hebrews 11:13-16.

60. A translation popularized by the Sojourners Community in Washington,
D.C. and the *Sojourners* magazine.

61. A translation popularized by the titles of two recent books by Hauerwas
and Willimon, *Resident Aliens* (referred to above) and *Where Resident Aliens
Live* (Nashville: Abingdon, 1996).

Chapter 7

1. Substantial anecdotal evidence is supported by studies such as Derek
Allen's *Planted to Grow.*

2. Michael Fanstone, *The Sheep That Got Away* (Tunbridge Wells, UK:
MARC, 1993).

3. Gibbs, *Winning*, pp. 275-281.

4. Robin Gamble, *The Irrelevant Church* (Eastbourne, UK: Monarch,
1991).

5. Morris Stuart, *So Long, Farewell and Thanks for the Church?* (Milton Keynes, UK: Scripture Union, 1996); first published in Australia by Hodder & Stoughton, 1992.

6. David Tomlinson, *The Post-Evangelical* (London: Triangle, 1995).

7. Arguably this has been the case throughout history. One example of this is the identification of the issues of the shape of monastic tonsure and the proper way of calculating the date of Easter that were ostensibly at stake at the Synod of Whitby in 664, when Roman and Celtic approaches to mission and church life clashed. The dispute was really about more fundamental questions of ethos.

8. Since this is also the tradition to which I belong, this section is self-critical rather than an excuse to criticize others. It is preferable if questions of ethos are raised from within (although the observations of outsiders may be helpful). It is encouraging to read of others involved in church planting who recognize the importance of this matter of ethos. See, for example: Scotland, *Recovering*, pp.13-14.

9. Quoted in Robinson and Christine, *Planting*, p. 130.

10. Tomlinson, *Post-Evangelical*, p. 15 (italics mine). The increasing confluence of evangelical and charismatic "streams" is detailed in a recent book by Peter Hocken, *The Strategy of the Spirit?* (Guildford: Eagle, 1996).

11. The English Church Census revealed that this was the section of the church which was growing most rapidly. The survivalist mentality of the first half of the twentieth century has given way to increased evangelical confidence, but there are signs that the pendulum has swung too far into smugness and triumphalism.

12. See Mark Noll, David Bebbington, and George Rawlyk, *Evangelicalism* (Oxford, UK: OUP, 1994), especially, pp. 75-79.

13. See, for example, the critique of Guinness, *Dining*, passim.

14. The roots of postmodernity have been traced back to the early twentieth century, but its impact on popular culture dates from the 1960s. There are indications that issues connected with postmodernity as well as post-evangelicalism and related phenomena will result in articles and books from various perspectives in coming years. Early examples include Nick Mercer, "Postmodernity and Rationality" in Anthony Billington, Tony Lane, and Max Turner, *Mission and Meaning* (Carlisle, UK: Paternoster Press, 1995) and Graham Cray et al, *The Post-Evangelical Debate* (London: SPCK, 1997). Also see more on such issues throughout this chapter

15. Harvey Cox, *Fire From Heaven* (London: Cassell, 1996), p. 300.

16. Shenk and Stutzman, *Creating*, pp. 103-104.

17. Ibid., 104.

18. Finney, *Recovering*, p. 40.

19. Finney, *Finding*, p. 24.

20. See *The Search for Faith* report, pp. 29-30, and Cox, *Fire*, pp. 300-320.

21. Cray, *From Here to Where?*, p. 17.

22. Acts 9:2; 19:9,23; 22:4; 24:14,22.

23. John 20:24-28.

24. Unkindly but provocatively described by R. E. O. White as "a monstrous monologue by a moron to mutes," quoted in Klaus Runia, *The Sermon*

Under Attack (Exeter, UK: Paternoster, 1983), pp. 9-10. Runia examines several reasons why monologue preaching is poorly suited to contemporary culture.

25. For example: Acts 9:27-29; 17:2-4,17; 18:4,19,28; 19:8-9; 24:25; 28:23-24.

26. A helpful introduction to this topic is Peter May, *Dialogue in Evangelism* (Nottingham, UK: Grove, 1990).

27. On this, see below in chapter 9.

28. On this, see Stuart Murray, *Spirit, Discipleship, Community: The Contemporary Significance of Anabaptist Hermeneutics* (Open University Ph.D. diss., 1992), pp. 224-258, 420-443.

29. Some very basic guidelines for communal reflection are suggested in Tomlinson, *Post-Evangelical*, p. 136.

30. Cray, *From Here to Where?*, p. 18.

31. Finney, *Finding*, p. 20.

32. Finney, *Recovering*, p. 43.

33. To explore the use of story further, see John Drane, *Evangelism for a New Age* (London: Marshall Pickering, 1994), pp. 64-72.

34. Walter Wink, *Engaging the Powers* (Minneapolis: Fortress Press, 1992), p. 263.

35. MTAG, *Search*, pp. 28-29.

36. It has been suggested that the notion of "membership" is unhelpful in contemporary society, giving an institutional flavor to community life (Warren, *Building*, p. 12), and that "regular attendance" no longer means at least once a week (Warren, *Signs*, p. 46).

37. Robert Warren acknowledges: "All too often we have to admit that what started as a 'new way of being church' has degenerated into a whole new set of meetings to attend" (Warren, *Building*, p. 11). He urges churches to "encourage the networking of individuals that by-passes the organizational" and to "let a good number of institutional forms of being church die with dignity" (p. 25).

38. Robinson, Win, p. 227.

39. Drane, *Evangelism*, pp. 53 54.

40. For a fascinating and detailed discussion of this, see Alan Kreider, "Worship and Evangelism in Pre-Christendom" *Vox Evangelica* XXIV (1994): 7-38.

41. John 7 is a classic example of shifting opinions and incompatible explanations.

42. On this theme, see the excellent book by Donald Kraybill, *The Upside-Down Kingdom*, rev. ed. (Scottdale: Herald Press, 1990).

43. Luke 4:18-19.

44. See Stuart, *So*, pp. 75-76.

45. As in Galatians 3:10.

46. On the role of prophets in this context see Warren, *Building*, p. 21; Gamble, *Irrelevant*, pp. 131-145.

47. Stuart, *So*, pp. 76-77.

48. Leviticus 25.

49. Acts 4:34.

50. Martin Hengel, for example, in his influential and extensive survey, *Property and Riches in the Early Church* (London: SCM Press, 1973), refers to

a range of ideas current among the churches concerning the redistribution of resources and care of the poor—but he makes no mention at all of tithing. A careful survey of writings between the first and third centuries fails to unearth any evidence that tithing was practiced or taught.

51. Augustine, for example, after teaching at length that Christ required his disciples to give up everything superfluous and to share their resources with the poor, acknowledged that few would do this and suggested tithing as a concession, and as a minimum measure. See Justo Gonzales, *Faith and Wealth* (New York: Harper & Row, 1990), pp. 219, 227.

52. Ramachandra, *Recovery*, p. 273 (italics his).

53. See Finney, *Recovering*, pp. 38-49; Drane, *Evangelism*, pp. 149-180; Laurence Singlehurst, *Sowing, Reaping, Keeping* (Leicester, UK: Crossway, 1995).

54. A helpful fresh approach is provided by Peter Cotterell in *Mission and Meaninglessness* (London: SPCK, 1990), pp. 75-83.

55. Some of the dangers are spelled out in Veith, *Guide*, pp. 210-216.

56. John 1:17.

57. 1 Corinthians 12:10. For a helpful introduction to this gift, see Douglas McBain, *Eyes That See* (Basingstoke, UK: Marshall Pickering, 1986).

58. Warren, *Building*, p. 53.

59. David Bosch, *A Spirituality of the Road* (Scottdale: Herald Press, 1979), especially, pp. 9-24.

60. Stuart, *So*, p. 28.

Chapter 8

1. Acts 2:46.

2. Acts 19:9.

3. On this movement, see W. Frend, *The Donatist Church* (Oxford, UK: Clarendon Press, 1971).

4. On this movement, see Roy Coad, *A History of the Brethren Movement* (Exeter, UK: Paternoster, 1976).

5. Gill, *Myth*, passim.

6. See chapter 10 for further discussion of LEP's.

7. We introduced this issue in chapter 2. The use of church buildings for mission purposes tends to reveal the underlying missiological convictions of the church.

8. Nodding, *Local*, p. 4.

9. This was a major concern in his seminal work, *The Bridges of God* (1955) and reappears in later writings.

10. Newbigin, *Open*, p. 136.

11. For example, Isaiah 2:2-5.

12. For example, Matthew 28:19; Acts 1:8.

13. See Finney, *Finding*, p. 43 and Warren, *Signs*, p. 75.

14. WCC, *Church*, p. 28.

15. Eddie Gibbs, *I Believe in Church Growth* (London: Hodder & Stoughton, 1981), p. 297.

16. In his paper "Divide and Conquer" at the Annual General Meeting of the Archbishop's Council on Evangelism, in November 1975.

17. Graham Dow, "Living with a Vision" in Scotland, *Recovering*, p. 125.

18. Robinson, *Win*, p. 233.

19. Guinness, *Dining*, p. 29.

20. David Tomlinson argues that large churches present to postmodern people what they "reject in the outside world: hierarchies, bureaucracies, and power struggles. . . . This is not a time for churches to be working toward 'bigger,' 'better' and 'more powerful'" (Tomlinson, *Post-Evangelical*, p. 144).

21. A brief consideration of this issue can be found in Chaney, *Church*, p. 66.

22. We will explore this further in chapter 10.

23. As we argued in chapter 2.

24. For example, Martin Robinson and David Spriggs, *Church Planting: The Training Manual* (Oxford, UK: Lynx, 1995), pp. 122-128

25. See, for example: Acts 2:4; 2:17-8; 4:24; 1 Corinthians 14 passim; Hebrews 10:24-25.

26. 1 Corinthians 14:26.

27. 1 Corinthians 14:29-31.

28. 1 Corinthians 14:35.

29. Quoted in Walter Klaassen, *Anabaptism in Outline* (Scottdale: Herald Press, 1981), p. 127.

30. For a summary of these and for a detailed exploration of the subject, see Stuart Murray, *Explaining Church Discipline*.

31. The notorious example of the Nine O'clock Service in Sheffield is best understood in terms of inadequate accountability rather than excessive creativity.

32. Matthew 18:17.

33. It has been calculated that the average church size throughout history and throughout the world is about 125 members.

Chapter 9

1. Lyle Schaller, *Survival Tactics in the Parish* (Nashville: Abingdon, 1977), p. 53.

2. Wagner, *Leading*, p. 59.

3. Gibbs, *Believe*, pp. 380-384.

4. For example, in Mark 10:42-45.

5. Perhaps the same is true of secular "mission statements."

6. Speech recorded in *Hansard*, 11 November 1947, col 206.

7. Newbigin, *Gospel*, p. 235.

8. Hauerwas and Willimon, *Resident*, p. 115 (italics theirs).

9. Robinson and Christine, *Planting*, p. 32.

10. Ellis and Mitchell, *Radical*, p. 115.

11. For example Luke 15:4. The commission to Peter to "take care of my sheep" (John 21:16) was given to someone who was already exercising and continued to exercise an evangelistic ministry.

12. See Roger Hayden, *English Baptist Heritage and History* (Didcot, UK: BUGB, 1990), p. 75.

13. This is not the place to enter the debate about the relationship between the Twelve and others named as apostles in the New Testament. Our interest

here is in the wider group rather than those referred to as the "apostles of the Lamb," whose role is evidently unique.

14. Another leadership role recovered within several church planting movements, but which we have insufficient space to explore in detail here.

15. Ellis and Mitchell, *Radical*, p. 120.

16. Although not insignificant. Recognizing this leadership role may provide greater scope for those involved to exercise their ministries and make easier the identification of those with appropriate gifts.

17. Hayden, *English*, p. 75.

18. Graham Dow recognizes the relevance of this ministry among Anglicans, in Scotland, *Recovering*, p. 124; Nigel Wright advocates its recovery among Baptists in Nigel Wright, *Challenge to Change* (Eastbourne, UK: Kingsway, 1991), pp. 172-190.

19. See Christine Trevett, *Montanism: Gender, Authority and the New Prophecy* (Cambridge, UK: CUP, 1996). The marginalization of prophecy was a further factor.

20. Some of the best known are contained in Thieleman van Braght, *Martyrs' Mirror* (Scottdale: Herald Press, 1950). See also a recent book edited by Arnold Snyder and Linda Hecht, *Profiles of Anabaptist Women* (Waterloo, Ont.: Wilfrid Laurier University Press, 1996).

21. Some examples are given in an unpublished paper by Rosie Nixson, "Women and Church Planting" (June 1996). I am grateful to her for permission to draw on her research in this section. See further her recent book, *Liberating Women for the Gospel* (London: Hodder & Stoughton, 1997).

22. Harvey Cox's fascinating account of the worldwide Pentecostal movement, *Fire from Heaven*, comments extensively on the role of women within this movement.

23. The only exceptions of which I am aware are three chapters written by women in the volume edited by Bob Hopkins: *Planting New Churches* (Guildford, UK: Eagle, 1991) and the volume edited by Monica Hill, *How to Plant Churches* (London: MARC, 1984), which includes two chapters written by the editor.

24. Rosie Nixson notes especially the chapter on leadership entitled "Give Me a Hundred Men" in Charlie Cleverley, *Church Planting Our Future Hope* (London, SU: 1991), and the assumption made of men-only reading in Chaney.

25. Only two speakers at the Challenge 2000 conference in 1995 were women: one led a workshop on "How Women Plant Churches," the other shared a workshop on "New Forms of Church."

26. Nixson, *Women*, p. 22.

27. Of relevance also for church planting, where team ministry is often given renewed emphasis, is the perception that women often function better than men in teams.

28. Scotland, *Recovering*, p. 47.

29. Ellis and Mitchell, *Radical*, p. 29, quoted in Scotland, *Recovering*, p. 47. A similar conclusion is expressed in Howard Synder, *The Community of the King* (Downers Grove, Ill.: InterVarsity Press, 1977), p. 95.

30. Scotland, *Recovering*, p. 48.

31. Ibid., p. 87.

32. Ibid., p. 25.

33. Ibid., pp. 50-62.

34. Warren, *Building*, p. 15.

35. Paul Beasley-Murray, *Anyone for Ordination?* (Turnbridge Wells, UK: MARC, 1993).

36. This is apparent, for example, in Lesslie Newbigin's otherwise helpful discussion of ministerial leadership for missionary congregations. See Newbigin, *Gospel*, p. 235.

37. See, for example, Wagner, *Harvest*, p. 72.

38. Margaret Kane, *Theology in an Industrial Society* (London: SCM, 1975), pp. 31-32. Kane uses the terminology of clergy and laity, which I have adapted here in line with the foregoing discussion.

39. Newbigin, *Gospel*, p. 231.

40. One example is the Evangelism and Church Planting course run by Oasis Trust, Spurgeon's College, Church Army, and Northern Baptist College.

41. Bosch, *Transforming*, pp. 15-16.

Chapter 10

1. Graham Horsley (*Planting*, p. 5), for example, notes that "most of the [church planting] literature assumes either an Anglican parish model or a congregational model and this is not always easily applied within the Methodist system."

2. A good summary, using popular terminology, is found in Wagner, *Harvest*, pp. 59-75.

3. A recent example is Martin Robinson and David Spriggs' *Church Planting: The Training Manual*. This is an excellent manual, which identifies ten different church planting models, but then appears to assume that the reader's interest is in the mother/daughter model. Some of its practical guidelines are applicable also to other models, but the concentration of attention on this one model undermines the claim of the subtitle that this manual provides "everything you need to train your church planting team." If the mother/daughter model is not used, this manual may be less helpful and even misleading.

4. Although advocates sometimes regard this as a positive factor. Graham Horsley writes: "Perhaps an important contribution of the church planting movement is to encourage Christians to risk failure for the sake of the kingdom of God" (Horsley, *Planting*, p. 9).

5. Indeed, there is evidence that there has been no increase during the 1990s on the rate of church planting in the 1980s. Roughly six churches per week have been planted from 1980 until 1997. The Challenge 2000 movement does not appear to have achieved any significant progress in the speed at which churches are planted, although it has certainly ensured that church planting is on the agenda of a much wider constituency than previously.

6. Some examples are noted in issue 1 of the newsletter of Anglican Church Planting Initiatives (Autumn 1996).

7. An article on page 1, Friday, May 26, begins: "New Anglican churches are being established at a faster rate than any time this century, but most 'church plants' are not appearing where they are most needed." Fifteen years earlier, the article continues, almost half the church plants were in urban priority areas, whereas "the trend now is that a higher proportion are in the middle class areas."

Some figures presented at the Anglican Church Planting Conference in June 1997 suggested that there had been more recent church planting in UPAs, but the report to the conference concluded that the overall trend was still toward planting in the "easier" areas.

8. *Faith in the City* (London: Church House, 1985).

9. None of the 38 recommendations to the church contained in *Faith in the City* deals with evangelism or church growth.

10. The terminology used in relation to urban mission varies from "inner city" to "urban priority areas" to "the urban poor" to "working class." Some terms are geographical; some are demographic; some are concerned with powerlessness and deprivation. Urban mission refers in this section to any and all of these dimensions and includes not only large inner city communities but areas of deprivation in more affluent areas and large overspill council housing estates into which inner city communities have periodically been decanted.

11. Bob Mayo, *Gospel Exploded* (London: Triangle, 1996) p. ix.

12. See, for example, Tony Walter, *A Long Way From Home* (Exeter, UK: Paternoster, 1979).

13. On this, see Wilson, "Colonies," p. 44.

14. An example of colonization planting is the Breakthrough Church in Tooting, South London, planted from Cobham in Surrey and now operating in four congregations. The story is told briefly in Cleverley, *Church*, pp. 49-51.

15. For example, David Hesselgrave, *Planting Churches Cross-Culturally* (Grand Rapids: Baker 1980); Charles Brock, *Indigenous Church Planting* (Nashville: Broadman 1981); Tom Steffen, *Passing the Baton: Church Planting that Empowers* (La Habra: Centre for Organizational Ministry Development, 1993).

16. For example, Seed teams (Methodist), TIE teams (Pioneer), YWAM mission teams.

17. Described in Johan Lukasse, *Churches with Roots* (Bromley, UK: MARC/STL, 1990).

18. Other books on planting teams include James Feeney, *Church Planting by the Team Method* (Anchorage, AK.: Abbott Loop Christian Centre, 1988) and Bruce Patrick, *The Church Planter and the Church Planting Team* (Auckland, New Zealand: BUNZ, 1991).

19. Oasis Trust and Spurgeon's College developed an initiative, known as "Urban Expression," in 1997, to train and deploy such teams to plant churches in inner London.

20. Kirk Hadaway, *Church Growth: Separating Fact from Fiction*, pp. 167-168.

21. See, for example, Gamble, *Irrelevant*, p. 149.

22. MTAG, *Search*, p. 32.

23. Raymond Fung, *The Isaiah Vision* (Geneva, Switzerland: WCC, 1992).

24. *Mission and Evangelism: An Ecumenical Affirmation* (1983), quoted at greater length in chapter 2.

25. A helpful book on this issue is Robert Linthicum, *Empowering the Poor* (Monrovia: MARC, 1991).

26. Williamson, *Such*, p. 180.

27. It may also be relevant in other areas. Some rural communities are quite deprived in terms of local facilities and church planting via social action may be appropriate here also.

28. I am indebted to Helen Wordsworth for this summary.

29. Graham Licence, *Rural Church Planting?* (Bedford, UK: BCGA, 1991). The question mark in the title indicates that the legitimacy of rural church planting is not accepted by all.

30. An evocative term used in Gamble, *Irrelevant*, p. 183.

31. If this model also involves the use of smaller groups within some of the satellites, the problems associated with three-level churches, considered in chapter 8, become relevant.

32. Graham Licence describes the relationship between Tonbridge Baptist Church in Kent and five village churches as an example of this strategy. See Licence, *Rural*, pp. 23-24.

33. A helpful chapter on adoption planting is contained in *Nodding*, Local, pp. 127-136, telling the story of such a plant and indicating the issues to be considered.

34. See Welby, *Replanting*, for a useful summary of the issues.

35. See Appendix A.

36. For example, those noted in Robinson and Christine, *Planting*, p. 131, and Licence, *Rural*, pp. 21-22. It may be that ecumenical planting is more appropriate in rural contexts than elsewhere.

37. Lings, *New*, p. 18. See also Robinson and Christine, *Planting*, p. 131.

38. Whether this movement is traced to the 1910 Edinburgh Conference or further back to examples of practical cooperation in pioneering contexts.

39. See WCC, *Church*, p. 35; Hocken, *Strategy*, p. 67; Robinson, *Win*, pp. 33, 48; Finney, *Finding*, p. 80.

40. Collaboration of this kind in Guildford, Surrey is described in Nodding, *Local*, pp. 137-152.

41. WCC, *Church*, p. 31.

42. Warren, *Building*, p. 52.

43. Ephesians 4:12.

44. Matthew 18:20—the conclusion of one of the two passages where Jesus speaks about the church.

Chapter 11

1. Finney, *Recovering*, p. 47.

2. Drane, *Evangelism*, p. 19.

SELECT BIBLIOGRAPHY ON CHURCH PLANTING

Reports

Allen, Derek. *Planted to Grow.* Didcot, UK: Baptist Union, 1994.

Archbishop's Commission on Urban Priority Areas. *Faith in the City.* London: Church House, 1985.

Ashdown, James. *A Guide to Ethnic Christianity in London.* London: Zebra Project, 1993.

Brierley, Peter. *"Christian" England.* London: MARC Europe, 1991.

Brierley, Peter. *Nominal Christians in the 1990s* in Gibbs, Eddie: *Winning Them Back.* Tunbridge Wells, UK: MARC, 1993.

Church of England. *Breaking New Ground.* London: Church House, 1994.

Davie, Grace. *Religion in Britain since 1945.* Oxford: Blackwell, 1994.

Finney, John. *Finding Faith Today.* Swindon, UK: Bible Society, 1992.

Mission Theological Advisory Group. *The Search for Faith and the Witness of the Church.* London: Church House, 1996.

Warren, Robert. *Signs of Life.* London: Church House, 1996.

World Council of Churches. *The Church for Others.* Geneva: WCC, 1967.

Accounts of Church Planting

Carey, George et al. *Planting New Churches.* Guildford, UK: Eagle, 1991.

Cleverly, Charlie. *Church Planting Our Future Hope.* London: SU, 1991.

Forster, Roger, ed. *Ten New Churches.* Bromley, UK: MARC Europe, 1986.

Montgomery, Jim and Anderson, Donald, *Discipling a Nation*. Colorado Springs: *Global Church Growth Bulletin*, 1980.

Manuals and Handbooks

Amberson, Talmadge. *The Birth of Churches: A Biblical Basis for Church Planting*. Nashville: Broadman, 1979.

Chaney, Charles. *Church Planting at the End of the Twentieth Century*. Wheaton: Tyndale House, 1986.

Ellis, Roger and Mitchell, Roger. *Radical Church Planting*. Cambridge: Crossway, 1992.

Feeney, James. *Church Planting by the Team Method*. Anchorage: Abbott Loop, 1988.

Hill, Monica, ed. *How to Plant Churches*. London: MARC, 1984.

Logan, Robert. *The Church Planter's Checklist*. Pasadena: Fuller, 1978.

Lukasse, Johan. *Churches with Roots*. Bromley, UK: MARC, 1990.

Montgomery, Jim. *DAWN 2000*. Crowborough, UK: Highland, 1989.

Nodding, Peter. *Local Church Planting*. London: Marshall Pickering, 1994.

Patrick, Bruce. *The Church Planter and the Church Planting Team*. Auckland: BUNZ, 1991.

Redford, Jack. *Planting New Churches*. Nashville: Broadman, 1978.

Ridley, Charles. *How to Select Church Planters*. Pasadena: Fuller, 1988.

Robinson, Martin and Christine, Stuart. *Planting Tomorrow's Churches Today*. Crowborough, UK: Monarch, 1992.

Robinson, Martin and Spriggs, David. *Church Planting—The Training Manual*. Oxford: Lynx, 1995.

Schaller, Lyle. *44 Questions for Church Planters*. Nashville: Abingdon, 1991.

Wagner, C. Peter. *Church Planting for a Greater Harvest*. Ventura: Regal, 1990.

Weatherley, Harry. *Gaining the Ground*. Didcot, UK: Baptist Union, 1994.

Booklets

Hopkins, Bob. *Church Planting: Models for Mission in the Church of England*. Nottingham, UK: Grove Booklets 4 and 8, 1988-89.

Horsley, Graham. *Planting New Congregations*. London: Methodist Church Home Mission, 1994.

Licence, Graham. *Rural Church Planting?* Bedford, UK: BCGA, 1992.

Lings, George. *New Ground in Church Planting*. Nottingham: Grove, 1994.

Welby, Alex. *Replanting*. Self-published, 1992.

Church Planting and Ecclesiology

Banks, Robert and Julia: *The Home Church*. Tring, UK: Lion, 1986.

Fanstone, Michael. *The Sheep That Got Away*. Tunbridge Wells, UK: MARC, 1993.

Gamble, Robin. *The Irrelevant Church*. Eastbourne, UK: Monarch, 1991.

George, Carl. *Prepare Your Church for the Future*. Chicago: Revell, 1991.

Hauerwas, Stanley and Willimon, William. *Resident Aliens*. Nashville: Abingdon, 1991.

Hybels, Lynne and Bill. *Rediscovering Church*. Grand Rapids: Zondervan, 1995.

Malphurs, Aubrey. *Planting Growing Churches for the Twenty-First Century*. Grand Rapids: Baker, 1992.

Nee, Watchman. *The Normal Christian Church Life*. Washington, D.C.: International Students Press, 1962.

Neighbor, Ralph. *Where Do We Go From Here?* Houston: Touch, 1990.

Pytches, David and Skinner, Brian. *New Wineskins*. Guildford: Eagle, 1991.

Robinson, Martin. *A World Apart*. Crowborough: Monarch, 1992.

Scotland, Nigel, ed. *Recovering the Ground*. Chorleywood: Kingdom Power Trust, 1995.

Shenk, David and Stutzman, Ervin. *Creating Communities of the Kingdom*. Scottdale: Herald, 1988.

Snyder, Howard. *The Community of the King*. Downers Grove, Ill. InterVarsity Press, 1977.

Stuart, Morris. *So Long, Farewell and Thanks for the Church?* Milton Keynes, UK: Scripture Union, 1996.

Tomlinson, David. *The Post-Evangelical.* London: Triangle, 1995.

Warren, Robert. *Being Human, Being Church.* London: Marshall Pickering, 1995.

Warren, Robert. *Building Missionary Congregations.* London: Church House, 1995.

Church Planting and Missiology

Bosch, David. *Transforming Mission.* Maryknoll, N.Y.: Orbis, 1991.

Bosch, David. *Witness to the World.* London: Marshalls, 1980.

Cray, Graham. *From Here to Where?.* London: Board of Mission, undated.

Finney, John. *Recovering the Past.* London: Darton, Longman & Todd, 1996.

Gibbs, Eddie. *Winning Them Back.* Tunbridge Wells, UK: MARC, 1993.

Newbigin, Lesslie. *The Gospel in a Pluralist Society.* London: SPCK, 1989.

Robinson, Martin. *To Win the West.* Crowborough, UK: Monarch, 1996.

Shenk, Wilbert, ed. *The Transfiguration of Mission.* Scottdale: Herald Press, 1993.

Yates, Timothy. *Christian Mission in the Twentieth Century.* Cambridge, England: CUP, 1994.

Cross-Cultural Church Planting

Brock, Charles. *Indigenous Church Planting.* Nashville: Broadman, 1981.

Hesselgrave, David. *Planting Churches Cross-Culturally.* Grand Rapids: Baker, 1980.

Hodges, Melvin. *The Indigenous Church.* Springfield: Gospel Publishing, 1976.

Steffen, Tom. *Passing the Baton.* La Habra: Centre for Organizational Ministry Development, 1993.

The Author

Stuart Murray was born in London and has lived there all but three years of his life. Raised in a Plymouth Brethren family and church, he was baptized at thirteen. He studied law at London University but decided in 1977 to become involved in inner city mission work rather than becoming a lawyer.

He spent twelve years in East London, planting and leading what is now Tower Hamlets Community Church, a multiracial charismatic church which also founded a small community school. During that time he pursued theological studies and encountered the Anabaptist tradition through contact with the London Mennonite Centre.

In 1989 Murray moved with his family to Nottinghamshire, where he wrote his first book, *City Vision* (Darton, Longman & Todd, 1989) and spent three years under the auspices of the Whitefield Institute, Oxford, working on a Ph.D. in Anabaptist hermeneutics. He worked part-time with a charitable trust serving homeless people. He also participated in forming and developing the UK Anabaptist Network, which sponsors study groups, runs conferences, and offers resources to the growing number of British Christians drawn to the Anabaptist tradition. He is now chair of this network and editor of the journal *Anabaptism Today*.

In 1992 Murray moved back to London to become Oasis Director of Church Planting and Evangelism at Spurgeon's College, the largest English Baptist seminary. During the past decade he has been responsible for developing this course, through which Baptist ministers and leaders from several other denominations have been trained. He is also responsible for postgraduate courses in Urban Ministry and Baptist/Anabaptist Studies as well as supervising research students.

Murray has continued to write, producing further books, numerous articles on mission themes, and a number of open learning workbooks. He has traveled widely in Britain, Europe, and the United States, preaching, training, and providing consulting services, especially on issues of urban mission and church planting.

Since 1997 he has been responsible for the development of Urban Expression, an urban church planting initiative in East London that recruits teams to plant new churches in one of the least churched and most culturally diverse parts of Britain. He has recently moved to Oxford with his wife, Sian, and two sons, Neal and Robert.